The Art of Minding Your Own Business

by

Alander L Pulliam

Minding Your Own Business

Breaking Free From Foolish Living

Alander Lee Pulliam Jr

Published by Alander Lee Pulliam Jr, 2025.

MINDING YOUR OWN BUSINESS

First edition. July 20, 2025.

ISBN: 979-8231631445

Written by Alander Lee Pulliam Jr.

This book is dedicated to every soul yearning for a life less ordinary—a life brimming with peace, purpose, and the quiet strength that comes from aligning oneself with God's divine plan. It is for those who feel the weight of the world on their shoulders, the incessant clamor of distractions pulling them in a thousand different directions, leaving them feeling depleted and adrift. It is for those who have been wounded by gossip, burdened by the weight of others' expectations, or tangled in the messy webs of impulsive actions.

It is for those wrestling with procrastination, battling unruly passions, and struggling to set healthy boundaries, finding themselves constantly pulled into the dramas of others, neglecting their own precious inner garden of growth and development. It is for the weary hearts who long for respite, the quiet souls seeking solace, and the courageous spirits determined to cultivate a life rooted in faith, self-mastery, and the unwavering love of our Creator.

This work is a testament to the power of intentional living, the wisdom of silence, and the transformative potential found in focusing on one's own spiritual journey. It is a beacon of hope, a guidepost on the path toward a life less fractured, more grounded, and profoundly more fulfilling. May these words serve as a gentle nudge, a loving invitation to embark on a journey inward, to discover the quiet strength residing within, and to embrace the peace, purpose, and power that await those who choose to live intentionally, guided by faith and empowered by the Holy Spirit. May this book serve as a reminder that your unique assignment from God is waiting for you – waiting to be discovered, nurtured, and finally, shared with the world. May your journey be filled with grace, wisdom, and abiding peace.

Sarah felt adrift. At 25, her peers were settling into careers, marriages, even families. She, however, felt a gnawing emptiness, a sense of being unmoored. She'd graduated with honors, landed a decent job, yet a persistent question echoed in her heart: What was her purpose? What was God's plan for her life? The comfortable routine felt like a gilded cage, trapping her in a life that felt...incomplete. She'd prayed, she'd searched, but the answer remained elusive.

Her frustration grew. She envied the seeming clarity of others' paths. Her friend Emily was thriving as a pediatrician, her passion for healing children evident in every conversation. Another friend, David, found immense satisfaction in his work as a missionary, dedicating his life to serving others. Sarah felt a pang of jealousy, tinged with self-doubt. Was she simply destined for a life of quiet mediocrity? Was she lacking something inherent, a spark that others seemed to possess?

One Sunday, after a particularly disheartening sermon on fulfilling God's will, Sarah found herself lingering after the service. Pastor Michael, a kind, elderly man with a warm smile and eyes that seemed to see straight into your soul, noticed her. He gently approached, his voice a calming balm against the turmoil in her heart. "Sarah," he began, his voice quiet yet resonant, "you seem troubled. May I offer some counsel?"

Sarah, surprised by his perception, poured out her heart. She confessed her doubts, her anxieties, her feeling of being lost in a sea of uncertainty. Pastor Michael listened patiently, offering nods of understanding and occasional words of encouragement. When she finished, he smiled gently. "Sarah," he said, "your feeling of being lost isn't unusual. Many of us wrestle with this question of purpose, of our place in God's grand design."

He leaned forward, his eyes twinkling. "But the key," he continued, "is to remember that God doesn't give us a blueprint for our lives. He gives us gifts, talents, passions – the building blocks, if you will. It's up to us to discern how to use these gifts to build something beautiful, something that glorifies Him."

He paused, then launched into a familiar yet profoundly relevant parable: the parable of the talents. He spoke of the master who entrusted his servants with varying amounts of talents, according to their abilities. He highlighted the servant who, through diligence and wise investment, doubled his master's investment. He spoke of the servant who buried his talent out of fear and laziness, and the devastating consequences that followed.

"Sarah," Pastor Michael concluded, "God has given you talents. Perhaps you haven't yet recognized them, or maybe you've been too afraid to use them. But they are there, waiting to be discovered, waiting to be used for His glory. Think about your strengths, your passions, the things you enjoy doing. Where do you feel a sense of fulfillment, even in small things? Those are often clues to the bigger picture."

Sarah pondered his words. She reflected on her life, her skills, her inclinations. She was a gifted writer, always finding solace in expressing herself through words. She possessed a knack for organizing, for bringing order out of chaos. And she had a deep compassion for those struggling with similar feelings of uncertainty and discouragement. These weren't just hobbies; they were gifts, talents God had given her.

Pastor Michael suggested a plan. He encouraged her to start small, to volunteer at a local homeless shelter, where she could use her organizational skills to help those in need. He suggested she start a blog, sharing her writing talents with a wider audience, using her words to offer encouragement and hope. He emphasized the importance of prayer, of seeking God's guidance in every step.

Over the next few months, Sarah diligently followed his advice. She started volunteering at the shelter, finding immense satisfaction in organizing supplies and providing administrative support. She launched a blog, hesitantly at first, sharing her thoughts, her struggles, and her journey of self-discovery. The response was overwhelmingly positive. She connected with readers who felt similarly lost and found immense fulfillment in sharing her experiences and offering encouragement.

Her writing began to attract attention. She was invited to speak at local women's groups, sharing her story and her newfound understanding of her divine assignment. She discovered a passion for mentoring young women, helping them navigate their own journeys of self-discovery. The quiet emptiness she'd felt before was replaced by a sense of purpose, a profound joy in using her gifts to serve others. She realized that her divine assignment wasn't a grand, singular event, but a continuous unfolding, a journey of faith and service.

Sarah's journey underscored a crucial truth: God's plan for our lives is not a pre-determined path, but a tapestry woven from the unique threads of our individual talents and passions. It's not about achieving some grand, singular accomplishment, but about faithfully using the gifts God has given us, no matter how small they may seem. It's about embracing our unique strengths and weaknesses, using them in service to others, and allowing God to guide us along the way. It's about understanding that the "divine assignment" isn't a single, momentous revelation, but a continuous unfolding, a process of growth, discovery, and faithful stewardship of the gifts we've been given. It's a quiet strength, born not of grand gestures, but of consistent, faithful action, fueled by a deep trust in God's plan.

This understanding transformed Sarah's perspective. The envy she once felt evaporated, replaced by a sense of gratitude for her own unique gifts and the opportunities to use them. She realized that everyone has a divine assignment, a unique purpose woven into the fabric of their being. The challenge wasn't to find a pre-ordained path, but to discern and develop the talents God had already bestowed, and to use them to serve and glorify Him. The feeling of being lost gave way to a profound sense of belonging, of being exactly where God wanted her to be, using her gifts in ways that brought joy to herself and blessing to others.

Sarah's journey became a testament to the power of self-discovery, a testament to the quiet strength that comes from understanding and embracing one's divine assignment. It wasn't a dramatic, life-altering event, but a gradual, transformative process, a continuous journey of faith, fueled by prayer, guided by discernment, and strengthened by service to others. It was a reminder that our true purpose isn't found in external validation or societal expectations, but in the faithful use of the gifts God has given us, a quiet strength blossoming in the service of others, a testament to the power of living a life fully surrendered to God's will.

This understanding wasn't just a philosophical concept for Sarah; it became a lived reality. The quiet strength she cultivated allowed her to navigate the complexities of life with grace and resilience. The struggles she faced, once overwhelming, became opportunities for growth, for deepening her faith, and for strengthening her relationship with God. Her journey became a beacon of hope, a testament to the transformative power of discovering and embracing one's divine assignment, a reminder that the most fulfilling life is one lived in service to God and to others. It was a life of quiet strength, a life of purpose, a life of peace. And that, she realized, was the greatest gift of all. A gift that far surpassed any earthly success or accomplishment.

The parable of the talents continued to resonate deeply within her. She understood now, not just intellectually, but viscerally, the importance of stewardship, of diligently using the gifts God had entrusted to her. She learned that burying her talents out of fear or self-doubt would not only rob her of joy and fulfillment, but would also deny others the benefits of her unique gifts. It was a profound realization, one that shaped not only her career and relationships, but the very essence of her being.

Her journey wasn't without its setbacks. There were days when doubt crept in, when the weight of responsibility felt overwhelming. But she learned to lean on her faith, to seek guidance through prayer and mentorship, and to draw strength from the community she had cultivated. She learned that the journey of self-discovery was a lifelong process, a continuous unfolding, a journey of faith, growth, and service. It was a journey she embarked upon not with a sense of self-reliance, but with a deep reliance on God's grace and guidance.

And so, Sarah's story became a powerful illustration of the quiet strength that emerges when we discover and embrace our divine assignment. It's a strength that is not loud or boastful, but quietly powerful, radiating from a life lived with intention, purpose, and a deep trust in God's plan. It's a strength that empowers us to navigate life's challenges with grace, resilience, and unwavering faith. A quiet strength that transforms not only our own lives but the lives of those around us. A strength that blossoms in the quiet corners of faithful service, a strength that is the very essence of a life lived for God's glory.

The quiet strength Pastor Michael spoke of resonated deeply within Sarah, but a new challenge emerged – a persistent struggle with procrastination that threatened to derail her newfound purpose. The enthusiasm of her initial efforts began to wane, replaced by a familiar inertia. The daunting task of writing regular blog posts, coupled with the demands of volunteering at the homeless shelter, felt overwhelming. She found herself delaying tasks, putting off writing until the last minute, leaving important administrative duties at the shelter unfinished. The familiar voice of self-doubt whispered insidious suggestions: "You're not good enough," "It's too much," "You'll fail anyway."

This battle with procrastination wasn't just a matter of laziness; it stemmed from a deeper-seated fear of failure, a fear of not living up to the expectations she had placed upon herself. The pressure to maintain the momentum she'd built felt suffocating, causing her to retreat into a familiar cycle of delay and guilt. The joy she'd initially found in her work began to diminish, replaced by a nagging sense of inadequacy and frustration.

One evening, feeling particularly discouraged, Sarah opened her Bible, searching for solace and guidance. She landed on Proverbs 16:3: "Commit to the Lord whatever you do, and he will establish your plans." The verse struck a chord. It wasn't enough to simply

intend to use her gifts for God's glory; she needed to actively *commit* to the process, trusting in His strength to overcome her weakness.

This realization prompted a shift in her approach. She began to pray before starting each task, asking God for guidance and strength to overcome her procrastination. She recognized the importance of breaking down large tasks into smaller, more manageable steps. Instead of facing the daunting prospect of writing a whole blog post at once, she would set smaller goals: writing an outline one day, composing the introduction the next, and so on. This strategy helped to alleviate the feeling of being overwhelmed, transforming a seemingly insurmountable task into a series of achievable milestones.

She also discovered the power of setting realistic goals. Instead of aiming for perfection, she focused on progress, celebrating small victories along the way. This approach shifted her perspective from one of self-criticism to one of self-compassion, fostering a sense of encouragement rather than discouragement.

Recognizing the importance of accountability, Sarah shared her struggles and her new plan with Pastor Michael. He became her mentor and confidante, offering encouragement and practical advice. He suggested she find an accountability partner – someone who would share her commitment to her goals and help her stay on track.

Sarah found such a partner in Emily, the pediatrician friend she'd initially envied. Initially hesitant to share her struggles, Sarah found that opening up to Emily fostered a sense of camaraderie and mutual support. They met regularly to discuss their progress, celebrate their successes, and offer encouragement when challenges arose. This mutual accountability proved invaluable, helping Sarah to overcome procrastination and stay focused on her goals.

The integration of scripture into her daily life proved transformative. She began to memorize verses that spoke to diligence, perseverance, and faith. Proverbs 10:4, "Lazy hands make for poverty, but diligent hands bring wealth," served as a constant reminder that procrastination was not merely a matter of convenience but a choice with tangible consequences. Colossians 3:23, "Whatever you do, work at it with all your heart, as working for the Lord, not for human masters," instilled in her a sense of purpose and dedication that transcended earthly rewards.

The change wasn't immediate or effortless. There were days when the old habits resurfaced, when procrastination threatened to consume her. But with each setback, Sarah learned to be more compassionate towards herself, recognizing that progress, not perfection, was the key to success. She learned to forgive herself for her lapses, to dust herself off, and to recommit to her goals with renewed determination. She embraced the power of prayer, recognizing that it wasn't a magical solution but a pathway to dependence on God's strength.

As Sarah consistently applied these strategies, she witnessed a marked improvement in her productivity and overall well-being. She began to meet her deadlines consistently, both at the shelter and with her blog. Her writing improved in quality, reflecting a deeper understanding of her purpose and a greater sense of confidence in her abilities.

Her blog continued to attract a growing readership, and her influence extended beyond the digital realm. She was invited to speak at larger conferences and workshops, sharing her story and inspiring others to overcome their own struggles with procrastination. She realized that her journey was not just about personal growth; it was about empowering others to discover their own quiet strength and to overcome the obstacles that hindered their path to fulfilling God's purpose for their lives.

The story of Sarah's journey emphasizes the essential role of self-discipline in realizing our divine assignments. It highlights the need for realistic goals, the power of breaking down tasks, the importance of accountability, and the sustaining strength found in prayer and scripture. It underscores that our struggles with procrastination are not insurmountable, but rather opportunities for growth, for deepening our faith, and for drawing closer to God.

The transformation wasn't merely about increased productivity; it was a spiritual awakening, a deepening of Sarah's faith and a strengthening of her relationship with God. She discovered that her divine assignment wasn't a passive reception of God's will but an active participation in His work, a collaboration with God in building His kingdom on earth. This understanding instilled in her not just self-discipline, but a deep sense of purpose, a quiet confidence that empowered her to overcome obstacles and to persevere in her calling.

The journey, however, wasn't without its bumps in the road. There were times when the old habits reasserted themselves, when the weight of responsibility felt too heavy, or when the voice of doubt whispered its familiar lies. But Sarah, armed with her newfound understanding and spiritual tools, learned to navigate these challenges with greater grace and resilience. She discovered the power of forgiveness, both for herself and for others, recognizing that perfection was not the goal, but progress.

She learned the importance of self-compassion. There were days when she would fall short, when she would fail to meet her self-imposed deadlines. But instead of wallowing in self-criticism, she would take a moment to acknowledge her feelings, to ask for God's grace, and then to gently redirect her focus towards her goals. This self-compassion proved crucial in preventing her from slipping back into the destructive cycle of procrastination.

The power of community also played a significant role in Sarah's continued success. She continued to meet with Emily, her accountability partner, regularly. Their shared journey became a source of encouragement and mutual support. They celebrated each other's successes and offered words of comfort and encouragement during times of struggle. This community served as a constant reminder that she was not alone in her journey and that God had placed people in her life to help her along the way.

Sarah's story serves as a powerful example of how self-discipline, intertwined with faith and community, can empower us to overcome obstacles and achieve our goals. It's a story of a young woman who transformed her life, not through dramatic upheaval, but through consistent, faithful action, guided by God's grace and fueled by a deep understanding of her own unique gifts and calling. It's a testimony to the power of quiet strength, a strength that blossoms in the service of others and in the faithful pursuit of God's will. It's a journey that continues to unfold, a testament to the enduring power of faith, resilience, and unwavering commitment to one's divine assignment. Her journey is a powerful reminder that even seemingly insurmountable challenges can be overcome through prayer, perseverance, and a deep trust in God's plan for our lives. The quiet strength she cultivated became the foundation upon which she built a life of purpose, fulfillment, and lasting peace.

Sarah's journey, while deeply personal, illuminated a critical element often overlooked in the pursuit of self-mastery: discernment. The ability to distinguish between wise and foolish choices, between paths leading to flourishing and those leading to destruction, proved as crucial as self-discipline in her transformation. Pastor Michael, recognizing this, gently guided Sarah toward cultivating this vital spiritual gift. He often spoke of discernment not as a mystical ability, but as a disciplined practice, honed through prayer, scripture, and wise counsel.

One evening, during a particularly challenging week where even her meticulously planned schedule felt overwhelming, Sarah confided in Pastor Michael about a new dilemma. Her younger brother, Mark, was facing a significant crossroads. He'd received an enticing job offer in a distant city, a lucrative opportunity that promised financial security but also meant leaving their aging parents largely alone. Mark, caught between his ambition and his familial responsibilities, was paralyzed by indecision. The family was deeply divided, with some urging Mark to seize the chance for advancement, others emphasizing his duty to support their parents in their twilight years. Sarah, amidst her own struggles, felt a growing sense of responsibility to help her family navigate this challenging situation.

Pastor Michael listened patiently, offering words of comfort and encouragement. He then gently guided the conversation towards the importance of discernment. "Sarah," he began, "this isn't just about making a career choice for Mark; it's about discerning God's will for your family. It's about seeking His wisdom in navigating a complex situation where there are no easy answers." He then shared a parable from the Bible, the story of the wise and foolish builders in Matthew 7:24-27. He explained how the wise builder, who diligently prepared a firm foundation, represented a life built on prayer, careful consideration, and a reliance on God's guidance. The foolish builder, who neglected these crucial elements, illustrated the danger of making decisions based solely on fleeting emotions or worldly ambitions.

"Discernment," Pastor Michael continued, "isn't about avoiding risks; it's about evaluating them prayerfully, seeking God's wisdom in each step. It's about listening to the still, small voice within, the voice of the Holy Spirit." He emphasized the importance of examining the motives behind Mark's desire for this new job. Was it driven by a genuine yearning for growth and fulfillment, or by a desire for worldly success and recognition? The same principles applied to the family's opposing viewpoints. Were their arguments rooted in love and concern for Mark and their parents, or driven by selfish desires and fears?

Pastor Michael suggested a family prayer meeting, a time dedicated to seeking God's guidance. He emphasized the importance of approaching the situation with humility, acknowledging their own limitations and biases. He encouraged them to study relevant scriptures, specifically passages that spoke of wisdom, faithfulness, and family responsibility. He advised them to spend time in quiet reflection, individually journaling their thoughts and feelings, and seeking clarity through prayer.

The family prayer meeting proved to be a pivotal moment. Initially, tensions were high, emotions raw. But as they began to pray together, something shifted. They began to listen to each other with greater empathy, acknowledging the validity of each other's concerns. They confessed their own biases and prejudices, humbly asking God for forgiveness and wisdom. They read aloud passages from Proverbs, seeking guidance in their decision-making.

Through prayer and scripture study, they discovered a shared concern for their parents' well-being. Mark realized the potential strain his absence could place upon them, not just physically but emotionally. The family, guided by God's Spirit, began to brainstorm alternative solutions. They explored the possibility of Mark working remotely, negotiating a more flexible schedule, or delaying the job offer until a more suitable time. This collaborative approach, guided by prayer and discernment, transformed a potentially divisive situation into an opportunity for deeper understanding and family unity.

The process, however, wasn't without its challenges. There were moments of doubt, disagreements, and setbacks. But through consistent prayer, honest communication, and a willingness to seek wise counsel, they navigated these hurdles. They learned to discern between impulsive actions and thoughtful responses, between fleeting emotions and enduring values. They discovered that true discernment wasn't about having all the answers upfront but about seeking God's guidance with humility and persistence.

Mark ultimately decided to postpone the job offer, choosing to remain closer to his family for a while longer. This wasn't a decision born out of fear or resignation, but a choice rooted in love, responsibility, and a clear understanding of his priorities. The experience drew the family closer, strengthening their bond and deepening their faith. It was a testament to the power of discernment, a gift cultivated through prayer, scripture, and wise counsel.

The process of discernment wasn't confined to the family crisis. Sarah applied these principles to her own life, increasingly aware of the subtle voices vying for her attention. She learned to discern between the genuine promptings of the Holy Spirit and the insidious whispers of self-doubt or worldly distractions. She became more discerning in choosing her friendships, recognizing the importance of surrounding herself with people who would encourage her spiritual growth and hold her accountable. She even became more discerning in her reading and media consumption, choosing sources that nurtured her faith rather than undermining it.

The path to discernment, like the path to self-mastery, is a lifelong journey, a process of continuous learning and refinement. It involves a constant striving to align our will with God's will, to make choices rooted in wisdom rather than impulse. It's a journey that requires patience, humility, and a willingness to seek guidance from trusted sources – mentors, spiritual advisors, and supportive communities. The reward, however, is a life lived with greater clarity, purpose, and peace. A life shaped not by the fickle winds of circumstance but by the steadfast hand of God. It's a life where quiet strength blossoms into a powerful expression of God's love and grace, a life that bears fruit for the glory of God. For Sarah, the quiet strength she discovered wasn't just about personal success; it was about cultivating the spiritual wisdom to discern God's will and live a life that truly reflected His purpose. And this discernment, more than anything else, became the bedrock of her ongoing journey of self-mastery.

The quiet strength Sarah had cultivated through discernment wasn't merely a shield against external pressures; it was also a powerful tool for navigating the turbulent waters of her own inner world. The next challenge, Pastor Michael recognized, lay not just in discerning God's will for others, but in conquering the unruly passions within herself. This was a far more personal battle, one that required a different kind of courage, a deeper level of self-awareness, and a willingness to confront uncomfortable truths.

Sarah had always been a driven individual, striving for perfection in every aspect of her life. This drive, while initially a source of strength, had become a relentless internal pressure cooker. It manifested in a relentless pursuit of achievement, a fear of failure that often paralyzed her, and a crippling perfectionism that left her perpetually exhausted. Beneath this veneer of control, however, lurked a deeper struggle – a tendency towards unhealthy coping mechanisms. She confessed to Pastor Michael a hidden battle with emotional eating, a pattern that escalated during periods of stress or self-doubt. Food, she admitted, had become a temporary solace, a way to numb the pain and silence the critical voice within.

Pastor Michael listened with compassion, offering words of understanding and encouragement. He acknowledged the complexity of her struggle, recognizing that it wasn't simply a matter of willpower, but a deeper issue rooted in emotional wounds and unmet needs. "Sarah," he said gently, "this is a journey that requires both spiritual and psychological healing. We need to address the root causes of your emotional eating, not just the symptoms." He recommended that she seek professional counseling, suggesting a therapist experienced in treating eating disorders and integrating faith-based principles into therapy.

This suggestion, at first, met with resistance. Sarah, accustomed to relying on her own strength and discipline, found the idea of seeking external help daunting. The vulnerability it required felt like a betrayal of her hard-won independence. Pastor Michael patiently addressed her concerns, emphasizing the importance of humility and acknowledging that seeking help wasn't a sign of weakness, but a testament to her strength and willingness to confront her struggles honestly. He reassured her that seeking professional help wasn't a rejection of her faith, but rather a complement to it – a way of utilizing all available resources in her pursuit of healing and wholeness.

The therapist Pastor Michael recommended was a woman named Dr. Emily Carter, a compassionate and insightful practitioner who skillfully blended psychological approaches with a deep understanding of Christian faith. Through therapy, Sarah began to explore the root causes of her emotional eating. She discovered that her relentless pursuit of perfection stemmed from a deep-seated insecurity, a fear of not being good enough. This insecurity had its roots in childhood experiences, subtle yet significant wounds that had shaped her self-perception and her coping mechanisms.

The therapy sessions weren't always easy. They often involved confronting painful memories and difficult emotions. But through Dr. Carter's guidance, Sarah learned to process these experiences in a healthy way, developing strategies for managing her emotions and challenging her negative self-talk. Dr. Carter helped her understand the connection between her thoughts, feelings, and behaviors, empowering her to make conscious choices rather than reacting impulsively to her emotions. She introduced Sarah to mindfulness techniques, teaching her to observe her thoughts and feelings without judgment, creating space between herself and her impulsive urges.

Mindfulness, Sarah discovered, was a powerful tool. It allowed her to become more aware of her triggers, recognizing the physical sensations and emotional cues that preceded episodes of emotional eating. This awareness provided her with a crucial window of opportunity, a moment to pause, breathe, and make a conscious choice rather than succumbing to impulse. Combined with regular prayer and Bible study, mindfulness became a spiritual practice, a way of connecting with God in the present moment and finding solace in His presence.

In addition to therapy and mindfulness, Sarah embraced other strategies to manage her emotions and desires. She began a daily practice of meditation, finding quiet moments throughout the day to center herself and connect with her inner peace. She explored different forms of exercise, finding activities she genuinely enjoyed – gentle yoga, long walks in nature, and even dancing. These activities helped her release pent-up energy, manage stress, and improve her overall well-being.

She also focused on cultivating healthy relationships. She sought out supportive friends and family members who encouraged her growth and held her accountable. She learned to set boundaries, saying no to situations or activities that might trigger her unhealthy eating patterns. She consciously cultivated gratitude, focusing on the positive aspects of her life, fostering a sense of contentment and appreciation.

The journey wasn't linear. There were setbacks, moments of weakness where old patterns resurfaced. But Sarah learned to view these setbacks not as failures, but as opportunities for growth and learning. With each challenge, she drew upon the resources she had cultivated – her faith, her therapy sessions, her mindfulness practice, and her supportive community. She learned to be kind to herself, recognizing that healing takes time and that progress is often incremental rather than dramatic.

Slowly, steadily, Sarah began to experience a transformation. The relentless drive for perfection began to ease, replaced by a more balanced approach to life. The fear of failure lessened, replaced by a sense of self-acceptance and self-compassion. The emotional eating subsided, replaced by healthier ways of coping with stress and managing emotions.

She developed a deeper understanding of the interconnectedness of her spiritual, emotional, and physical well-being. She realized that conquering unruly passions wasn't about suppressing her emotions or denying her desires, but about managing them in a healthy and God-honoring way. It was about integrating faith and psychology, using both spiritual and psychological tools to create a life characterized by wholeness, balance, and peace. The quiet strength she had discovered through discernment now blossomed into a profound inner peace, a resilience that enabled her to navigate life's challenges with grace and courage. It was a testament to the power of self-mastery, a journey fueled by faith, guided by wisdom, and sustained by the unwavering love and grace of God. It was a journey that transformed her from a woman driven by inner turmoil to a woman empowered by God's love, a woman who found true strength not in relentless striving, but in the quiet, unwavering peace of a life surrendered to His will. And in that surrender, she found not just self-mastery, but a deeper understanding of God's love and the incredible capacity for healing that exists within the human heart, a healing that extends far beyond the individual, transforming relationships and leaving a ripple effect of grace in its wake. This journey of healing became a testament to the transformative power of faith, the enduring resilience of the human spirit, and the boundless grace of God.

Sarah's journey toward self-mastery wasn't solely about conquering her emotional eating; it was a holistic process encompassing every facet of her life. Dr. Carter, astutely recognizing this, introduced the crucial concept of boundaries. "Sarah," she explained one day, "your relentless pursuit of perfection often stems from a fear of disappointing others, a fear that prevents you from saying no." This resonated deeply with Sarah. She had always prioritized the needs of others, often neglecting her own well-being in the process. She'd found herself overcommitted to church activities, volunteer work, and even social engagements, leaving herself perpetually drained and vulnerable to emotional eating as a coping mechanism.

Dr. Carter used the analogy of a garden. "Imagine your life as a garden," she said. "You have limited time, energy, and resources. If you plant too many seeds, overcrowd the space, and neglect the soil, nothing will thrive. Similarly, if you overcommit yourself without setting boundaries, you'll inevitably burn out." This resonated profoundly with Sarah. She had been so busy tending to the needs of everyone else that she'd neglected the essential nourishment her own soul required.

The Bible, Dr. Carter pointed out, is full of examples of setting boundaries. Jesus himself, despite his tireless ministry, frequently withdrew to quiet places for prayer and solitude. He understood the importance of rest and rejuvenation. He knew his limitations and respected them. He prioritized his relationship with God, recognizing that it was the foundation upon which all else rested. This resonated deeply with Sarah, who often felt guilty about taking time for herself.

Dr. Carter helped Sarah identify specific areas where she needed to set stronger boundaries. One example was her involvement in the church's women's ministry. While she deeply valued her role and the relationships she had built, she realized that she was consistently overextending herself. She had taken on the responsibility of coordinating various events, managing the group's finances, and often offering personal counsel to members, often late into the night. This left her feeling overwhelmed, resentful, and exhausted.

Dr. Carter gently suggested that Sarah delegate some of her responsibilities and learn to say no to additional requests. This was incredibly difficult for Sarah initially. She felt guilty about letting others down, afraid of appearing selfish or incapable. But Dr. Carter helped her reframe her perspective. "Saying no to one commitment," she explained, "allows you to say yes with greater intention and energy to the things that truly matter – both to yourself and to God."

Sarah started small. She politely declined a request to coordinate the upcoming church fundraiser, explaining that she needed to prioritize her well-being. To her surprise, the other women in the ministry understood and readily stepped up to share the responsibility. It was a liberating experience. She realized that she wasn't indispensable, and that others were capable of handling things without her.

This newfound freedom extended to other areas of her life. She began to protect her personal time, setting aside specific hours each day for prayer, meditation, and simply being alone with her thoughts. She established routines that prioritized her physical and emotional well-being, such as regular exercise and healthy meals. She consciously limited her social engagements, saying no to invitations that left her feeling drained or stressed.

Setting boundaries wasn't always easy. There were moments of resistance, times when she felt the pull to revert to her old patterns of overcommitment. But each time, she reminded herself of the importance of self-care and the lessons she had learned. She also found great support in her faith community. The women in her church ministry not only understood her struggle but also celebrated her progress. They held her accountable, gently reminding her when she started to overextend herself.

The concept of Sabbath also gained a new significance for Sarah. She began to view the Sabbath not merely as a day of rest, but as a sacred boundary, a time specifically set aside to honor God and to replenish her own soul. It became a time for prayer, meditation, spiritual reflection, and relaxation – a refuge from the demands of everyday life.

This deliberate practice of setting boundaries resulted in a remarkable transformation in Sarah's life. She felt more balanced, less stressed, and more fulfilled. Her relationships became more meaningful, as she was able to engage with people with greater presence and intention. The constant feeling of overwhelm dissipated, replaced by a sense of peace and calm. Her emotional eating significantly subsided as she learned healthier ways of managing stress and self-soothing.

The key, she discovered, was not to eliminate all commitments, but to choose them wisely and intentionally. It was about prioritizing her well-being, recognizing that she couldn't pour from an empty cup. It was about understanding that setting boundaries wasn't selfish, but an act of self-love and an essential part of living a life pleasing to God. She found support in Proverbs 16:3: "Commit your work to the Lord, and your plans will be established." She learned to carefully discern which tasks and commitments were truly in alignment with God's purpose for her life and to let go of those that were not.

Sarah began to apply the principle of boundaries to her professional life as well. She learned to politely but firmly decline requests that encroached on her personal time or exceeded her capabilities. She learned to delegate tasks effectively, trusting others to do their part. She also created clear expectations for her work, setting boundaries to prevent burnout and maintain a healthy work-life balance. This allowed her to excel in her work while protecting her emotional and physical well-being.

She started to realize that setting boundaries was a continuous process, not a one-time event. It required ongoing vigilance and self-awareness. But the rewards far outweighed the effort. The peace and joy she experienced as a result of setting healthy boundaries was immeasurable.

Sarah's transformation serves as a powerful testament to the importance of boundaries, not just in personal relationships but in every aspect of life. It's a reminder that self-care is not selfish; it's a spiritual necessity. It's a recognition that we are not meant to carry the weight of the world on our shoulders. It's a pathway to a more balanced, fulfilling, and God-honoring life. It is a demonstration of the quiet strength that comes from embracing self-mastery, not through relentless striving, but through the gentle art of saying "no" and prioritizing what truly matters. The journey of self-mastery, Sarah learned, is not a solo endeavor. It's a journey undertaken with God's guidance, supported by a loving community, and fueled by a deeper understanding of self and a commitment to living a life of purpose and peace. The serenity she found wasn't simply an absence of turmoil but a conscious choice, a testament to the power of boundaries and the transformative grace of God. This quiet strength, this gentle self-assertion, became the foundation upon which she built a life of genuine wholeness, a life lived in harmony with God's plan and her own true self. Her journey highlights that true strength isn't found in superhuman effort but in the wise cultivation of boundaries, leading to a life of both profound personal peace and impactful service to others. It's a profound lesson that echoes throughout scripture and resonates in the hearts of all those who seek a life of authentic self-mastery, guided by faith and sustained by grace.

The quiet strength Sarah cultivated through setting boundaries didn't shield her from the complexities of community life. Her newfound peace was occasionally tested, particularly by the insidious undercurrents of gossip and meddling that, like weeds, threatened to choke the flourishing garden of her soul. Living in a close-knit church community, she witnessed firsthand the destructive power of idle words and intrusive actions.

One Sunday afternoon, after a particularly fulfilling service filled with uplifting hymns and a powerful sermon on forgiveness, a storm of whispers erupted in the church hallway. It started subtly, a hushed exchange between two women, their faces close, their voices low. But like a ripple in a pond, the whispers spread, widening into a torrent of speculation and judgment. The subject? Martha, a young single mother struggling to make ends meet while raising two young children.

Initially, Sarah remained distant, choosing to remain silent amidst the swirling rumours. She had learned the value of quiet observation, understanding that often, the truth reveals itself in time. She had also learned to protect her own heart, refusing to engage in conversations that felt toxic or judgmental. She knew that gossip was a poison, slowly eroding trust and fracturing relationships. Proverbs 11:13, "A gossip betrays confidences, but a trustworthy person keeps a secret," resonated deeply within her. She saw the truth of this proverb unfolding before her eyes. The whispers were betraying Martha's confidence, shattering the trust within the community.

However, the whispers escalated. The initial concerns about Martha's financial struggles transformed into accusations of irresponsibility and moral failings. The murmurs turned into outright pronouncements, laced with condemnation and harsh judgment. Sarah felt a growing unease. She recalled the parable of the wheat and the tares (Matthew 13:24-30), where Jesus cautioned against prematurely judging others. Martha, she knew, was struggling, and rather than extending compassion and support, her fellow church members were tearing her down with their words.

One evening, during a women's fellowship group, the gossip reached a fever pitch. Several women were openly discussing Martha, their comments ranging from speculation about her personal life to harsh criticism of her parenting skills. Sarah felt a wave of sadness wash over her. She felt a deep sense of responsibility to intervene, remembering James 3:5-6, which speaks to the power of the tongue to both build up and tear down. Her silence now felt like complicity in Martha's suffering. She knew she could no longer remain passive.

Taking a deep breath, Sarah spoke up. Her voice was calm but firm. "Sisters," she began, "I've been listening to this conversation, and it grieves my heart. We are called to love one another, to support each other, especially those who are struggling. Martha is facing challenges, yes, but she is also a child of God, deserving of our compassion and grace, not our judgment."

Her words hung in the air, breaking the flow of gossip. A heavy silence settled over the room. Some women looked ashamed, their faces flushed with guilt. Others remained defensive, unwilling to relinquish their judgments. Sarah continued, drawing on the teachings of Jesus, who consistently emphasized forgiveness and compassion. She reminded them of the parable of the prodigal son, highlighting God's boundless love and forgiveness even in the face of great mistakes. She spoke of the importance of bearing each other's burdens (Galatians 6:2), and how gossip is the opposite of bearing burdens—it adds weight to the already struggling.

The conversation shifted. Some women apologized for their part in spreading the rumors. Others remained hesitant, but the tone of the discussion had changed. Sarah's intervention, rooted in biblical principles and infused with genuine compassion, had begun to heal the wounds inflicted by gossip. She explained that while it's important to address concerns, it should always be done with love, care, and a desire to help, rather than to condemn.

The following Sunday, Sarah approached Martha after the service. She expressed her sorrow for the hurtful gossip and offered her support. Martha, visibly relieved, shared her struggles with Sarah, acknowledging her financial difficulties but also expressing her determination to overcome them. Sarah's act of kindness and empathy became a catalyst for healing within the community.

The incident served as a powerful lesson for Sarah and the entire congregation. It highlighted the destructive consequences of gossip and meddling, revealing how these actions damage relationships, hinder spiritual growth, and violate the principles of Christian love. It also underscored the importance of confronting such behavior with grace and truth, and the transformative power of sincere repentance and forgiveness.

The experience deepened Sarah's understanding of the wisdom of silence, not as passive avoidance but as a strategic tool for discernment and self-preservation. She learned that silence could be a powerful act of resistance against negativity, a refuge from the noise of judgment, and a space for cultivating inner peace. It became a sanctuary where she could listen to the voice of God, discern His will, and respond with love, compassion, and wisdom.

The incident with Martha also highlighted the importance of boundaries in community life. Sarah realized that setting boundaries wasn't just about protecting her own emotional well-being, but also about protecting the well-being of others. By choosing to speak up, she set a boundary against gossip, a boundary that protected Martha from further harm.

Over time, the gossip subsided, replaced by a renewed commitment to kindness, compassion, and understanding. Martha's situation improved, not just financially, but also spiritually and emotionally, thanks to the support and encouragement she received from the church community, once they had repented of their gossip. The incident reminded the entire church community that every individual is worthy of respect and compassion. It emphasized that we are called to be a community that builds up and encourages one another, rather than tearing each other down.

The journey toward spiritual maturity, Sarah learned, wasn't a solitary pursuit but a communal one. It involved setting boundaries, choosing silence wisely, and engaging in difficult conversations with grace and truth. It was a journey marked by both personal growth and the cultivation of healthier relationships within the context of a supportive, faith-based community. This journey underscored the profound interconnection between self-care, community well-being, and spiritual growth, all grounded in the timeless wisdom of Scripture. It was a journey, not without its challenges, but one that ultimately led to a deeper sense of peace, fulfillment, and a stronger connection with God and with others. The serenity she had discovered through setting personal boundaries extended to the wider context of her community life, enriching her relationships and fostering a more loving and supportive environment for everyone. It was a testament to the power of intentional living, guided by faith and fuelled by love.

The quiet strength Sarah had cultivated, born from setting healthy boundaries, extended beyond her personal life. It became a bulwark against the insidious erosion of trust that threatened to unravel the fabric of her close-knit church community. She'd learned the hard way that not every confidence shared was treated with the sacredness it deserved. The wisdom of silence, once a tool for self-preservation, now became a vital element in safeguarding not only her own heart but also the hearts of others.

This understanding grew from a painful experience, a sharp lesson in the perils of misplaced trust. She recalled a man from her small town, David, a man known for his generosity and unwavering faith. David, a pillar of the community, had confided in a close friend, Elias, about a deeply personal struggle – a family crisis that threatened to tear his world apart. Elias, outwardly a man of strong faith, had promised discretion, the unspoken covenant of brotherhood binding them together. He swore to keep David's secret safe, a promise made under the watchful gaze of their shared faith.

But Elias's promise proved as fragile as a winter's ice. Within weeks, the whispers began. They started subtly, like the rustling of leaves in a gentle breeze – a vague rumour here, a hushed aside there. But soon, the whispers escalated into a torrent of speculation, twisting David's private pain into a public spectacle. His family crisis, once a private burden, became the subject of community gossip, distorted and magnified with each retelling.

The betrayal ran deeper than simple gossip. It was a violation of trust, a shattering of the sacred bond of friendship. David, already grappling with immense emotional turmoil, found himself burdened by the added weight of public shame and judgment. The very community he'd served faithfully for years turned on him, their whispers laced with unwarranted speculation and harsh judgment.

Sarah witnessed this unfolding tragedy with a growing sense of sorrow and unease. She saw the stark contrast between Elias's outward piety and his callous disregard for the sanctity of trust. The event served as a stark reminder of the parable of the wicked servant (Matthew 24:45-51) – how those entrusted with responsibility and knowledge can misuse it, inflicting deep wounds upon others. David's story became a cautionary tale, etched deeply in Sarah's heart.

This incident illuminated a crucial aspect of guarding one's heart: the careful selection of confidants. Not everyone who claims friendship possesses the wisdom and discretion to handle sensitive information. The proverb, "He who trusts in his own heart is a fool, but he who walks wisely will be delivered" (Proverbs 28:26), resonated deeply with Sarah. She realised that wisdom wasn't about withholding all secrets, but about discerning who was worthy of carrying the burden of another's vulnerability.

Proverbs 16:23 further clarified the importance of discernment: "The heart of the wise makes his speech judicious, and his lips promote learning." This isn't about being silent at all costs, but about choosing when and how to speak. It is about knowing that some things are best left unsaid, particularly to those who lack the maturity, empathy, or discretion to handle them responsibly.

The need for discernment wasn't limited to close friends; it extended to all relationships. Sarah realized that even within the church community, not every individual possessed the integrity to protect confidential information. Some were prone to gossip, others driven by a thirst for drama, and still others simply lacked the capacity for empathy and understanding. Choosing wisely about whom to confide in, therefore, became a vital aspect of spiritual protection.

The story of David and Elias also highlighted the insidious nature of gossip. Sarah reflected on the damage caused by loose tongues, the way seemingly innocent whispers can escalate into devastating accusations, destroying reputations and fracturing relationships. The power of words, both to build up and tear down, became increasingly clear to her. She saw how easily rumours could distort the truth, transforming a crisis into a character flaw, a private struggle into a public spectacle.

She recalled the words of James 3:5-6: "Likewise the tongue is a small part of the body, but it boasts great things. Consider what a great forest is set on fire by a small spark. The tongue also is a fire, a world of evil among the parts of the body. It corrupts the whole body, sets the whole course of one's life on fire, and is itself set on fire by hell." The imagery of fire, she realized, vividly captured the destructive potential of careless speech and gossip.

The experience led Sarah to develop a heightened awareness of her own communication style. She became more intentional in her speech, choosing her words carefully, considering the impact they might have on others. She practiced listening more than speaking, letting empathy guide her interactions. She learned to recognize the early signs of gossip and to gently redirect conversations towards more constructive paths.

The lesson extended beyond mere silence. It was about proactive love. It was about choosing to speak words of encouragement, offering support instead of judgment. It was about confronting harmful gossip with truth and grace, as she had done with the women discussing Martha.

In the wake of David's ordeal, Sarah became a champion of discretion. She shared his story with others, not to condemn Elias, but to caution them against the dangers of misplaced trust and the destructive nature of gossip. She emphasized the importance of guarding their hearts and choosing their confidants wisely, recognizing that some secrets, particularly those bearing the weight of personal struggles, should be shared only with those who possess the maturity, empathy, and discretion to handle them with the utmost care and respect. She stressed the spiritual implications of betraying confidence, reminding them that true friendship involves fidelity, loyalty, and a deep commitment to protecting the vulnerable.

Sarah's journey taught her that the wisdom of silence was not about isolation or fear, but about careful discernment and responsible stewardship of another's heart. It was a profound lesson in self-preservation and in the cultivation of truly meaningful relationships built on a foundation of trust, respect, and mutual care. It was about safeguarding not only her own heart but also the hearts of others, a lesson woven into the very fabric of her faith and her life. It was a journey of learning, growing, and becoming a more compassionate and discerning steward of her own words and the confidences of others.

The aftermath of David's ordeal left a profound mark on Sarah, shaping not only her understanding of silence but also her approach to communication. She realized that true wisdom wasn't merely about choosing when to remain silent; it was equally, if not more importantly, about the art of listening. Silence, she now understood, was a powerful tool, but it was only one piece of the puzzle. Active, empathetic listening was the other, equally crucial component.

Her newfound appreciation for listening stemmed from witnessing the devastating consequences of inattentive hearing. In David's case, Elias's failure to truly listen to his friend's pain had led to a tragic breach of trust and a profound wounding of the community. Elias, caught up in his own perspectives and perhaps even fueled by a desire for drama, had failed to grasp the depth of David's suffering. He'd heard the words, but he hadn't listened to the heart behind them.

Sarah began to see active listening not as a passive activity, but as a powerful act of love. It was a way of showing others that their feelings and experiences mattered, that they were truly seen and heard. This understanding resonated deeply with her faith, reminding her of the parable of the Good Samaritan (Luke 10:25-37), where compassion is expressed not through words alone, but through attentive care and selfless action. Listening, she realized, was a vital part of that compassionate response.

To illustrate the transformative power of attentive listening, Sarah often recounted the story of two close friends within her congregation, Martha and Esther. Martha, a woman known for her strong opinions and forthright manner, had clashed with Esther, a more reserved and introspective individual. Their conflict stemmed from a misunderstanding over a church event, escalating into a bitter disagreement that threatened to fracture their long-standing friendship.

The tension between Martha and Esther had become palpable, a silent chasm dividing two women who had once shared a deep bond. Sarah, sensing the rift, approached them separately, offering her support and suggesting they engage in a facilitated conversation. She emphasized the importance of listening, not just to respond, but to truly understand the other's perspective.

Their initial meeting was fraught with tension. Both women initially clung to their positions, each convinced of the righteousness of their own views. But Sarah gently guided them toward a different path. She encouraged them to take turns speaking, with the other attentively listening without interruption. She reminded them of the biblical principle of "be quick to listen, slow to speak, and slow to anger" (James 1:19).

As Martha began to speak, sharing her feelings of frustration and hurt, Sarah noticed a subtle shift in Esther's demeanor. Her initial defensiveness began to melt away as she listened intently, not just to Martha's words, but to the emotion behind them. She saw the pain in Martha's eyes, the vulnerability in her voice. For the first time, Esther truly heard Martha, not as an opponent in a conflict, but as a friend in distress.

Similarly, as Esther shared her perspective, Martha listened with newfound empathy. She heard the fear and insecurity that lay beneath Esther's quiet demeanor. She understood that Esther's actions hadn't been born of malice, but of a different understanding of the situation. The initial clash of personalities dissolved as each woman listened to the other's heart.

The conversation wasn't without its moments of emotional intensity. There were tears, apologies, and a shared recognition of their respective roles in the misunderstanding. But through it all, active listening served as a bridge, connecting two hearts that had been drifting apart. The power of attentive hearing transcended the mere exchange of words, forging a deeper bond between them than before. They realized that their conflict hadn't been caused by irreconcilable differences, but by a failure to truly listen to one another.

Sarah highlighted several key elements of active listening that helped Martha and Esther find resolution. First, she stressed the importance of

empathetic listening, the ability to understand and share the feelings of another person. This involves not only hearing the words being spoken, but also paying attention to body language, tone of voice, and emotional cues. It requires setting aside one's own biases and perspectives and stepping into the other person's shoes. This echoed the Golden Rule, to treat others as you would want to be treated.

Secondly, Sarah emphasized the need for

uninterrupted listening. She encouraged Martha and Esther to take turns speaking without interruption, ensuring each felt heard and validated. This act of giving one's full attention demonstrated respect and created a safe space for vulnerability. Interruptions, even well-intentioned ones, can derail the listening process and undermine the speaker's trust.

Thirdly, Sarah promoted

reflective listening, where the listener paraphrases or summarizes what the speaker has said to ensure understanding. This clarifies points, avoids misunderstandings and shows the speaker that they are being heard correctly. It also gives the speaker an opportunity to clarify their thoughts and feelings.

Finally, Sarah stressed the importance of

non-judgmental listening. This involves avoiding interruptions, criticisms, or unsolicited advice. It calls for a commitment to hear the speaker without trying to change their mind or impose one's own opinions. This aspect aligns with biblical teachings on forgiveness and compassion, fostering an environment of acceptance rather than judgment.

The story of Martha and Esther became a powerful illustration of the transformative power of active listening within the community. It highlighted how attentive listening could not only resolve conflicts but also deepen relationships, fostering mutual understanding, empathy, and forgiveness. It underscored the fact that active listening is a way of showing love in action. It's about being present, both physically and emotionally, to listen not just to words but to the heart of the speaker.

Sarah's experience with Martha and Esther cemented her understanding of the art of listening as a crucial aspect of both personal growth and spiritual development. It reinforced her belief that effective communication is not just about what we say, but also how we listen. By actively listening to others, we demonstrate love, build trust, and create a space for genuine connection. This isn't merely a communication skill; it is a spiritual discipline, a form of service to God and neighbor. Her experiences, shaped by the wisdom of silence and the art of listening, became a beacon guiding her own life and the lives of those around her. She continued to share these lessons, weaving them into her sermons, her counseling sessions, and her daily interactions, transforming a quiet strength into a vibrant testament to the power of empathetic engagement. She learned that silence, combined with truly attentive listening, could heal wounds, mend broken relationships, and build a community grounded in love and understanding.

The gentle hum of conversation filled the small, warmly lit room. Sarah, surrounded by the familiar scent of old books and brewing coffee, observed the faces gathered in her weekly support group. Tonight's theme: forgiveness. The weight of the word hung heavy in the air, a palpable tension interwoven with the quiet hope that flickered in each person's eyes.

"Forgiveness," she began softly, her voice carrying the quiet authority that came from years of pastoral care and a deep understanding of the human heart, "is not about condoning wrongdoing. It's not about forgetting the hurt. It's about releasing the burden we carry when we refuse to let go of anger, resentment, or pain."

A woman named Emily, her face etched with weariness, spoke first. "I struggle with that," she confessed, her voice trembling slightly. "My sister, she... she stole from me. Not a small amount either. Years of savings, gone. And she hasn't even apologized."

Sarah nodded, her expression empathetic. "The betrayal is immense, Emily. The violation of trust, the financial hardship...it's understandable that you're struggling to forgive." She paused, giving Emily space to process her emotions. "But I want you to consider this: Holding onto that anger, that resentment, it's like carrying a heavy stone in your heart. It weighs you down, prevents you from moving forward, from experiencing the joy and peace God offers."

She shared a passage from Matthew 6:14-15: "For if you forgive other people when they sin against you, your heavenly Father will also forgive you. But if you do not forgive others their sins, your Father will not forgive your sins." The words hung in the silence, a powerful reminder of the interconnectedness of forgiveness—both human and divine.

"Forgiveness isn't just for the other person," Sarah continued. "It's also for you. It's about setting yourself free from the prison of bitterness. Imagine that stone, Emily. How much easier would your life be if you could lay it down? It doesn't mean you forget what happened. It means you choose to release the power it has over you."

Another member, a man named Daniel, chimed in. His voice was quiet, almost hesitant. "I've been trying to forgive myself. I made a terrible mistake years ago, a decision that hurt someone I loved deeply. Even though they've forgiven me, I can't seem to forgive myself."

Sarah's gaze was gentle, her voice soothing. "Self-forgiveness is often the hardest kind, Daniel. We are so quick to judge ourselves, more harshly than we would ever judge another. Remember that God's love is unconditional. He sees your repentance, your remorse. His grace is sufficient, even when we stumble."

She spoke of the parable of the Prodigal Son (Luke 15:11-32), highlighting the father's unwavering love and forgiveness despite the son's egregious actions. "God's forgiveness isn't based on our merit, but on His boundless grace. We must extend that same grace to ourselves."

The conversation flowed, each individual sharing their unique struggles and triumphs. A young woman named Jessica spoke of forgiving a parent for years of emotional neglect. An elderly gentleman, Thomas, shared his journey of forgiving a former business partner who had cheated him out of his life's savings. Each story was different, yet each echoed the universal struggle with forgiveness and the profound transformation that comes from releasing the weight of unforgiveness.

Sarah guided the discussion, weaving in biblical principles and practical strategies for practicing forgiveness. She emphasized the importance of prayer, seeking God's guidance and strength. She also highlighted the value of journaling, allowing emotions to flow freely onto paper as a way of processing hurt and anger. The concept of writing a "forgiveness letter," not necessarily to be sent, but as a tool for personal catharsis, was also explored.

"Sometimes," Sarah said, "forgiveness is a process, not a single event. It's a journey, not a destination. There will be moments of doubt, moments of anger, moments when the pain resurfaces. That's okay. Acknowledge those feelings, but don't let them define you. Keep moving forward, one step at a time."

She encouraged the group to practice empathy, to try and understand the perspective of the person who hurt them, even if it didn't excuse their actions. "Understanding doesn't equate to condoning. It simply means seeking to see the situation from a different angle. Perhaps they were hurting, too, struggling with their own demons. That doesn't diminish your pain, but it can help you to release some of the bitterness."

Sarah also stressed the importance of seeking professional help when needed. "Forgiveness is a deeply personal and sometimes challenging process. Don't hesitate to reach out to a therapist or counselor if you need support."

As the evening drew to a close, a sense of peace settled over the room. The weight of the initial tension had lifted, replaced by a quiet strength and a shared understanding. They had shared vulnerabilities, offered support, and found comfort in the collective journey of healing and forgiveness.

Sarah concluded the session with a prayer, asking for God's grace and guidance in their ongoing journey of forgiveness. She emphasized that forgiveness isn't a sign of weakness, but a testament to the power of love, a reflection of God's own boundless mercy. It is a journey of releasing the past, embracing the present, and stepping into a future free from the chains of unforgiveness. A future where hearts, once wounded, could finally find healing and peace. The silence that followed the prayer was not empty, but full of a quiet understanding, a shared hope for a future unburdened by the weight of the past. A future where forgiveness, both of others and of self, could become the foundation of a life lived in grace and freedom. A future where the transformative power of God's love could truly flourish.

The quiet hum of the support group's afterglow lingered as Sarah, alone in her study, reflected on the evening's discussion. The theme of forgiveness had resonated deeply, but a subtle undercurrent of judgment, often self-inflicted, remained. This, she realised, was a crucial aspect of true healing and freedom – breaking the cycle of judgment. It was a battle fought not only against others' harsh criticisms but, more often, against the relentless inner critic that whispered doubts and condemnation.

She recalled a particular conversation from years ago, a story that had shaped her understanding of this insidious cycle. A close friend, Martha, had confided in her about a strained relationship with her daughter, Clara. Clara, a talented artist, had chosen a path that clashed dramatically with Martha's traditional values. Martha, despite her outward expressions of love, struggled with silent disapproval, a subtle judgment that poisoned their interactions. The judgment wasn't overt; it was woven into the fabric of their conversations, in the unspoken expectations, the subtle sighs, and the missed opportunities for genuine connection.

Sarah had gently guided Martha towards self-reflection, encouraging her to examine the root of her judgment. Was it fear for Clara's future? Disappointment that Clara wasn't following the path Martha had envisioned? Or perhaps a deeper insecurity about her own choices and life path? As Martha explored these questions, the weight of her judgment began to lift, replaced by a burgeoning empathy and understanding.

The cycle of judgment, Sarah realised, often begins with a perceived threat to our own beliefs or self-image. We judge others because it makes us feel superior, safer, or more in control. It's a defensive mechanism, a way of protecting ourselves from perceived vulnerabilities. But in reality, it creates a barrier, isolating us from genuine connection and hindering our ability to experience true joy and peace. It's a subtle form of self-protection, but it builds walls rather than bridges.

Imagine a ripple effect. Martha's judgment of Clara created a distance, a chasm between mother and daughter. This distance, in turn, fueled Martha's own self-doubt and insecurity, deepening the cycle. The judgment wasn't just harming Clara; it was slowly eroding Martha's own well-being. This insidious pattern is replicated countless times in our lives, affecting relationships, communities, and even our relationship with God.

Breaking this cycle demands a conscious effort, a willingness to step outside of our self-centered perspective and embrace empathy and compassion. It requires a deep dive into self-awareness, confronting the root causes of our judgments – our insecurities, fears, and prejudices. This often involves difficult introspection, acknowledging our own flaws and imperfections, and recognizing that others are navigating their own struggles, just as we are.

One of the most effective tools in breaking the cycle of judgment is the practice of active listening – truly hearing and understanding another person's perspective without interruption or judgment. It's about putting aside our own opinions and biases, and creating a safe space where others can share their thoughts and feelings without fear of condemnation. Active listening not only fosters deeper connections but also reveals the humanity behind the actions we may initially judge harshly.

Consider the parable of the Good Samaritan. The priest and Levite, both religious leaders, saw the injured man and passed him by. They judged the situation as too dangerous, too messy, too inconvenient. But the Samaritan, a member of a despised group, disregarded societal prejudices and extended compassion and aid. He didn't judge; he acted. His actions broke the cycle of indifference and judgment, offering a powerful example of unconditional love.

Furthermore, extending grace to ourselves is just as critical. We often hold ourselves to impossibly high standards, constantly judging our shortcomings and failures. This inner critic can be relentless, whispering doubts and undermining our self-worth. But God's grace is boundless, a gift freely offered, not earned. Just as we extend grace to others, we must extend it to ourselves, acknowledging our flaws without letting them define us. This is not self-indulgence; it's self-compassion, a recognition of our inherent worthiness of love and forgiveness.

Practicing forgiveness, as discussed earlier, is intertwined with breaking the cycle of judgment. Forgiveness is not condoning harmful actions; it's about releasing the burden of resentment and anger that fuels judgment. It's about choosing to let go of the need to control or punish, and instead, to focus on healing and moving forward. Forgiveness, both of others and of ourselves, sets us free from the chains of bitterness and allows for genuine connection and peace.

Consider a scenario: Imagine a workplace dispute. Two colleagues, Mark and Lisa, are embroiled in a conflict fueled by miscommunication and differing opinions. Mark perceives Lisa as incompetent and lazy, while Lisa views Mark as arrogant and dismissive. Their judgments create a hostile environment, hindering productivity and affecting team morale. By practicing active listening, they could discover the root of their misunderstandings. Perhaps Mark is overwhelmed and feeling pressured, projecting his stress onto Lisa. Perhaps Lisa feels undervalued and unheard, leading her to appear less engaged. Understanding these underlying issues allows for empathy and compassion to emerge, breaking the cycle of judgment and paving the way for productive collaboration.

Beyond individual relationships, the cycle of judgment extends to societal levels. We often judge entire groups of people based on stereotypes and prejudices, failing to see the individuals within those groups. This collective judgment fosters division, discrimination, and injustice. Breaking this cycle requires a commitment to education, critical thinking, and seeking diverse perspectives. It involves actively challenging our own biases and preconceived notions, and striving for a more inclusive and just society.

Journaling can be a powerful tool for self-reflection. Writing down our judgments, exploring their root causes, and examining our reactions can be profoundly illuminating. It allows us to identify recurring patterns of judgment and to develop strategies for responding differently. It's a process of unpacking the emotional baggage that fuels our judgmental attitudes.

Prayer, too, plays a crucial role. Through prayer, we connect with God, seeking guidance, strength, and wisdom to navigate the challenges of breaking the cycle of judgment. We can ask God to help us cultivate empathy, compassion, and forgiveness – for ourselves and for others. Prayer provides a space for self-reflection and a source of strength in facing our own judgments and those of others.

In conclusion, breaking the cycle of judgment is a lifelong journey that demands conscious effort, self-awareness, and a commitment to empathy and compassion. It's not a quick fix but a process of transformation, requiring ongoing work on our attitudes, behaviors, and inner critic. By actively practicing active listening, extending grace, embracing forgiveness, and seeking guidance through prayer and journaling, we can dismantle the walls of judgment and build bridges of understanding, compassion, and peace, both within ourselves and in our relationships with others. This is the pathway to true freedom – freedom from the burden of judgment and the limitations it imposes, a freedom found in the boundless love and grace of God. A freedom that allows us to embrace the inherent worth of every human being, ourselves included.

The quiet hum of forgiveness lingered in Sarah's mind, a gentle counterpoint to the persistent thrum of self-judgment. She understood now that true healing wasn't just about forgiving others; it was about extending that same grace to herself, a process intricately woven with the tapestry of healthy relationships. The support group had illuminated this, highlighting the crucial role of trustworthy friendships in navigating life's complexities. But how did one identify these true friends, these anchors in the storms of life?

The answer, Sarah mused, wasn't a simple checklist, but rather a nuanced understanding of what constitutes genuine connection. It wasn't about the number of friends one had, but the quality of the relationships. Superficial friendships, often plentiful in the early years, were like fleeting summer butterflies – vibrant, attractive, but ultimately ephemeral. True friendships, on the other hand, were like sturdy oak trees, weathering the fiercest storms, their roots digging deep into the soil of mutual respect, unwavering support, and honest accountability.

Sarah recalled her college days, a whirlwind of new faces and fleeting connections. She had surrounded herself with a vibrant group, always laughing, always busy, always on the go. These friends filled her social calendar, but they left an emptiness in her heart. Their conversations were shallow, focused on trivial matters – the latest fashion trends, upcoming parties, gossip about others. They offered little in the way of genuine support or understanding. When Sarah faced personal challenges – a family crisis, academic struggles – their empathy felt thin, their offers of help fleeting. They were present for the celebrations, but absent during the struggles.

One particular incident stood out. During a difficult breakup, she had reached out to several of these "friends," seeking solace and understanding. Their responses were dismissive, peppered with clichés and unsolicited advice that felt judgmental and uncaring. Their focus wasn't on her pain; it was on how her situation might impact their own lives, their carefully constructed social circles. This experience became a pivotal moment for Sarah, a harsh but necessary lesson in discerning true friendship.

True friendship, she realized, was defined not by constant presence or boisterous laughter, but by unwavering support during times of adversity. It was about the quiet acts of kindness, the listening ear, the shoulder to cry on, the hand extended in times of need. It was about a mutual understanding, a shared journey through life's joys and sorrows. It was about accountability, the willingness to offer constructive criticism and honest feedback, even when it was uncomfortable. It was about empathy, the ability to understand and share the feelings of another.

In contrast to her college friendships, Sarah now cherished a small circle of close friends – women who had walked alongside her through thick and thin. These friendships were not always easy; they were marked by disagreements, misunderstandings, and occasional hurts. But these challenges were navigated with honesty, respect, and a commitment to reconciliation. They were friendships built on a foundation of trust, where vulnerability was embraced, not exploited. These friends celebrated her successes, comforted her in her grief, and challenged her to grow. They held her accountable, gently guiding her back onto the right path when she strayed. They offered unwavering support, even when she made mistakes, believing in her inherent goodness even when she doubted herself.

She thought of Emily, a friend since childhood. Their friendship had weathered countless storms, from teenage heartbreak to career setbacks, from family conflicts to personal struggles with faith. Emily had never judged Sarah's choices, even when they differed from her own. She had offered unwavering support, a listening ear, and practical help when needed. Their friendship wasn't characterized by dramatic displays of affection, but by a quiet, consistent presence, a steadfast loyalty that transcended time and circumstance.

Then there was Jessica, a friend she'd met through a shared ministry project. Jessica's sharp wit and unwavering faith had challenged Sarah to grow spiritually. She pushed Sarah to examine her own beliefs, to delve deeper into scripture, to confront her own prejudices and assumptions. Their friendship wasn't always comfortable; Jessica's honesty could be blunt, her criticisms direct. But Sarah knew that her criticisms stemmed from a place of love and concern, a genuine desire to see Sarah thrive. Jessica held her accountable, challenging her to live up to her potential.

These friendships, Sarah realized, were not simply relationships based on shared interests or social convenience. They were bonds forged in the fires of shared experiences, strengthened by mutual respect, support, and a shared commitment to growth. They were relationships where vulnerability was embraced, where imperfections were acknowledged, and where love persisted even in the face of conflict. These were the friendships that nourished her soul, sustained her spirit, and guided her toward a deeper understanding of herself and her relationship with God.

The qualities of these true friendships extended beyond the individual level, impacting Sarah's overall well-being. She found greater resilience in the face of adversity, knowing that she had a support system to lean on. Her sense of self-worth was enhanced by the unconditional love and acceptance she received from her friends. She felt a deeper sense of belonging, a connection to something larger than herself. These friendships provided her with a safe space to be vulnerable, to share her fears and insecurities without judgment. They offered a sanctuary from the harsh realities of the world, a refuge where she could rest and recharge.

The contrast between her superficial and genuine friendships highlighted a critical lesson: True friendships are not merely social transactions, but deep, meaningful connections based on mutual respect, support, and shared values. They are built on a foundation of trust, honesty, and empathy, and they require effort, commitment, and a willingness to nurture the relationship over time. Identifying these friendships requires self-awareness, a clear understanding of one's own values and needs, and the ability to discern genuine connection from superficial pleasantries. It's about recognizing the friends who lift you up, challenge you to grow, and support you through life's inevitable trials and tribulations. It's about recognizing those who see the real you, not just the persona you project to the world. These are the friendships that truly matter, the friendships that enrich your life and nurture your soul. These are the friendships that reflect the kind of love God offers to each of us—unconditional, steadfast, and eternally faithful. And as Sarah learned, cultivating such friendships is not merely a social pursuit, but a spiritual one—a pathway to a richer, fuller life rooted in love and grace.

The air in the small, book-lined room hummed with a quiet intensity. Sunlight streamed through the stained-glass window, painting the faces of the gathered group in shifting hues of gold and crimson. This wasn't a casual gathering; it was a covenant, a weekly commitment to mutual support and accountability within their faith journey. Sarah, having navigated the treacherous waters of superficial friendships, found herself deeply grateful for this sanctuary, this space where vulnerability wasn't a weakness, but a pathway to deeper connection and spiritual growth.

Tonight's focus was accountability, a concept that initially felt uncomfortable, even threatening. The idea of being held to a standard, of having one's flaws exposed to others, had once felt like a profound invasion of privacy. But through the shared experiences and open hearts within this group, she had come to see accountability not as judgment, but as a crucial element of authentic Christian living, a reflection of God's own loving discipline.

Pastor Michael, a gentle soul with a keen understanding of the human heart, led the discussion. "Brothers and sisters," he began, his voice a warm baritone, "accountability isn't about condemnation; it's about compassionately guiding one another toward wholeness. It's about mirroring God's own love, His patient, persistent encouragement as we strive toward His likeness."

He paused, letting his words sink in. "Think of the parable of the shepherd searching for the lost sheep. Does the shepherd condemn the sheep for straying? No. He rejoices when he finds it, carries it back to the flock with tenderness and care. That, my friends, is the essence of accountability within the body of Christ."

The group nodded, a silent affirmation of his words. Each member had their own experiences to share, their own struggles and triumphs in navigating the path of discipleship. Maria, a mother of three, spoke of her struggle to maintain consistent prayer amidst the chaos of daily life. She confessed to feeling overwhelmed, tempted to let her devotional time slide, her spirit lagging behind her demanding schedule.

"But," she added, a hint of triumph in her voice, "thanks to the support of this group, I've found ways to adapt. John reminded me of the power of short, focused prayer times, scattered throughout the day – little moments of connection with God, even amidst the laundry and the school runs." John, a quiet, thoughtful man, simply smiled, his eyes twinkling with genuine satisfaction.

Then came David, a young man wrestling with doubts about his vocation. He felt called to ministry but was plagued by fear of failure, the weight of responsibility pressing heavily on his shoulders. He confessed his anxieties, admitting his reluctance to share his doubts with anyone outside this safe space. The group listened patiently, offering words of encouragement, sharing similar experiences, and reminding him of God's unwavering presence and guidance. They challenged him to discern God's will, to step out in faith, reminding him of the verse: "Do not be afraid, for I am with you; do not be anxious, for I am your God. I will strengthen you, I will help you, I will uphold you with my righteous right hand." (Isaiah 41:10)

Sarah shared her own journey, her struggle with self-doubt and perfectionism. She spoke of how her friends within the group had gently challenged her to embrace her imperfections, reminding her that God's grace extended even to her failures. They had helped her to set realistic goals, to celebrate small victories, and to approach her spiritual journey with kindness and self-compassion, a concept that had previously felt foreign and almost heretical.

The conversations continued, weaving a rich tapestry of shared experiences, honest confessions, and mutual encouragement. Each member offered their unique gifts – a listening ear, a word of wisdom, a practical suggestion, a heartfelt prayer. The space was filled with the palpable sense of camaraderie, a shared commitment to spiritual growth, bound together by the adhesive of grace and accountability.

The importance of accountability was not just about holding each other accountable for specific actions or goals, it extended to the broader aspect of spiritual formation. It was about consistently seeking feedback on our spiritual disciplines, examining our hearts, and ensuring that our lives reflected the values we professed to uphold. The group actively encouraged each other to delve deeper into scripture, to engage in spiritual practices like prayer and meditation, and to serve others in tangible ways. They challenged each other to examine their actions in the light of scripture, confronting blind spots and nurturing spiritual maturity.

Accountability also encompassed the challenge of maintaining integrity in everyday life. The small group offered support and guidance when faced with ethical dilemmas, providing a sounding board for discerning God's will in complex situations. They offered perspective when dealing with conflict, reminding each other of the importance of forgiveness and reconciliation. They prayed for each other when facing difficult decisions, seeking wisdom and strength in God's promises.

The emphasis on accountability wasn't simply a set of rules or regulations, but a dynamic process of mutual growth. It involved confronting uncomfortable truths with grace and sensitivity, acknowledging mistakes without self-recrimination, and celebrating progress with genuine enthusiasm. It was about creating a space where weakness became a source of strength, and vulnerability led to deeper connection.

As the meeting drew to a close, a sense of peace settled over the group. They had shared their burdens, celebrated their victories, and committed themselves to continued growth, strengthened by the bonds of mutual support and accountability. Sarah felt a deep sense of gratitude, a recognition that true friendship wasn't simply about shared laughter and pleasantries. It was about a commitment to walking alongside one another, to bearing each other's burdens, to holding each other accountable, and to nurturing each other's spiritual growth in the grace of God. It was about reflecting the very essence of Christ's love, a love that is both challenging and unconditionally sustaining. It was, she realised, the kind of friendship that transcended time and circumstance, a reflection of the eternal bond between God and His people. And as the gentle strains of a closing hymn filled the room, Sarah knew that her journey towards genuine friendship, towards a deeper connection with God and others, was far from over, but it was a journey she was now confidently taking, hand in hand with her community of faith.

The quiet hum of the evening lingered even after the group dispersed, the lingering scent of old books and brewing coffee a comforting presence in Sarah's memory. The lessons of accountability, so powerfully illustrated that night, resonated deeply. But even within the supportive confines of their small group, the reality of conflict remained. True friendship, she was beginning to understand, wasn't a utopian ideal free from friction; rather, it was a crucible where authentic relationships were forged in the fires of disagreement, refined by the grace of forgiveness, and strengthened by the commitment to reconciliation. This, she realized, was the next crucial step in her journey towards building trustworthy friendships – learning to navigate conflict constructively.

Pastor Michael had often spoken of the inevitability of conflict, drawing parallels to the storms that buffet a ship at sea. A storm doesn't necessarily signal a sinking vessel; it often reveals the strength of the hull, the skill of the captain, and the solidarity of the crew. Similarly, conflicts within friendships weren't indicators of failure but opportunities for growth, deepening the bonds of understanding and empathy. The key, he emphasized, lay not in avoiding conflict, but in confronting it with grace, wisdom, and a willingness to understand the other's perspective.

This was easier said than done. Sarah vividly remembered a past friendship, one that had foundered on the shoals of unspoken resentment. A seemingly minor disagreement – a difference of opinion regarding a shared project – had festered, left unaddressed, eventually poisoning the well of their relationship. Neither of them had possessed the communication skills, or the willingness, to bridge the gap, to understand the other's point of view. The silence, heavy with unspoken accusations, had become a chasm too wide to cross.

This experience, however, had become a valuable lesson. She now understood that open, honest communication was the bedrock of resolving conflict. It wasn't enough to simply state one's position; it required actively listening, truly hearing what the other person was saying, even when their perspective differed sharply from her own. This involved setting aside personal biases, emotional defensiveness, and the urge to interrupt. It meant consciously creating a space where both parties felt safe to express themselves without fear of judgment or ridicule.

Sarah found herself reflecting on a conversation between two friends, Emily and Jessica, from her church community. Emily, a meticulous planner known for her unwavering adherence to schedules, and Jessica, a free-spirited artist who thrived on spontaneity, had recently experienced a conflict regarding their collaborative art project. The project, a vibrant mural for the church hall, had faced delays due to differing artistic visions and management styles.

Emily, initially upset by Jessica's seemingly casual approach to deadlines, had expressed her frustrations in a way that felt accusatory. Jessica, in turn, had reacted defensively, feeling misunderstood and unjustly criticized. The situation had escalated into a hurtful exchange, leaving both feeling hurt and frustrated.

However, unlike Sarah's past experience, Emily and Jessica had decided to address their conflict directly. They chose a neutral setting – a quiet corner of the church garden – and committed to a conversation focused on understanding, not blame. Emily began by expressing her feelings, using "I" statements to avoid sounding accusatory. "I felt anxious when the deadlines weren't met," she said, "because I worry about letting the church down."

Jessica listened patiently, offering empathetic nods. When it was her turn, she shared her perspective, acknowledging Emily's concerns but explaining her own artistic process, which thrived on improvisation and spontaneous inspiration. "I understand your concerns about deadlines, Emily," Jessica said gently, "but my creative process isn't linear. I need that freedom to let the art flow."

What followed was a remarkable demonstration of compromise and mutual respect. They agreed to establish a more flexible timeline, incorporating elements of both their approaches. They established regular check-in points, allowing for adjustments and feedback along the way. The collaborative process transformed from a source of conflict into an enriching experience of mutual learning and creative synergy.

This example highlighted another crucial element in resolving conflict – compromise. It wasn't about one person winning and the other losing; it was about finding common ground, a mutually acceptable solution that respected the needs and perspectives of both individuals. Compromise required a willingness to relinquish some personal preferences, to see beyond one's own needs and consider the other person's point of view.

Finally, the power of forgiveness played a pivotal role in resolving conflict and rebuilding trust. Holding onto resentment, harboring anger, only perpetuated the hurt and prevented healing. Forgiveness wasn't about condoning hurtful behavior; it was about releasing the burden of anger and bitterness, allowing oneself to move forward.

The biblical concept of forgiveness, deeply rooted in the parable of the Prodigal Son, underscored the transformative power of extending grace, even to those who have wronged us. Jesus' teachings emphasized the importance of extending forgiveness not just seven times, but seventy times seven – a limitless capacity for compassion and reconciliation. This didn't mean ignoring or minimizing harmful actions; it meant choosing to break the cycle of hurt, choosing love over retribution.

Forgiveness, Sarah realized, wasn't a single act but a continuous process, requiring ongoing effort and a willingness to let go of anger and bitterness. It might involve seeking reconciliation, engaging in restorative conversations, or simply praying for the other person's well-being.

In navigating conflict within her own friendships, Sarah learned to implement these principles: to practice active listening, to seek mutual understanding, to be willing to compromise, and to extend forgiveness. She understood that these weren't quick fixes; they were ongoing practices, requiring self-reflection, empathy, and a steadfast commitment to nurturing the bonds of friendship.

The journey wasn't always easy. There would be times when emotions ran high, when misunderstandings deepened, and when the temptation to retreat into silence loomed large. But through it all, Sarah discovered that the path of resolving conflict, while challenging, ultimately led to a richer, deeper, and more authentic connection with her friends. It was in the crucible of disagreement, in the shared experience of overcoming conflict, that true friendship was forged. It was a testament to the transformative power of grace, compassion, and the unwavering commitment to love, even in the midst of conflict. And it was a journey, she knew, that would continue to shape and strengthen her friendships for years to come, a testament to the enduring power of faith and friendship.

The quiet strength of those friendships, forged in the fires of conflict and refined by forgiveness, provided a solid foundation. However, Sarah soon discovered that navigating conflict wasn't the only challenge in building trustworthy friendships. Another crucial element, equally important, was establishing and maintaining healthy boundaries. This realization dawned on her during a conversation with Pastor Michael, who spoke of the delicate balance between intimacy and independence within friendships.

He used the analogy of a vine and a trellis. The vine, representing the friendship, needs the support of the trellis (boundaries) to grow strong and healthy. Without the structure of the trellis, the vine might sprawl uncontrollably, becoming tangled and weak. Similarly, friendships without healthy boundaries risk becoming codependent, where one person's needs consistently overshadow the other's, leading to resentment and emotional exhaustion.

Pastor Michael shared a story from his own life. He had once been close friends with a fellow seminarian, a man named David who possessed an incredibly generous spirit. However, David's generosity often blurred into a lack of boundaries, leaving Pastor Michael feeling emotionally drained and overwhelmed. David would call him at any hour, often venting about his anxieties and insecurities for hours on end. He would frequently drop by unannounced, expecting Pastor Michael to drop everything to listen and offer support. While Pastor Michael genuinely cared for David, he found himself constantly sacrificing his own time, energy, and emotional well-being to meet David's seemingly endless needs.

"I loved David," Pastor Michael confessed, "but I was slowly being suffocated by the lack of boundaries. I felt like a lifeline, not a friend. I was always giving, but I wasn't receiving the reciprocal support and consideration I needed." He explained how he eventually realized the necessity of establishing clear boundaries, not to distance himself from David, but to preserve the friendship and protect his own mental health. He learned to politely decline some calls, to suggest alternative times for conversations, and to set aside specific times for meeting, rather than always being on-call.

He began to politely but firmly assert his needs, explaining that he needed time for his own responsibilities and self-care. It wasn't easy. David initially reacted with hurt and confusion. He felt rejected and misunderstood, believing that Pastor Michael was abandoning him. However, Pastor Michael patiently explained his perspective, emphasizing his continued friendship and care, while also highlighting the importance of mutual respect and balance within their relationship.

Through open communication, David gradually came to understand the need for boundaries. He learned to respect Pastor Michael's time and space, and their friendship transformed from a one-sided burden to a healthier, more mutually beneficial relationship. This experience taught Pastor Michael the profound importance of setting boundaries, not as a means of rejection, but as a way of preserving the genuine connection and ensuring the long-term well-being of the friendship.

Sarah found this analogy incredibly helpful. She realized that she too had struggled with setting boundaries in some of her friendships. She had a tendency to overextend herself, wanting to please everyone and always being available, resulting in a feeling of being constantly overwhelmed. She recalled a friendship with a woman named Lisa, who was always confiding in Sarah about her personal struggles, often dwelling on negativity and self-pity. Sarah, deeply empathetic, listened patiently and offered support, often sacrificing her own time and energy to help Lisa.

However, after a while, Sarah found herself feeling drained and emotionally exhausted. Lisa's constant negativity started impacting her own mood and well-being. While Sarah cared deeply for Lisa, she realized she needed to establish some boundaries to protect herself. This wasn't about abandoning Lisa; it was about setting healthy limits that allowed for both support and self-preservation.

She started by gently suggesting to Lisa that she might benefit from seeking professional help, offering to help her find resources. She also began limiting the amount of time she spent listening to Lisa's continuous complaints, suggesting they take breaks or focus on more positive aspects of their lives during their conversations. She learned to say no to requests that felt overwhelming or interfered with her own commitments, explaining her limitations calmly and respectfully. Lisa, initially resistant, gradually came to understand Sarah's need for boundaries, recognizing that Sarah's well-being was vital to their friendship's health.

Setting boundaries, Sarah discovered, wasn't a sign of selfishness; it was a necessary act of self-respect and self-preservation. It allowed her to maintain friendships while protecting her own emotional and mental well-being. It required courage, assertiveness, and clear communication. It meant learning to say "no" without feeling guilty, to prioritize her own needs without feeling selfish, and to communicate her limits without fear of damaging the relationship.

She also learned that setting boundaries wasn't a one-time event; it was an ongoing process, requiring continuous self-awareness and mindful adjustments. As friendships evolved, her needs and boundaries might also change, requiring open communication with her friends to ensure mutual understanding and respect. It was a testament to the ongoing work of nurturing healthy relationships, where both parties feel respected, supported, and empowered.

Establishing healthy boundaries in friendships wasn't about erecting walls; it was about building a sturdy, well-constructed trellis that allows the vine of friendship to grow strong and flourish, reaching towards the sun, supported yet independent, a testament to the beauty of mutual respect and the enduring power of a balanced friendship – a friendship rooted in grace, grounded in truth, and blossoming in mutual love and support. This journey of building trustworthy friendships, Sarah found, was a lifelong process of growth, learning, and constant refinement – a journey guided by faith and strengthened by the enduring principles of love, forgiveness, and grace. And it was, she realized, a journey richly worth taking.

The aroma of roasted lamb mingled with the sweet scent of wildflowers, a fitting perfume for the celebration unfolding beneath the sprawling oak tree. Laughter, lighthearted banter, and the clinking of glasses filled the air as Sarah, along with her closest friends, marked a significant milestone – ten years of unwavering friendship. It wasn't just a decade of shared experiences; it was a testament to the enduring power of genuine connection, a bond forged in mutual trust and nurtured by a shared faith.

As the evening deepened, a quiet contemplation settled over the group. The celebratory mood shifted, subtly, into a reflective one. Each friend, in turn, shared their thoughts, their memories, their gratitude for the profound impact this friendship had woven into the fabric of their lives. Their stories intertwined, a tapestry woven with threads of support, encouragement, and unwavering love – a living illustration of Proverbs 17:17, "A friend loves at all times, and a brother is born for adversity."

Mark, a quiet, contemplative soul, spoke first. He recounted a time of deep personal struggle, a period of profound doubt and uncertainty that threatened to consume him. "I was lost," he admitted, his voice husky with emotion, "spiritually adrift, emotionally exhausted. But you, my friends, you were my anchors. You didn't judge, you didn't offer simplistic solutions, you simply loved me, flaws and all, and held me up when I couldn't stand." His words resonated deeply, echoing the profound truth that true friendship offers a safe haven during life's storms. It's a place of unconditional love, where vulnerability is embraced, and imperfections are celebrated.

Emily, a vibrant and energetic woman, shared a different perspective. She spoke of the joyous times, the shared laughter, the adventures that had strengthened their bonds. "It's not just about the difficult times," she said, her eyes sparkling with mirth. "It's about the joy, the celebration, the shared moments of pure, unadulterated happiness. This friendship has amplified my joys, making them even more vibrant and meaningful. It's like having a chorus of voices singing along to the symphony of my life, making the music richer and fuller." Her words highlighted another vital aspect of true friendship: the amplification of joy, the shared celebration of life's victories.

David, a man known for his wisdom and spiritual insight, offered a biblical lens through which to view their friendship. He spoke of the deep, abiding love exemplified in the relationship between David and Jonathan, a bond so profound that it transcended even the pressures of royal courtly life (1 Samuel 18:1-4). "Their friendship," David explained, "was a testament to the transformative power of genuine love, a love that offered unwavering support, loyalty, and unconditional acceptance. It reminds us that true friendship is a gift from God, a blessing intended to enrich our lives and draw us closer to Him." He emphasized the importance of prayer and mutual spiritual support within their friendship circle, highlighting how their shared faith had strengthened their bonds and guided them through times of adversity.

Sarah, reflecting on the past decade, acknowledged the challenges they had faced – disagreements, misunderstandings, and times when their individual paths diverged. Yet, she emphasized that it was through these experiences that their friendship had deepened and matured. "We've learned to forgive, to communicate openly and honestly, and to navigate conflict with grace and understanding," she said. "It's in the midst of these challenges that the true strength of our friendship has been revealed. It's not the absence of conflict, but our ability to overcome it together, that has forged this unbreakable bond." Her words underscored the vital role of forgiveness and open communication in maintaining healthy, lasting friendships. It's the ability to navigate disagreements constructively, to extend grace and understanding, and to maintain a willingness to mend broken bridges that builds resilience and deepens intimacy within the relationship.

As the evening drew to a close, the friends sat in comfortable silence, each contemplating the profound blessing of their mutual friendship. They had shared laughter and tears, victories and defeats, joys and sorrows – a complete tapestry of life's experiences woven together by the strong threads of love, support, and unwavering loyalty. Their gathering wasn't just a celebration of a decade of friendship; it was an acknowledgment of the enduring power of genuine human connection, a bond that had enriched their lives in countless ways, drawing them closer to God and one another.

The blessing of true friendship extends far beyond mere companionship. It's a profound spiritual gift, a source of immense emotional sustenance, and a powerful catalyst for personal growth. True friends are like family chosen by the heart, individuals who understand us, accept us, and support us unconditionally. They challenge us to grow, to become better versions of ourselves, and to live more fully into the lives God intended for us. They become companions on our journey of faith, offering encouragement, prayer, and a steadfast presence when we falter.

The Bible is replete with examples of profound and transformative friendships – David and Jonathan, Ruth and Naomi, Paul and Silas, to name but a few. These relationships highlight the vital role that genuine connection plays in our spiritual and emotional well-being. They demonstrate how the love and support of true friends can sustain us through adversity, inspire us to reach our full potential, and deepen our relationship with God. These relationships weren't without their challenges; yet, their enduring strength lay in their mutual love, loyalty, and commitment to each other.

Think about the friendship between David and Jonathan. Their bond was characterized by unwavering loyalty, mutual respect, and a deep understanding of each other's hearts. Jonathan, the crown prince, stood by David, a young shepherd boy, even when it meant risking his own position and safety. He offered David unwavering support, both emotionally and strategically, demonstrating the selflessness and commitment that define true friendship.

The friendship between Ruth and Naomi is another powerful example of unwavering loyalty and selfless love. Ruth chose to remain faithful to Naomi, her mother-in-law, despite facing hardship and uncertainty. She stood by Naomi's side through adversity, demonstrating the strength and depth of a friendship grounded in compassion and unwavering commitment.

Paul and Silas's friendship, forged in the midst of imprisonment, showcases the power of shared faith and mutual support. Despite facing harsh conditions, they found strength in each other, singing praises to God even in the depths of despair. Their experience serves as a testament to how faith and friendship can sustain us through even the most difficult circumstances.

These biblical examples highlight several key aspects of true friendship: unconditional love, unwavering loyalty, mutual respect, open communication, forgiveness, and shared faith. These elements are essential for building strong, lasting relationships that enrich our lives and draw us closer to God. True friendship is not merely a social connection; it's a profound spiritual gift that strengthens our faith, enhances our emotional well-being, and helps us live more fully into God's plan for our lives.

Cultivating and maintaining true friendships requires effort, commitment, and a willingness to invest time and energy into nurturing these precious relationships. It involves extending grace, offering forgiveness, communicating openly and honestly, and being willing to put the needs of our friends ahead of our own. It requires a commitment to building trust, offering unwavering support, and celebrating the joys and sorrows of our friends' lives. In essence, it demands a commitment to living out the teachings of Christ – love, compassion, and selflessness.

In the midst of our busy lives, it's easy to neglect the importance of nurturing our friendships. But by prioritizing these relationships, by making time for connection and meaningful interaction, we invest in a profound source of spiritual and emotional sustenance. We enrich our lives, and the lives of our friends, in ways that cannot be measured. The blessings of true friendship are immeasurable, and the rewards far outweigh the effort required to cultivate and maintain these precious bonds. They are, ultimately, gifts from God – testaments to His love, grace, and unwavering commitment to our well-being. As Sarah and her friends discovered that evening, celebrating a decade of enduring friendship, these gifts are among the most valuable we will ever receive.

The lingering warmth of the evening, the echoes of laughter and shared stories, faded as Sarah drove home. The celebration had been beautiful, a testament to the enduring power of friendship, but a subtle unease stirred within her. David's words about prayer and mutual spiritual support resonated deeply, highlighting an area where she felt she was falling short. Her life, consumed by the relentless demands of her high-powered career, had left little room for consistent spiritual disciplines. She was a successful marketing executive, juggling multi-million dollar campaigns, international travel, and the constant pressure to outperform expectations. Her faith, once a vibrant and central part of her life, had become a quiet, almost apologetic whisper amidst the clamor of her demanding schedule.

The following week felt like a whirlwind. Presentations, conference calls, and endless emails blurred into an indistinguishable mass. Sarah found herself functioning on autopilot, fueled by caffeine and adrenaline, her spiritual life relegated to fleeting, hurried prayers before sleep. This wasn't the intentional life she yearned for, the life she knew, deep down, God had intended for her. She recognized the discrepancy between her outward success and her inward emptiness. The celebratory feeling from the weekend had been fleeting, leaving her feeling more depleted than ever. She needed to prioritize her spiritual disciplines if she was going to truly live with intentionality.

The first step, she decided, was prayer. Not the rushed, mumbled requests before sleep, but deliberate, focused time spent in conversation with God. She began by setting aside just five minutes each morning, before the deluge of emails and phone calls began. Even five minutes, she discovered, was enough to create a sense of calm and focus, to center herself before diving into the chaos of her day. She found a quiet corner of her apartment, opened her Bible, and simply spoke to God. She didn't worry about eloquent phrasing or perfectly formed sentences. She just talked, pouring out her heart, her anxieties, her gratitude, her hopes, and her fears.

Initially, it was difficult. Her mind would wander, her thoughts drifting back to work deadlines and unanswered emails. But gradually, with persistent practice, she found herself becoming more present, more attuned to God's presence. She started noticing small moments of grace throughout her day, little blessings that she had previously overlooked in her relentless pursuit of professional success. A kind word from a colleague, a smooth-running project, a beautiful sunset – these became moments of quiet gratitude, reminders of God's constant presence and loving care.

Next, she tackled Bible study. She had always enjoyed reading scripture, but her approach had been sporadic, driven by fleeting moments of inspiration rather than consistent discipline. Now, she committed to reading a specific passage each day, taking time to meditate on its meaning and relevance to her life. She started with the Gospels, allowing the words of Jesus to sink deeply into her heart. She realized how much she had missed by allowing her busy life to neglect this source of comfort and wisdom. She began journaling her reflections, writing down her insights and prayers. This process helped her internalize the scriptures, to see their relevance not just as abstract teachings, but as a roadmap for her daily life.

Meditation, too, presented its own challenges. The stillness required felt almost alien after years of living in a whirlwind of activity. Her mind raced, filled with thoughts, worries, and to-do lists. But she persevered, gradually learning to quiet her thoughts, to find a place of inner peace and reflection. She discovered that even short periods of meditation – just ten or fifteen minutes – had a profound effect on her ability to focus and manage stress. Her energy levels improved, and the constant feeling of being overwhelmed began to subside.

But integrating these disciplines wasn't just about adding more tasks to her already packed schedule. It was about reshaping her priorities, about consciously choosing to make space for God in her life. This meant learning to say "no" to certain commitments, to delegate tasks, and to prioritize her well-being above the relentless demands of her career. It was a process of gradual transformation, of learning to live with intentionality, placing God at the center of her life.

Sarah started incorporating mindfulness into her daily routine. She became more aware of the present moment, appreciating the small things - the taste of her morning coffee, the feel of the sun on her skin, the laughter of a child. This heightened awareness extended to her interactions with others, allowing her to connect more deeply with her colleagues, her friends, and even strangers. She began to see her job not just as a source of stress and pressure, but as an opportunity to serve others, to use her skills and talents to make a positive impact on the world.

Her newfound spiritual discipline wasn't always easy. There were days when she felt overwhelmed, when the pressure to succeed seemed unbearable. There were days when the temptation to abandon her new routines was strong. But she found strength in her community of faith, in her friends who supported and encouraged her journey. They understood the challenges she faced, and they offered her words of encouragement, prayer, and practical assistance.

The change wasn't just internal; it became evident in her relationships. Her friendships deepened, as she had more time and energy to invest in them. Her relationships with colleagues improved, as her stress levels decreased and her ability to connect with others increased. Even her relationship with her family became richer, as she was able to be more present and engaged. The spiritual disciplines weren't just about her personal growth; they were transforming her interactions with the world around her.

One evening, she found herself reflecting on the past few months. She had gone from a woman barely clinging to her faith amidst the chaos of her career to someone who actively sought God in every aspect of her life. The change wasn't dramatic or sudden, but a steady, persistent movement towards a more intentional and fulfilling life. She realized that her success wasn't just about achieving professional goals, but about living a life that honored God and served others.

The process was ongoing, a continuous journey of growth and refinement. She still faced challenges and temptations to revert to her old habits. But now she had a framework, a set of spiritual practices to help her navigate the complexities of life. The quiet moments of prayer, the thoughtful study of scripture, the peaceful practice of meditation – these had become anchors in her life, grounding her amidst the storms and reminding her of the enduring presence of God's love. She understood now that living with intentionality wasn't just about making a list of goals and checking them off. It was about aligning her life with God's purpose, and her spiritual disciplines were the tools that allowed her to do so. It was a journey, a continuous striving to live more fully into the life God had created for her. And in that continuous striving, she found a deeper peace and a more profound sense of purpose.

The success she had craved, the recognition she had pursued, now felt secondary to the deeper fulfillment she found in her relationship with God and her commitment to living intentionally. The busy professional life remained, but now it was infused with a different perspective, a sense of purpose and direction that transcended the demands of her career. The spiritual disciplines were not just additions to her life, but transformative forces shaping her priorities, her relationships, and her understanding of herself and her place in the world. Her life, once a chaotic whirlwind, was now a tapestry woven with threads of faith, intentionality, and a profound sense of God's unwavering love. The journey continued, but now, it was a journey she walked with a renewed sense of purpose, a deeper understanding of God's grace, and a heart filled with gratitude.

Sarah's newfound spiritual disciplines had brought a sense of calm amidst the storm of her demanding career, but she realized that true intentionality required more than just daily practices. It demanded a conscious setting of goals—goals aligned not just with her professional ambitions, but with her deepest spiritual values. She understood that setting goals wasn't about creating a rigid checklist, but about charting a course toward a life lived in accordance with God's will.

The first step was introspection. She spent a quiet evening, her Bible open beside her, journaling and reflecting. She asked herself profound questions: What did God truly want for her life? What were her unique talents and gifts, and how could she use them to serve Him? What areas of her life needed healing or transformation? She prayed for discernment, asking God to illuminate her path and guide her toward meaningful objectives.

The answers didn't come in a sudden flash of revelation, but gradually emerged through prayer, meditation, and careful reflection on scripture. She recognized a recurring theme: generosity. She had always been a hard worker, but her focus had been largely self-oriented, driven by a desire for professional achievement and personal recognition. Now, she saw the need to channel her energy and talents towards serving others.

This revelation led to the first concrete goal: volunteering at a local homeless shelter. The idea felt daunting at first. Her schedule was already packed, and the thought of adding another commitment felt overwhelming. But she prayed for strength and clarity, reminding herself that God didn't call the equipped, He equipped the called.

The initial experience was humbling. The shelter was filled with people struggling with poverty, addiction, and mental health issues. Sarah, used to the polished world of marketing, felt out of her depth. Yet, she found a surprising sense of fulfillment in serving others. The simple act of handing out food, offering a listening ear, or helping with cleaning tasks brought her a deeper sense of purpose than any successful marketing campaign ever could. She realized that true success wasn't measured in dollars or accolades, but in the positive impact she had on others.

Her next goal stemmed from her desire to deepen her relationships. She realized that her career had often placed a strain on her friendships and family connections. She committed to scheduling regular time with loved ones, not just for quick catch-ups, but for meaningful engagement and quality time. This meant learning to say "no" to some work commitments, to protect the space needed for genuine connection. She planned regular dinners with her family, coffee dates with friends, and weekend retreats with her close spiritual community. The result was a strengthening of bonds, a deeper sense of belonging, and a richer emotional life.

Another goal she set was to improve her financial generosity. She had always tithed to her church, but now she felt compelled to give more. She started by increasing her regular contributions, and then she began exploring other avenues of giving. She volunteered to mentor young women entering the marketing field, offering her professional expertise and experience without expecting anything in return. She also began donating regularly to charities that aligned with her spiritual values.

Setting these goals wasn't a one-time event; it was an ongoing process of discernment and refinement. Sarah regularly reviewed her goals, assessing her progress and making adjustments as needed. She understood that life was a journey, not a destination, and her goals were intended to guide her along the path, not confine her to a rigid framework. She prayed for flexibility and adaptability, recognizing that God might lead her in unexpected directions.

She incorporated a system of accountability into her goal-setting. She shared her goals with trusted friends and mentors within her church community, asking them to pray for her and offer support and encouragement. She also scheduled regular check-ins with her spiritual advisor, who helped her stay focused and on track. Knowing that others were invested in her journey helped her remain committed to her goals, even when faced with challenges and setbacks.

Setting intentional goals wasn't always easy. There were times when she felt overwhelmed, discouraged, or tempted to abandon her efforts. But she reminded herself of the reason behind her goals—to live a life that honored God, served others, and reflected her deepest spiritual values. She found strength in her faith, in her community, and in the knowledge that God was walking alongside her, guiding her every step of the way.

Her increased intentionality brought about a profound shift in her perspective. She began to see her daily tasks not merely as obligations, but as opportunities for spiritual growth and service. Even mundane activities, like grocery shopping or commuting, became occasions for mindfulness and prayer. She practiced gratitude for small blessings, recognizing God's presence in the everyday details of her life.

As the months progressed, Sarah's life became a beautiful tapestry woven with threads of faith, intentionality, and purpose. She continued to excel in her professional career, but her success was now measured not only by financial gains and professional recognition, but by the positive impact she had on others and the depth of her relationship with God. The sense of fulfillment she experienced was profound and lasting, a testament to the power of living with intentionality.

The process taught her the importance of self-compassion. There were times when she stumbled, when she fell short of her goals. She learned to forgive herself, to dust herself off, and to keep moving forward. She understood that growth was a process, a continuous journey of learning and refinement. She embraced imperfection as part of the process, knowing that her worth wasn't contingent on her achievements but on her unwavering relationship with her Creator.

The transformation extended to her relationships. Her interactions with colleagues, friends, and family became richer and more meaningful. She listened more deeply, offered more empathetic support, and cultivated genuine connections. Her life, once dominated by the relentless demands of her career, now embraced a healthier balance of work, rest, and spiritual disciplines.

Sarah's story became a powerful example within her church community. She shared her journey openly, inspiring others to set their own meaningful goals, to integrate their faith into their daily lives, and to live with intentionality. She facilitated workshops on goal-setting and spiritual disciplines, empowering others to embark on their own journeys of transformation. She discovered that true fulfillment comes not from achieving external goals alone, but from aligning her life with God's purpose and living a life that reflects His love. This journey wasn't simply about personal growth; it was about becoming a vessel through which God's love could flow abundantly into the world. The ongoing journey toward intentional living, therefore, became not only a source of personal enrichment for Sarah, but also a powerful witness to the transformative power of faith. Her life became a living testament to the beauty and grace of a life lived purposefully, guided by faith and shaped by a deep commitment to God's will.

The crisp mountain air, scented with pine and damp earth, filled Sarah's lungs as she sat cross-legged on the yoga mat. The retreat center, nestled amongst towering redwoods, felt a world away from the frenetic energy of her marketing career. This wasn't a vacation; it was a deliberate retreat, a time carved out for spiritual reflection and the cultivation of mindful living. The previous weeks had been a whirlwind of goal-setting, a conscious effort to align her life with God's purpose. But true intentionality, she was learning, wasn't just about setting goals; it was about *living* those goals, moment by moment. And that required a deep dive into the present.

The retreat facilitator, a gentle woman named Sister Agnes, with eyes that held the wisdom of decades spent in contemplation, had emphasized the insidious nature of the mind's tendency to wander. "Our minds," she'd explained, "are like restless monkeys, constantly leaping from branch to branch of thought, flitting between past regrets and future anxieties, rarely settling on the present moment." Sister Agnes had introduced a variety of techniques to tether the mind to the "now," to cultivate a state of present-moment awareness.

One technique was mindful breathing. Sarah closed her eyes, focusing her attention on the sensation of her breath entering and leaving her body. She noticed the gentle rise and fall of her chest, the cool air filling her lungs, the warmth of the exhaled breath against her lips. At first, her thoughts drifted – to an upcoming presentation, to a conversation she'd had with her mother, to anxieties about the upcoming holiday season. But each time she caught herself wandering, she gently redirected her attention back to her breath, to the simple, grounding reality of the present moment.

Another technique was body scan meditation. Sister Agnes guided them through a systematic awareness of their physical sensations, starting with the toes and slowly moving upward to the crown of their head. Sarah noticed the tingling in her fingers, the pressure of the mat beneath her, the subtle tension in her shoulders. She acknowledged these sensations without judgment, simply observing them as they were. The process revealed hidden areas of tension, both physical and emotional, that she hadn't been consciously aware of.

Mindful walking was another practice. They walked slowly, deliberately, paying attention to the sensation of their feet making contact with the ground. They focused on the rhythm of their steps, the movement of their bodies, the sights, sounds, and smells around them. The rustling of leaves, the chirping of birds, the scent of pine needles – each became a rich source of sensory experience, anchoring Sarah in the present.

Over the course of the retreat, Sarah discovered the power of simply being. It wasn't about achieving something, or planning something, or even reflecting on something. It was about existing fully in the present moment, without striving, without judgment, simply being present. This, she realized, was the foundation upon which intentional living could truly flourish. It was the fertile ground from which her carefully cultivated goals could grow and bear fruit.

She reflected on her previous attempts at mindful living – the sporadic meditation sessions, the hurried attempts at prayer, the fleeting moments of gratitude. Now, she understood that mindfulness wasn't a separate practice to be squeezed into a busy schedule; it was a way of being, a lens through which she could view the entire tapestry of her life.

One evening, as the sun dipped below the horizon, painting the sky in hues of orange and purple, Sarah sat by the lake, her Bible open in her lap. She read Psalm 23, focusing on each word, allowing the ancient verses to sink deep into her soul. She wasn't merely reading words on a page; she was experiencing the peace and comfort of God's presence in that moment.

The experience transcended the intellectual understanding she had gained from her scripture studies. The serenity of the setting, the gentle lapping of the water against the shore, the breathtaking beauty of the sunset – all contributed to a deepening of her spiritual connection. The Psalm wasn't just a collection of words; it was a living expression of God's love and faithfulness, experienced in the here and now.

The retreat challenged her previous notion of intentionality as a series of carefully planned actions. It showed her that true intentionality wasn't merely about the "doing," but about the "being" – being present, being mindful, being fully engaged in each moment. It was about aligning her actions with her deepest values, not just as a future goal, but as a present reality.

Returning to her busy life, she implemented her new-found mindfulness in every aspect of her day. She practiced mindful eating, savoring each bite of food, appreciating the nourishment it provided. She approached her work with greater awareness, focusing on the task at hand without letting her mind wander to other concerns. Even mundane tasks, like washing dishes or folding laundry, became opportunities for mindfulness.

She also became more aware of the impact of her words and actions on others. Her interactions became more genuine, more present, more empathetic. She listened more intently, offering a deeper level of understanding and compassion. She noticed how she previously would react impatiently to frustrating situations but now discovered a quiet inner stillness that allowed her to respond with greater grace and patience.

This newfound mindfulness was not a passive state, but rather an active engagement with life. It was a constant practice of bringing her awareness back to the present moment, again and again, even amid the distractions and challenges of daily living. She carried the quiet intensity of the retreat with her into the city's noise.

There were setbacks, of course. The demands of her career sometimes overwhelmed her, and her mind still occasionally slipped into the familiar patterns of worry and anxiety. But she now possessed a set of tools – mindful breathing, body scan meditation, mindful walking – that helped her gently redirect her focus back to the present moment.

The integration of mindfulness wasn't a quick fix; it was a journey. But it was a journey that transformed her relationship with herself, with God, and with the world around her. It was a journey that empowered her to live not just intentionally, but authentically, moment by moment, guided by the unwavering presence of God. Her life, previously a blur of activity and achievement, now possessed a richness and depth that transcended the superficial. She had discovered that true fulfillment wasn't found in the distant future, but in the sacred space of the present moment. And that sacred space, she realized, was filled with the abundant grace of God.

Her intentional living now encompassed a mindful present, the foundation upon which her future goals could securely stand. This mindful awareness became her compass, guiding her actions, shaping her interactions, and informing her decisions, ensuring her life was not only successful but also deeply meaningful and aligned with God's purpose, not just in the abstract, but in the concrete reality of each passing moment. The journey of intentionality had begun to reveal its true transformative power, woven into the fabric of daily life, one mindful breath, one present moment at a time. The mountain air, the quiet lake, the redwood forest, became symbols of this new reality, reminders of the peace and purpose found only in the present moment – a peace that transcended the worries of the past and the anxieties of the future, leaving her anchored firmly in God's loving presence, here and now.

The quiet hum of gratitude began to permeate Sarah's being, a subtle yet powerful shift in her perspective. The retreat, with its emphasis on present-moment awareness, had unlocked a new understanding of God's grace, not as a distant promise, but as a tangible reality woven into the fabric of each moment. This newfound awareness extended beyond her personal experiences, influencing her interactions with others and revealing the profound blessings hidden in the simplest of things.

One afternoon, during a shared meal with the other retreat participants, a quiet conversation sparked a profound revelation. A woman named Emily, a schoolteacher burdened by the weight of administrative tasks and demanding students, shared her anxieties about the upcoming school year. She felt overwhelmed, drained, and deeply discouraged. As Emily spoke, Sarah noticed the subtle tension in her shoulders, the tightness in her jaw, the weariness in her eyes. It mirrored Sarah's own struggles before the retreat.

However, instead of offering platitudes or problem-solving advice, Sarah instinctively leaned into her newly cultivated practice of gratitude. Instead of focusing on Emily's challenges, she shifted her attention to what she saw as blessings in Emily's life. "Emily," Sarah began softly, "looking at you, I see a woman dedicated to shaping young minds, to nurturing the potential within each child. That's a profound calling, a gift you possess, an incredible blessing."

Emily looked surprised, a flicker of uncertainty in her eyes. She hadn't considered her role in that light. Sarah continued, "Think of the countless moments of connection you have with your students, the laughter, the shared learning, the small victories you celebrate together. Those are blessings, Emily. Don't let the administrative burden overshadow the incredible impact you have on those young lives."

Other participants joined in, sharing their own perspectives, highlighting the blessings woven into Emily's challenging role. One mentioned the joy of witnessing students' 'aha' moments, another pointed out the satisfaction of contributing to the community through education. Gradually, Emily's posture softened, her shoulders relaxing. A small smile played on her lips as she acknowledged the validity of these observations. The weight of her anxieties seemed to lighten.

This experience underscored the transformative power of gratitude. It wasn't about denying the hardships or pretending they didn't exist. It was about shifting the focus, about acknowledging the good amidst the challenges, about recognizing God's hand in the seemingly mundane aspects of daily life.

Returning to her city life, Sarah made a conscious effort to cultivate gratitude in every facet of her existence. She began a gratitude journal, writing down three things she was thankful for each day, no matter how small. Sometimes it was the warmth of the sun on her face, other times it was the kindness of a stranger, or the simple comfort of a warm cup of tea. The act of writing it down, of consciously acknowledging these blessings, deepened her appreciation and shifted her perspective.

She also began to express her gratitude to others more frequently. A simple "thank you" to the barista who made her coffee, a heartfelt note to a friend who offered support, a phone call to her parents expressing her love and appreciation – these small acts of gratitude not only strengthened her relationships but also filled her heart with a sense of peace and contentment.

Sarah realized that practicing gratitude wasn't merely a spiritual exercise; it was a fundamental shift in her worldview. It challenged her tendency to focus on what was lacking and instead encouraged her to appreciate what she already possessed. It was a conscious decision to choose joy over complaint, to see the glass as half full rather than half empty.

This new perspective permeated her professional life as well. Previously, Sarah had focused on her accomplishments, measuring her success by external benchmarks like promotions and financial gains. Now, she found herself appreciating the smaller blessings in her work: the satisfaction of completing a challenging project, the collaborative spirit among her team members, the opportunity to use her skills and talents to serve others. This shift in perspective decreased her stress levels and improved her overall job satisfaction.

One evening, while walking her dog, Max, in a nearby park, Sarah noticed a homeless man sitting on a bench, his head bowed in apparent despair. In the past, she might have averted her gaze, feeling a mix of pity and discomfort. But now, a different impulse arose. She felt a stirring in her heart, a prompting to offer kindness and compassion.

Approaching the man cautiously, Sarah offered him a warm smile. She didn't offer money or unsolicited advice; instead, she simply acknowledged his presence. "Hello," she said gently. "It's a beautiful evening, isn't it?" The man looked up, his eyes conveying a deep weariness. Yet, there was a flicker of surprise at her kindness.

They engaged in a brief conversation. Sarah listened attentively, offering a space for him to share his experiences, his hopes, his disappointments. She didn't try to fix his problems; she simply offered her presence, her empathy, her quiet acknowledgement of his humanity. As they spoke, Sarah found herself feeling grateful for her own life, for the roof over her head, the food on her table, the loving relationships in her life.

The encounter wasn't without its challenges. The man's story was heart-wrenching, a testament to the struggles faced by many in society. But amidst the sadness, Sarah discovered a profound sense of gratitude for the simple blessings in her own life. She felt a deeper connection to humanity, recognizing the shared struggles and shared hopes that unite us. She left the park feeling enriched, humbled, and profoundly grateful.

Sarah's journey of gratitude became a continuous practice, a daily affirmation of God's grace in her life. It wasn't about ignoring the challenges or denying the difficulties. It was about choosing to see the good, to appreciate the blessings, to acknowledge God's hand in every aspect of her existence. It was about finding joy in the present moment, recognizing that even amidst hardship, there is always something to be grateful for.

This intentional practice of gratitude transformed Sarah's life, filling her heart with a quiet contentment that transcended external circumstances. It became a powerful antidote to anxiety and fear, replacing worry with peace, and despair with hope. It deepened her faith, reaffirming her belief in God's unwavering love and provision. The transformative power of gratitude, she discovered, wasn't just a feeling; it was a way of being, a way of seeing the world, a way of living a life deeply rooted in faith and appreciation. And it was a journey she knew would continue to unfold, revealing ever more blessings along the way, each a testament to God's immeasurable love and grace.

The gratitude wasn't passive; it spurred her to action. Seeing the needs of others, she felt compelled to give back, to share her blessings with those less fortunate. She volunteered at a local soup kitchen, spending time with the individuals she served, listening to their stories, and offering a listening ear and a warm meal. She found immense satisfaction in these acts of service, further deepening her understanding of gratitude as both a personal practice and a pathway to serving others.

Through this intentional practice of gratitude, Sarah discovered that true contentment wasn't about accumulating possessions or achieving external milestones. It was about recognizing and appreciating the abundance that already existed in her life – the love of family and friends, the beauty of nature, the gift of health, the opportunity to contribute to the world. These were blessings she had previously taken for granted, blessings she now cherished deeply.

Moreover, the practice of gratitude strengthened her relationship with God. Instead of viewing God as a distant figure to be appeased or a source of demands to be met, she perceived Him as a loving Father who constantly showered her with blessings, big and small. This intimate understanding fueled a deeper connection, one characterized by trust, intimacy, and unwavering faith. Her prayers shifted from petitions to expressions of thanks and praise, her heart overflowing with an ever-increasing awareness of God's generous provision and unfailing love.

In the bustling city, amidst the noise and demands of daily living, Sarah found solace and strength in her gratitude practice. It wasn't always easy; moments of frustration and despair still occurred. But now, she had a tool, a lens through which to view her challenges, a perspective that allowed her to find gratitude even in the midst of difficulties. Her life, once defined by striving and achievement, had taken on a new dimension, a depth and richness that transcended the superficial, a life marked by intentionality, mindfulness, and an abiding sense of gratitude.

The lessons learned at the mountain retreat had taken root, transforming her life into a tapestry woven with threads of gratitude, mindfulness, and a deepening relationship with God. The journey of intentional living continued, but now it was a journey characterized by a profound sense of gratitude, a journey that continually revealed the immeasurable abundance of God's grace, one thankful breath, one appreciative moment at a time.

The crisp morning light streamed through the large windows of Sarah's newly minimalistic home, illuminating dust motes dancing in the air. Gone were the overflowing bookshelves, the cluttered countertops, the accumulation of possessions that had once defined her space. In their place was a serene calm, a quiet elegance born of intentionality and a conscious embrace of simplicity. This wasn't a sudden, drastic upheaval; it was a gradual process, a shedding of excess that mirrored the inner transformation she had undergone.

The move had been prompted, in part, by a conversation with her husband, David, a successful architect known for his meticulous attention to detail. He, too, had been feeling the weight of their busy lives, the constant pressure to achieve more, to acquire more, to keep up with the relentless pace of modern existence. They had begun to notice a growing disconnect, a subtle distance creeping into their relationship, overshadowed by the demands of career, social obligations, and the ever-present pursuit of more.

One evening, amidst a pile of unopened mail and half-finished projects, David had voiced his concerns. "Sarah," he said softly, "I feel like we're drowning in stuff. All this... it's suffocating us. We're so busy acquiring things that we're forgetting to appreciate what truly matters."

His words struck a chord. Sarah, still basking in the afterglow of her gratitude practice, recognized the truth in his statement. The accumulation of possessions, once a symbol of success, now felt like a burden, a distraction from the richness of their lives. They had become slaves to their possessions, rather than masters of their own destinies. Together, they embarked on a journey of decluttering, not simply a physical cleansing but a spiritual one.

The process began slowly, with small steps. They started by sorting through their closets, donating clothes they hadn't worn in months, letting go of items that no longer served a purpose. Each item discarded felt like a weight lifted, a burden released, a step toward freedom. They sifted through drawers, kitchen cabinets, and forgotten corners of the house, purging items that held only sentimental value without practical use.

They learned to discern between true needs and mere wants. This wasn't about asceticism or deprivation; it was about cultivating a mindful appreciation for what they already possessed. They replaced the frantic energy of consumerism with the quiet joy of mindful living, appreciating the simplicity and elegance of their streamlined space.

Their children, eight-year-old Lily and ten-year-old Tom, were initially resistant to the changes. Lily clung to her collection of stuffed animals, each one a cherished companion. Tom hoarded his comic books, each panel a portal to a fantastical world. But Sarah and David patiently explained their intentions, emphasizing the importance of appreciating quality over quantity, of choosing experiences over possessions. They involved the children in the decluttering process, allowing them to choose which items to keep and which to donate.

The process became a family project, a shared experience that strengthened their bonds. They discovered the joy of letting go, the freedom that came from simplifying their lives. Lily learned to choose her favorite stuffed animals, appreciating each one more deeply. Tom carefully selected his most treasured comic books, understanding the value of owning less, but of higher quality. The children, once attached to material things, began to appreciate the intangible gifts of family, nature, and shared experiences.

Their home transformed into a haven of peace and tranquility. The walls, once adorned with a chaotic array of artwork and photographs, now featured a few carefully chosen pieces that evoked a sense of serenity. The open spaces allowed for more freedom, more movement, more connection. They rediscovered the joy of shared meals, of family games, of quiet moments together, uninterrupted by the distractions of a cluttered environment.

Their newfound simplicity extended beyond their home. They became more selective about their social engagements, choosing quality time over quantity. They said no to commitments that drained their energy, leaving space for meaningful connections. They learned the art of saying "no" without feeling guilty or inadequate. They embraced the quiet beauty of nature, spending weekends hiking in the woods, picnicking by the lake, and simply enjoying the simple pleasures of being outdoors.

The intentional simplification of their lives had a ripple effect on every aspect of their existence. Their finances became more manageable, freeing them from the burden of debt and the relentless pursuit of material wealth. They found themselves having more time for each other, their relationships deepening through shared experiences and meaningful conversations. Their stress levels decreased, their overall well-being improved.

David found that his creative energy was revitalized. The clutter that had once weighed on his mind now allowed him to focus on his work with renewed clarity and passion. He began to incorporate elements of minimalism into his architectural designs, creating spaces that were both functional and aesthetically pleasing, spaces that fostered a sense of calm and well-being.

Sarah, ever mindful of her gratitude practice, continued to find joy in the simplest things. The warmth of the sun on her skin, the laughter of her children, the quiet moments shared with David – these were the true treasures of her life. She started a blog, sharing her family's journey toward simplicity, inspiring others to embark on their own journeys toward a more intentional and fulfilling existence.

Their story became a testament to the transformative power of embracing simplicity. It wasn't about deprivation, but about abundance—an abundance of time, energy, and meaningful connections. It was about appreciating the inherent richness of life, unburdened by the weight of excess. It was about living with intention, each choice reflecting a conscious commitment to what truly matters. Their home became not merely a space to live in but a sanctuary, a reflection of their values, and a testament to the beauty of a life lived simply, intentionally, and gratefully.

The journey of simplifying their lives wasn't without its bumps in the road. There were moments of temptation, times when the allure of acquiring more seemed irresistible. They faced challenges in maintaining their minimalist lifestyle, especially as their children grew older and their needs and desires evolved. But they learned to adapt, to remain flexible and to view their minimalist lifestyle not as a rigid set of rules, but as a guiding principle that allowed for growth, change and adaptability. They regularly reassessed their possessions, ensuring that only items that served a genuine purpose remained, a continuous act of mindful curation.

Through this ongoing process, their family strengthened their bond, their relationships deepened and the shared experience of decluttering had created a newfound respect for their possessions and a deeper understanding of what truly matters. They realized simplicity wasn't just about getting rid of stuff; it was about creating space for meaningful connection, for intentional living, for gratitude and appreciation. It was a continuous process, a journey of mindful living that enriched their lives in ways they never could have imagined. They had traded a life of accumulation for a life of appreciation, a life of clutter for a life of connection. And in that exchange, they found an immeasurable abundance.

The quiet hum of contentment that had settled over Sarah and David's home was shattered one blustery November evening. A phone call, sharp and jarring, ripped through the peaceful atmosphere. It was David's brother, Mark, his voice choked with emotion, delivering news that sent icy tendrils of fear snaking around Sarah's heart. Mark's business, a small construction firm, had imploded. A major project had gone disastrously wrong, leaving him facing crippling debt and the very real possibility of bankruptcy. Worse still, he was facing a lawsuit that threatened to consume everything he owned.

The news hung heavy in the air, a suffocating blanket that extinguished the warmth of their recently found simplicity. The carefully curated calm of their home felt suddenly fragile, the quiet joy threatened by a storm of uncertainty. David, usually the pillar of strength and composure, felt the weight of responsibility crush him. He paced the room, his usually meticulous movements now frantic, a whirlwind of worry and helplessness.

Sarah, remembering the lessons she'd learned in her journey toward simplicity – lessons that extended beyond decluttering and into the realm of spiritual discipline – found herself unexpectedly calm amidst the turmoil. The inner peace she had cultivated wasn't extinguished; it was tested, refined, and, she felt, strengthened. This was a trial, a crucible that would test their faith, their resilience, and their trust in God's plan.

"David," she said softly, her hand resting gently on his arm, "let's pray."

That night, they knelt together, their voices joining in a prayer born not of desperation, but of quiet trust. They didn't plead for a miraculous solution, a sudden reversal of fortune. Instead, they poured out their hearts to God, acknowledging their fear, their anxieties, but also expressing their unwavering faith in His sovereignty. They asked for guidance, for strength, for the wisdom to navigate this crisis, and above all, for the grace to accept whatever outcome God had in store.

The following weeks were a blur of meetings with lawyers, financial advisors, and concerned family members. The weight of Mark's impending financial ruin settled heavily upon the family, casting a pall over even the brightest moments. The children, Lily and Tom, sensed the undercurrent of tension, their usual ebullient spirits dampened by the gravity of the situation.

Sarah, however, remained resolute. She drew strength from her daily gratitude practice, focusing on the small blessings that still permeated their lives. The warmth of the sun, the laughter of her children, the unwavering love of her husband – these were anchors in the storm, reminders of the abundant grace that surrounded them.

She also leaned heavily on her faith, studying scripture and seeking wisdom from her pastor. The passages about God's sovereignty, His unwavering love, and His promise to provide for His children became sources of comfort and strength. She learned to distinguish between God's permissive will (allowing events to unfold) and His perfect will (His ultimate purpose within those events), a concept that proved crucial in navigating the difficult emotions that arose.

The pastor emphasized the importance of prayer, not as a magical formula for changing circumstances, but as a means of connecting with God, pouring out one's heart, and aligning oneself with His will. He also stressed the importance of surrendering control, of letting go of the need to understand God's plan completely, and trusting that even in the midst of suffering, God was working all things together for good.

This understanding didn't magically erase their difficulties. There were tears, moments of doubt, and times when fear threatened to overwhelm them. But through it all, their faith, strengthened by prayer and their shared reliance on God's sovereignty, provided a steadfast foundation.

David, initially consumed by anxiety and self-blame, gradually found a new strength and resolve. He discovered a renewed purpose in supporting his brother, not just financially, but emotionally, practically assisting in navigating the legal intricacies and providing unwavering encouragement. He found a renewed depth in his faith, acknowledging that God's sovereignty extended to trials and that this experience was an opportunity for spiritual growth.

Lily and Tom, though young, also participated in this profound family experience. They learned about faith, perseverance, compassion, and empathy. Sarah took the time to explain the situation to them, avoiding sugarcoating but offering assurance that even in hard times, their family was bound by faith and love, and God's love was a steadfast anchor. They learned to pray, to express their fears, and their unwavering faith in God's plan. They participated in acts of service toward their uncle, learning lessons of compassion and empathy that could not be acquired in any classroom.

Remarkably, the legal battle didn't conclude in the catastrophic way everyone had feared. A settlement was reached, far less devastating than anticipated. Mark, humbled but resolute, began to rebuild his life, guided by lessons learned in the crucible of crisis. He discovered a new sense of purpose, a renewed perspective, and a deeper appreciation for the value of relationships and faith.

The experience transformed the entire family. It wasn't merely the financial aspects; the shared ordeal deepened their bond, strengthening their faith and creating an unshakeable foundation based on love, perseverance, and trust in God's sovereign plan. They had learned that true wealth wasn't measured in possessions, but in family, faith, and an unwavering trust in a loving God who works all things for good, even in the face of unimaginable difficulties. Their simplified lifestyle, initially a choice for inner peace, proved to be a valuable asset during their crisis, allowing them to focus on what truly mattered – their faith, their family, and their trust in God's unwavering love and sovereign plan. The lessons learned during this challenging time were immeasurable, a testament to the transformative power of faith and the enduring strength of a family united in their trust in God. The experience had forged a deeper, more resilient faith in God's sovereignty, a faith that extended beyond the confines of their home, shaping their lives in profound and lasting ways.

The settlement, while less devastating than predicted, still left a scar. The emotional toll was substantial, a lingering ache beneath the surface of their renewed calm. David, though relieved, wrestled with a subtle sense of disappointment. He had poured his heart and soul into helping Mark, sacrificing time, energy, and resources. He'd prayed fervently for a miraculous intervention, a complete reversal of fortune that would erase the debt entirely. The reality, while better than the worst-case scenario, felt like a compromise, a compromise with God's plan, a compromise that left him questioning.

Sarah noticed the subtle shift in David's demeanor. The quiet contentment that had returned after the initial shock was now tinged with a quiet dissatisfaction. He wasn't outwardly complaining, but the subtle slump of his shoulders, the way he'd avoid eye contact when she mentioned Mark's progress, spoke volumes. One evening, after the children were asleep, she sat beside him on the couch, his hand nestled in hers.

"David," she began gently, her voice barely above a whisper, "I've noticed something. You seem... unsettled. Is it still Mark?"

He sighed, a long, weary sound. "It's not just Mark, Sarah. It's... everything. I prayed so hard for a complete turnaround, a miracle. And while this outcome is better than bankruptcy, it still feels like... a failure. Like we didn't fully trust God's plan. Like we didn't completely surrender."

Sarah squeezed his hand, her heart aching for him. She understood his struggle. The human desire for control, for a clear path, for a guaranteed happy ending, is powerful. But surrendering to God's will, truly surrendering, wasn't about eliminating challenges; it was about relinquishing the need to dictate the outcome.

“David,” she said softly, “Remember what Pastor Michael said? God’s plan isn't about avoiding hardship, it’s about growing through it. It’s about refining us, shaping us, making us stronger and more compassionate.”

She reached for her well-worn Bible, turning to the book of James. She read aloud, her voice clear and steady, "Consider it pure joy, my brothers and sisters, whenever you face trials of many kinds, because you know that the testing of your faith produces perseverance. Let perseverance finish its work so that you may be mature and complete, not lacking anything." (James 1:2-4)

"We prayed for guidance, David," she continued. "And God guided us. He guided Mark through a difficult path. He guided us to support each other, to grow closer as a family, and to experience His unfailing love even in the midst of hardship. Did we get everything we wanted? No. But we received so much more. A deeper faith, a stronger family bond, and a renewed appreciation for God's grace. Wouldn't you say that's a victory?”

David looked at her, his eyes filled with a mixture of sadness and dawning understanding. "I guess...I guess I focused so much on the 'what' that I missed the 'why'. I wanted the problem solved, not the lessons learned.”

Sarah nodded, her heart overflowing with compassion. "We all do, sometimes. But the lessons, David, the growth, the strengthening of our faith... these are immeasurable treasures. Surrendering to God's will isn't about passive acceptance; it's about active trust, even when the path is unclear. It's about believing that He is working, even when we don't see it."

The following weeks were a time of reflection and renewed commitment. David and Sarah dedicated themselves to studying scripture, delving deeper into the concept of God's sovereignty. They learned about the difference between God's active and permissive will – the active will being His direct intervention, the permissive will allowing events to unfold according to natural consequences but ultimately working toward His good purpose. They realized that even in the midst of suffering, God's ultimate goal was their sanctification, their spiritual growth, and their deepening relationship with Him.

They started a new journal, a family journal, where they documented their journey, their struggles, their victories, and their faith. It became a powerful tool, not just for recording their experiences, but for processing emotions, for sharing vulnerabilities, and for reaffirming their shared commitment to trust in God's plan.

The children, Lily and Tom, joined in the journaling process. Though their understanding was limited, they participated in expressing their feelings, drawing pictures, and adding their own prayers for their uncle. They learned that faith wasn't a passive acceptance of whatever happens but an active participation in a journey guided by God's love.

The transformation was gradual, a gentle unfolding of understanding and acceptance. David's quiet dissatisfaction gave way to a sense of peace, a quiet confidence in God's plan. He understood that surrender wasn't about resignation; it was about releasing control, trusting God's wisdom even when the path was shrouded in uncertainty.

They began to see their journey not as a series of setbacks, but as a pilgrimage of faith, a refining process that sculpted their characters, strengthened their family bonds, and deepened their connection to God. They realized that true surrender wasn't about getting what we want, but about wanting what God wants for us, trusting that His plan, even amidst the trials, is ultimately good, perfect, and leads to a destiny far exceeding anything they could have imagined.

Their lives weren't magically transformed into a fairytale; the challenges remained. But their perspective had shifted. Their faith, once tested to its limits, had emerged stronger and more resilient. They had learned to see God's hand not only in the big events, but in the smallest details of their daily lives – the warmth of the sun, the laughter of their children, the unwavering love that bound them together as a family. The simplicity of their lives, once a choice, had become a way of life, a reflection of their inward peace and their unwavering trust in the sovereign plan of a loving God.

Their journey served as a powerful testament to the transformative power of faith, a reminder that even amidst the storm, even when the path is uncertain, the unwavering love and sovereign plan of God is our anchor, our guide, and our ultimate source of hope and peace. They learned that true surrender is not about giving up, but about giving in to God's grace, His guidance, and His ultimate plan for their lives, a plan that, though mysterious at times, ultimately leads to a destiny far grander than they could ever have imagined. The journey was far from over, but the foundation of their faith had been laid, strong and unyielding, built on a bedrock of trust in God's sovereign will. The lessons learned, the challenges overcome, and the faith that had been forged in the fires of trial would serve them well in the days, months, and years to come, shaping their lives in ways they could only begin to comprehend.

The crisp mountain air, scented with pine and damp earth, offered a welcome contrast to the turmoil brewing within David. The prayer retreat, nestled amidst towering pines, felt a world away from the anxieties that had clung to him like shadows. Sarah, ever perceptive, had recognized the lingering unease beneath his surface calm and insisted on this retreat, a silent plea for respite and spiritual renewal.

The first few days were a blur of quiet contemplation, of shared meals eaten in reverent silence, of walks along winding trails that seemed to mirror the twists and turns of their lives. The retreat leader, a gentle woman named Sister Agnes, spoke of surrender, not as a passive resignation but as an active trust, a conscious decision to release the reins of control to a higher power. She spoke of the serenity prayer, that simple yet profound plea for the serenity to accept the things we cannot change, the courage to change the things we can, and the wisdom to know the difference.

David, however, found himself wrestling with the "things we cannot change." He replayed the events of the past months, analyzing every decision, every prayer, searching for the point where he had deviated from God's plan, the point where things had gone wrong. He had meticulously documented every aspect of Mark's financial crisis in his journal, meticulously recording each conversation, each plea for help, each agonizing prayer. His journal had become a battlefield, a place where he relentlessly fought the battles already lost.

Sister Agnes, sensing his struggle, gently approached him after a morning meditation. "David," she said softly, her eyes reflecting the wisdom of years spent guiding souls through the valleys of despair, "Your journal is a testament to your devotion, your love for your brother. But it seems to have become a source of further anguish."

He nodded, unable to speak, the weight of his unspoken frustrations heavy in his chest.

"Sometimes," Sister Agnes continued, her voice a calming balm, "our attempts to control the outcome blind us to the blessings along the way. God's plan unfolds not in a straight line, but in a tapestry woven with threads of joy and sorrow, success and failure. We tend to fixate on the threads of sorrow, neglecting the beauty of the overall design."

She suggested a different approach to journaling – one focused on gratitude, on recognizing the small miracles, the unexpected graces that punctuated their lives. She asked him to write down, not just the challenges, but the ways God had sustained them, the moments of love and support they had received, the resilience they had discovered within themselves. She shared anecdotes from her own life, tales of hardship and loss, but also of unexpected blessings, of divine interventions that had seemed impossible at the time.

David initially resisted. It felt disingenuous to write about gratitude when the weight of his anxieties felt so overwhelming. But, slowly, he started to listen to her words. He started small, focusing on the beauty of the mountain scenery, the peace of the quiet mornings, the simple act of sharing a meal with his family. He wrote about the kindness of strangers, the comforting words of friends, the unwavering love of Sarah. He started noticing things he'd previously overlooked—the laughter of his children, the warmth of the sun on his face, the simple act of breathing.

This shift in perspective proved transformative. As he focused on gratitude, a quiet sense of peace began to settle within him. He discovered that gratitude was not merely a passive appreciation; it was an active engagement with God's grace, a recognition of His presence in every moment, even the challenging ones. He began to see the difficulties not as isolated incidents but as part of a larger narrative, a story orchestrated by a loving God who was guiding him towards a destiny he could not yet comprehend.

The retreat included guided meditations, designed to help participants connect with their inner selves, to still the racing thoughts, and to find a sanctuary of peace within. David found these meditations particularly helpful. He discovered the power of deep breathing, of focusing on his senses, of quieting his mind and allowing God's presence to fill the void.

One evening, during a session focusing on forgiveness, a wave of emotion washed over him. He realized that he hadn't truly forgiven himself for his perceived failures. He had been so focused on the outcome of Mark's situation that he had failed to appreciate the process, the lessons learned, the spiritual growth that had taken place.

He confessed his struggle to Sister Agnes, his voice choked with emotion. She listened patiently, offering words of compassion and understanding. She reminded him of God's boundless love and forgiveness, His willingness to embrace him even in his imperfections. She guided him in a simple prayer of confession and forgiveness, a letting go of the burden of self-recrimination.

The final day of the retreat arrived too soon. The mountain air, once a welcome escape, now felt like a parting embrace. David left with a renewed sense of purpose, a quiet confidence in God's plan. His journal, once a source of anxiety, now held a collection of reflections on gratitude, a testament to God's unwavering love and presence in every aspect of his life.

The journey back home wasn't without its challenges. The demands of daily life, the anxieties of the world, crept back into his consciousness. But the seed of peace planted at the retreat had taken root, nurtured by daily prayer and meditation, by a conscious focus on gratitude. He found himself less reactive, more centered, better able to navigate the inevitable storms of life.

He continued to practice the techniques learned at the retreat, integrating them into his daily life. He began each day with a quiet time of prayer and meditation, setting aside time for reflection and communion with God. He made a conscious effort to notice the small miracles in his daily life, expressing gratitude for the simple pleasures and the unexpected graces that came his way. He continued journaling, documenting not just the challenges but also the blessings, the moments of joy, the expressions of love.

He shared his newfound peace with Sarah, the quiet contentment radiating from within him. Their family life flourished, strengthened by their shared faith and their commitment to active trust in God's plan. They embraced the imperfections, the uncertainties, knowing that even amidst the storms, God's love was their constant anchor. Their lives, once defined by anxieties and uncertainties, were now guided by a quiet faith, a peaceful surrender to the divine will, and an unwavering trust in a future guided by a loving and all-powerful God. The challenges remained, but their perspective had changed. They had learned to find peace in the midst of the storms, knowing that even the darkest clouds eventually yielded to the radiant light of God's grace.

The drive home, though physically shorter than the journey to the retreat, felt strangely longer. The mountain air, once a balm to his soul, was now a fading memory, replaced by the familiar hum of the highway and the ever-present anxieties that seemed to cling to the fabric of daily life. Yet, something had shifted within David. The peace he'd found nestled amongst the pines hadn't vanished completely; it lingered, a faint but persistent ember in the hearth of his heart. This ember, he knew, was fueled by something more profound than simply a scenic change or a few days of quiet reflection. It was fueled by prayer, a consistent, heartfelt conversation with the God he had come to know in a new, more intimate way.

He had always prayed, of course. Prayers of thanksgiving for blessings received, prayers of petition for needs unmet, prayers of supplication for those he loved. But these prayers, he realized, had often been hurried, perfunctory, more like a checklist of requests than a genuine communion. At the retreat, he had discovered a different kind of prayer, a slower, deeper, more intimate conversation with God, a silent listening as much as a vocal asking.

This new approach began with a simple act: sitting quietly, breathing deeply, and focusing on his awareness of God's presence. He didn't need a secluded mountaintop; he could find this quiet space in the ordinary moments of his life—during his morning commute, amidst the chaos of family dinner, even while waiting in line at the grocery store. It wasn't about escaping the world, but about finding God within it.

His prayers transformed, becoming less about demanding answers and more about seeking guidance, about surrendering control and trusting in God's wisdom. He learned to phrase his requests not as demands but as humble entreaties, acknowledging his own limitations and dependence on a higher power. He stopped trying to force God's hand, to manipulate outcomes, and instead, focused on aligning his will with God's, asking for the strength and wisdom to discern His plan.

One evening, as he knelt beside his bed, a profound sense of gratitude washed over him. He prayed not just for himself and his family, but for Mark, for his brother's difficult journey, for the strength and resilience Mark was discovering in the midst of his trials. He prayed for those who had helped them—friends, family, even strangers who had extended a hand of compassion. It was in this moment of selfless prayer that he experienced a profound release of anxiety. He let go of the need to control the outcome of Mark's financial struggles and surrendered it to God's loving care.

This act of surrender, fueled by consistent prayer, became a recurring theme in his daily life. As he faced the daily challenges of work, family, and life's inevitable setbacks, he turned to prayer not as a last resort but as his first response. He found that the simple act of acknowledging God's presence, of sharing his burdens and anxieties, brought a sense of calm and perspective he had never experienced before.

His journal, once a chronicle of worries and anxieties, became a record of his prayers and the answers he received. He documented not just the problems he faced but also the small graces, the unexpected kindnesses, the moments of peace that punctuated his days. He saw these moments not as mere coincidences but as evidence of God's loving hand guiding and protecting him.

He discovered the power of intercessory prayer, praying for others, even those he didn't know. He prayed for peace in the world, for those suffering from illness and injustice, for those who were lost and searching for meaning. He found that these acts of selfless prayer brought a deeper sense of connection to God and to his fellow human beings.

One particularly challenging day at work, when a project seemed destined for failure, David found himself overwhelmed with stress and frustration. He paused, closed his eyes, and engaged in a short but powerful prayer. He didn't ask for the project to magically succeed; instead, he asked for the wisdom to make the best decisions possible, for the strength to persevere, and for the peace to accept the outcome whatever it might be. To his surprise, a solution presented itself – a simple, elegant solution that had somehow escaped his notice during the earlier frantic attempts. The project was salvaged, not by a miracle, but through a clarity of thought and purpose born of prayer.

He began to teach his children the importance of prayer, not as a ritualistic duty but as a natural expression of their faith. They started their days with a simple family prayer, thanking God for His blessings and asking for guidance. They prayed before meals, before school, before bedtime. It became a natural part of their family rhythm, a quiet reminder of God's constant presence and unwavering love.

Sarah noticed the transformation in David. She saw the quiet confidence that had replaced the anxiety that had once consumed him. She saw the patience and compassion he extended to others, the serenity with which he navigated the daily storms of life. Their relationship deepened, strengthened by their shared faith and their commitment to prayer as a way of life.

He started attending a small prayer group at his church, finding comfort and support in the fellowship of other believers. He learned from their experiences, sharing his own struggles and victories. The group became a source of encouragement and accountability, a reminder that he was not alone in his journey of faith.

Through prayer, David didn't merely receive answers to his problems; he discovered a deeper understanding of God's character, His love, His mercy, and His unwavering faithfulness. He learned that prayer wasn't about changing God's mind but about changing his own heart, about aligning his will with God's, about finding peace and purpose in the midst of life's uncertainties. The retreat on the mountain had been a catalyst, a spiritual awakening, but the ongoing power of consistent, heartfelt prayer was what truly transformed his life. It was the steadfast anchor in the storms, the gentle guiding hand in the darkness, the source of strength and hope that enabled him to navigate the challenges of life with a newfound sense of peace, purpose, and unwavering trust in God's plan. And as he continued to pray, he knew that this journey, this ongoing conversation with God, was a lifelong commitment, a source of strength and guidance that would sustain him through whatever life might bring. The prayer, he discovered, wasn't a one-time event, but a living, breathing relationship – a continuous dialogue with the God who loved him unconditionally.

The quiet strength David found wasn't a magic trick, a sudden erasure of worry. It was a gradual, almost imperceptible shift, a deepening of his relationship with God, a trust that bloomed not in the absence of uncertainty but in its very midst. He learned that faith wasn't a shield against life's storms, but a sturdy ship to weather them. His anxieties, once a roaring tempest, became manageable waves, each one met with a prayer, a surrender, a quiet acceptance of God's will.

His newfound peace wasn't merely personal; it rippled outwards, affecting his relationships. Sarah, his wife, felt the change. She didn't need words to understand; she saw it in his eyes, felt it in his touch, heard it in the gentle timbre of his voice. Their evenings, once filled with tension and hushed anxieties over Mark's precarious financial situation, now held a shared serenity, a quiet confidence grounded in their shared faith. They prayed together, not demanding solutions, but seeking comfort and strength in their shared journey.

Mark, David's brother, was the epicenter of much of their worry. His business had faltered, his savings dwindling, his future uncertain. He struggled with the temptation to despair, to lose hope in the face of mounting debts and dwindling prospects. He saw the quiet strength in his brother, the unwavering faith that refused to waver even amidst the storm. David didn't offer platitudes or easy answers; instead, he offered his unwavering support, his prayers, his presence. He listened without judgment, offering a listening ear, a strong shoulder to lean on, a constant reminder that he wasn't alone. He helped Mark identify his talents and strengths and encouraged him to seek new opportunities, to trust in God's guidance even in the midst of the overwhelming challenges.

One evening, after a particularly difficult day, Mark confided in David. "I feel like I'm drowning, David," he confessed, his voice thick with despair. "I don't know how much longer I can keep this up."

David, placing a comforting hand on his brother's shoulder, replied, "Mark, I don't have all the answers. But I know the One who does. Let's pray together." And they did. It wasn't a lengthy, formal prayer, but a heartfelt conversation with God, a pouring out of anxieties and fears, a humble request for guidance and strength.

The prayer wasn't a magical solution to Mark's financial problems. The debts remained, the uncertainty lingered. But something shifted within Mark. He felt a quiet strength, a peace that surpassed understanding. It was the peace that comes from surrendering one's anxieties to a loving God, the peace of knowing that even in the darkness, God's love is a constant light.

This wasn't just about David and Mark. Their faith extended to their community, their church, their wider circle of family and friends. They actively participated in their church's outreach programs, offering support to others facing various challenges. They saw acts of service as a tangible expression of their faith, a means to spread hope and love to those in need. They learned to pray for their enemies, for those who held different beliefs, praying for peace and reconciliation. This act of extending their faith beyond their personal concerns expanded their understanding of God's unconditional love. They discovered that prayer wasn't a self-centered act, but a means to connect with God and others, fostering a deep sense of community.

Their faith extended even to strangers. They regularly volunteered at a local soup kitchen, interacting with individuals from diverse backgrounds, listening to their stories, sharing their burdens, offering a helping hand. They learned to see the divine image reflected in every person they encountered, regardless of their circumstances. They discovered that their faith wasn't confined to the walls of a church, but was meant to be lived out in their daily interactions with the world.

The journey wasn't always easy. There were moments of doubt, of fear, of uncertainty. There were times when the weight of their problems seemed insurmountable. But even in those moments, they clung to their faith, relying on their prayers, their community, their shared belief in God's unwavering love and faithfulness.

They learned that faith is not the absence of doubt but a steadfast trust despite doubt. It's a constant conversation with God, a journey of continuous learning and growth. It's a journey of surrender, of letting go of control and trusting in God's plan, even when that plan is unclear. It's a journey of love, of compassion, of service, of extending God's grace and mercy to others.

David's journal became a testament to this journey, not just a record of his own struggles but a chronicle of God's faithfulness, a collection of prayers answered in ways he never expected. He documented the small miracles, the unexpected kindnesses, the moments of peace that punctuated the storms. He learned to recognize God's hand in the everyday occurrences of life, finding meaning and purpose in the mundane, seeing the divine in the ordinary.

One such entry read: "Today, Mark received a phone call. A potential investor. A glimmer of hope in the darkness. We prayed for this, but it doesn't erase the challenges. It's a step, a small victory in a long journey. Thank you, God, for your faithfulness. Thank you for your love. Thank you for the ongoing journey."

This journey of faith, nurtured by prayer, sustained by community, and grounded in unwavering love, transformed David, Mark, and their families. It didn't remove life's uncertainties, but it gave them the strength, the hope, and the unwavering trust to navigate them with grace, resilience, and an enduring faith in God's plan, however mysterious or challenging it might seem. The uncertainties remained, but their fear had lessened. They had learned to embrace the unknown with a confident trust in God's loving hands. The mountain retreat had been a beginning; the journey of faith, a lifetime's commitment. Their stories became a testament to the power of embracing faith in the face of uncertainty, a living example of trusting God's plan, even when the path ahead remained unclear. Their lives, once defined by anxiety and fear, now shone with a quiet strength, a radiant hope, fueled by a love that transcended the limits of human understanding. Their journey became a beacon, a testament to the unwavering power of faith, a light shining brightly in the darkness, inviting others to join them on the path towards a deeper, more meaningful relationship with God. The future, while still uncertain, held not fear, but a hopeful anticipation, a confident trust in the divine plan unfolding, step by step, prayer by prayer.

The quiet strength that had settled over David and Mark wasn't merely an absence of problems. Their lives still held challenges; Mark's financial struggles, for instance, continued to cast a shadow. But something profound had shifted within them, a deep wellspring of inner peace that allowed them to navigate their difficulties with a newfound resilience. This peace wasn't a magical solution, a sudden erasure of their anxieties. It was the fruit of a deep and abiding relationship with God, a trust that blossomed in the fertile ground of their faith, nurtured by prayer and sustained by a strong community.

Consider the story of Elizabeth. She wasn't a part of David and Mark's immediate circle, but her journey mirrored their own in many ways. Elizabeth, a successful businesswoman, had always strived for perfection. Her life was a carefully orchestrated symphony of achievement, a meticulously planned schedule of meetings, deadlines, and social engagements. She was admired by many for her drive, her accomplishments, but inwardly, she felt a gnawing emptiness. Her success felt hollow, her achievements unsatisfying. The constant pressure to maintain her image, to reach higher, to achieve more, left her perpetually exhausted, emotionally drained, and spiritually adrift.

She often found herself staring at the city lights from her high-rise apartment, feeling a profound sense of isolation despite her many connections. The applause of the crowd faded the moment she stepped away from the spotlight. Her meticulously curated life, once a source of pride, now felt like a gilded cage. She lacked the inner peace she so desperately craved. The constant striving, the relentless pursuit of external validation, had left her soul parched and empty. Sleep became elusive, replaced by a restless tossing and turning, her mind racing with anxieties, her heart heavy with a vague sense of unease. Her relationships suffered, strained by her perpetual busyness and her inability to truly connect with those around her. She felt like a stranger in her own life.

One day, while browsing in a bookstore, a small, unassuming volume caught her eye. The title, "Finding Peace in the Storm," resonated with her inner turmoil. She bought the book, and that night, she began to read. The words spoke to her soul, illuminating the darkness within. The book wasn't filled with lofty theological concepts or complicated spiritual practices; instead, it offered simple, practical steps towards finding inner peace, emphasizing the importance of slowing down, of cultivating gratitude, of connecting with God through prayer and meditation.

It spoke of surrender, of releasing the need for control, of trusting in a higher power. It emphasized the importance of self-compassion, of accepting one's imperfections, and of cultivating forgiveness – both for oneself and for others. Elizabeth found herself deeply moved by the honesty and vulnerability of the author's personal experiences. She recognized her own struggles mirrored in the author's journey, and it gave her a sense of hope, a feeling that she wasn't alone in her quest for inner peace.

This book became her guide, her companion on a transformative journey of self-discovery. She started by incorporating small changes into her daily routine. She began her day with a few minutes of prayer and meditation, focusing on expressing gratitude for the blessings in her life, both big and small. She made a conscious effort to slow down, to savor the simple pleasures, to appreciate the beauty of the world around her – the sunrise, the birdsong, the warmth of the sun on her face. She started to disconnect from her devices, giving herself time to just be, to be present in the moment.

She began to cultivate self-compassion, acknowledging her limitations, forgiving herself for her past mistakes, and treating herself with the same kindness and understanding she would offer a dear friend. She started journaling, pouring out her thoughts and feelings onto paper, releasing the weight of her anxieties and worries. She learned to identify her triggers, the situations or people that tended to push her emotional buttons, and developed strategies for managing her reactions in a healthier way.

Elizabeth also began to actively cultivate her relationships. She made time for meaningful conversations with her loved ones, prioritizing quality time over quantity. She learned to listen attentively, to empathize with others' experiences, and to offer support without judgment. She found a quiet joy in connecting with others on a deeper level, sharing her vulnerabilities, and experiencing the healing power of shared humanity. She joined a small prayer group at her local church, finding solace and encouragement in shared faith and prayer. This community became a source of strength, a safe haven where she could be herself, free from the pressure to maintain a perfect image.

The changes were gradual, almost imperceptible at first, but they were profound. Elizabeth began to notice a subtle shift in her perspective, a softening of her heart, a growing sense of inner peace. Her sleep improved, the anxieties that once plagued her became less intense, and her mood became more stable. She felt a deep sense of contentment that transcended her external circumstances. She realized that true happiness wasn't about achieving more, but about being more – more present, more compassionate, more connected to herself and to God.

She discovered that inner peace wasn't the absence of problems, but a state of being that allowed her to navigate challenges with grace, resilience, and a sense of hope. She still faced setbacks and difficulties, but her responses were different. Instead of reacting with anxiety and frustration, she met each challenge with a quiet strength, a trusting surrender to God's will. She found that her faith wasn't a shield against life's storms, but a sturdy ship to weather them.

Elizabeth's transformation wasn't about discarding her ambition or her drive. It was about aligning her ambitions with her values, ensuring that her pursuits contributed to her overall well-being rather than depleting it. She continued to be successful in her career, but her priorities had shifted. She valued her relationships more, prioritized her spiritual life, and practiced self-care with intentionality.

Her newfound peace became contagious, rippling outwards to touch the lives of those around her. She became a source of inspiration and encouragement to her colleagues, friends, and family. Her ability to remain calm and centered in the face of adversity became a testament to the power of inner peace. She discovered that true influence comes not from striving for power, but from radiating a quiet strength, a gentle love that inspires others to seek their own path to peace.

Elizabeth's journey underscores the truth that inner peace isn't a destination but a journey, a lifelong commitment to cultivating spiritual growth, self-awareness, and a deep connection with God.

It is a path paved with prayer, meditation, self-compassion, and meaningful relationships. It's a process of learning to surrender control, to trust in the divine plan, and to find contentment in the midst of life's uncertainties. It's a journey of letting go of the illusion of perfection, embracing our imperfections, and discovering the profound beauty of our authentic selves, reflecting the divine image within. It's a testament to the fact that true peace is not found in external circumstances, but in the depths of our hearts, where God resides. Elizabeth's journey, much like David and Mark's, showcases the transformative power of faith, demonstrating that even in the face of life's challenges, a profound and enduring inner peace is attainable through a deeper relationship with God and a commitment to living a life guided by faith, love, and service.

The aroma of roasted chicken and freshly baked bread filled the air, a comforting blanket against the crisp autumn evening. Laughter spilled from the open windows of the cozy farmhouse, a joyful symphony of shared moments and cherished memories. Inside, gathered around a long, wooden table laden with food, was the Miller family – a tapestry woven with threads of varying ages, personalities, and experiences, yet united by an unshakeable bond. This wasn't just a family dinner; it was a celebration, a quiet acknowledgement of the strength that had blossomed in their relationships, a strength directly related to the peace they had individually cultivated in their lives.

Their journey hadn't been without its storms. Years ago, the Millers had been a fractured family, plagued by misunderstandings, resentment, and unspoken hurts. Arguments had been frequent, silences heavy with unspoken grievances. Each member, consumed by personal struggles, had built walls around their hearts, isolating themselves from the very people they loved most. Their individual paths towards peace had been different, yet their convergence into a unified, loving family was a testament to the power of individual transformation.

John, the patriarch, a man weathered by years of hard work and responsibility, had been particularly resistant to change. He carried the weight of the world on his shoulders, believing his strength lay in control, in relentlessly shouldering the burdens of his family. He had difficulty expressing emotions, believing vulnerability was a weakness. His initial resistance to the spiritual practices his wife, Mary, had begun incorporating into their lives was significant. He found meditation tedious, prayer an unnecessary formality. However, witnessing the positive changes in Mary and their children, he gradually began to understand the power of surrendering his need for control to a higher power, allowing God to guide and comfort him. This surrender released a profound weight from his shoulders, allowing him to be present, to listen more attentively, to communicate openly and genuinely.

Mary, a woman of unwavering faith, had been the catalyst for change. Her journey toward peace began with a humble acknowledgment of her own imperfections, a willingness to forgive herself for past mistakes and to extend grace to those around her. This self-compassion allowed her to approach her family with greater patience and understanding, to see their struggles not as personal attacks, but as expressions of their own individual journeys. She became the anchor of their family, consistently offering love, support, and a safe haven for open communication. Her unwavering faith, exemplified in her consistent prayers and meditation, created an atmosphere of peace in the family home. She understood that building a peaceful family was not about suppressing conflict, but addressing it with grace and respect.

Their children, Sarah and Thomas, had their own battles to fight. Sarah, the elder, had struggled with anxiety and perfectionism, mirroring the pattern of Elizabeth's story. The relentless pursuit of academic excellence and social acceptance had left her emotionally depleted. Her path to peace involved learning to embrace her imperfections, forgiving herself for falling short of her self-imposed standards, and prioritizing self-care. The mindfulness practices that she incorporated into her daily routine—meditation and deep breathing—helped her manage her anxiety and reconnect with a sense of inner calm. Thomas, the younger sibling, had struggled with a rebellious spirit and a lack of direction. His journey toward peace involved a gradual acceptance of his responsibility in his actions, coupled with a re-evaluation of his values and ambitions. He discovered that true contentment lay not in external validation, but in aligning his choices with the values he believed in deeply. He found a renewed appreciation for the simple act of helping his family. His journey emphasized the importance of making amends for past behaviors.

The family dinner was a testament to their individual growth. Conversations flowed easily, each member comfortable sharing their experiences, their joys and struggles, without fear of judgment or criticism. The laughter was genuine, spontaneous, and heartfelt. There were no hidden agendas, no unspoken resentments; only a genuine appreciation for one another. The children openly expressed their love and gratitude to their parents. John, without hesitation, shared his vulnerability, acknowledging his past mistakes and expressing his love for his family. Mary, with gentle wisdom, offered encouragement and affirmation to her children. It was a night of true connection, a celebration of the peace that had transformed not only their individual lives but their relationships.

The strength of their bonds was evident in the small gestures, the shared glances, the comfortable silences. It was reflected in their ability to navigate disagreements with respect and understanding. Disagreements still arose, of course, but they were addressed without aggression or animosity, instead handled with mutual respect, a willingness to listen, and a desire to seek resolution. They practiced active listening, understanding each other's perspective, and finding common ground. They had learned to communicate their needs and expectations without blame or criticism. They had learned to forgive, both themselves and each other, recognizing that forgiveness is not condoning but releasing.

Their shared faith served as a foundation for this familial unity. Regular family prayers, both formal and informal, created a shared spiritual space where they connected not only to God but also to each other. They found solace and strength in their shared belief system, which strengthened their bonds. The church community also played a significant role in their transformation. The support they received from their fellow parishioners, the shared experiences of faith, provided a sense of belonging and mutual encouragement. They learned from each other, supporting each other in their individual journeys of faith. This shared journey helped them build a deeper appreciation for the importance of community, not only in their church but in their immediate family circle.

Their transformed relationships extended beyond their immediate family. Their newfound peace radiated outward, impacting their relationships with extended family, friends, and neighbors. Their ability to remain calm and centered in the face of adversity became a testament to the power of inner peace. They became a source of inspiration and encouragement to others, demonstrating the transformative power of living a life guided by faith, love, and service.

The Miller family's journey demonstrates the profound connection between individual peace and strong relationships. It's a testament to the fact that inner peace isn't just a personal pursuit, but a catalyst for creating deeper, more meaningful connections with those around us. By cultivating inner peace, we create an environment of love, respect, and understanding, paving the way for stronger, more fulfilling relationships. It's a journey that requires commitment, patience, and perseverance, but the rewards are immeasurable, transforming not only our individual lives but the lives of those we love. The fragrance of the roasted chicken, the warmth of the gathering, and the joyful laughter that filled the room on that autumn evening was a testament to the enduring power of peace, a peace that had permeated their hearts, their homes, and their relationships, creating a family bound together not by blood alone, but by a shared commitment to love, understanding, and a deep, abiding faith. It was a beautiful picture of the fruits of a peaceful life, a legacy woven with the threads of love, forgiveness, and the quiet strength that comes from a deep relationship with God. Their story is an inspiring reminder that the path to peace is not a solitary journey, but a journey that transforms ourselves and the relationships that define our lives.

The scent of woodsmoke and pine hung in the crisp air as Daniel stood on the precipice of his lifelong dream. Below him lay the sprawling vineyard, rows upon rows of ripening grapes stretching towards the distant mountains, a testament to years of hard work, unwavering dedication, and a healthy dose of stubborn perseverance. He'd achieved it, the vineyard he'd envisioned since he was a boy, his hands calloused and stained from years of toil, his heart overflowing with a pride that felt both exhilarating and...empty.

He'd climbed the ladder of success, rung by rung. He'd faced setbacks, endured financial strain, battled the capricious whims of nature, and outmaneuvered shrewd competitors. He'd poured his soul into this land, transforming barren hillsides into a flourishing testament to his ambition. Yet, as he stood there, gazing upon his achievement, a subtle unease stirred within him. The thrill of victory felt... muted. The satisfaction he expected was absent. He'd reached the summit, but the view, while spectacular, lacked the depth, the resonance he'd anticipated.

He'd always measured success by tangible achievements. A prestigious university degree, a lucrative business deal, the acquisition of this very vineyard – each milestone marked with a sense of accomplishment. He'd chased the American dream with relentless focus and had attained it. He had the vineyard, the house with a view, the comfortable lifestyle. He even had a loving family – his wife, Sarah, supportive and understanding, their children growing into responsible adults. But something was missing. A quiet hollowness echoed in the silence between the sounds of nature, a void that no amount of material success could fill.

His reflection that evening, staring at his weary face in the bathroom mirror, confirmed his unease. The lines etched around his eyes spoke of sleepless nights, not of joy, but of stress. The success he'd craved had brought not only wealth, but a relentless pressure to maintain it, a constant striving that left him feeling perpetually depleted. He found himself increasingly isolated, disconnected from the very people he loved, trapped in a gilded cage of his own making.

This was when he turned inward, to the spiritual practices he'd always considered ancillary. He'd been raised in a Christian household, attending church dutifully but without a deep, personal understanding of its tenets. He'd seen faith as something separate from his life, a weekend ritual rather than a daily guide. Now, staring into the emptiness of his achievement, he found himself drawn to the quiet solace of prayer and meditation, seeking answers to questions he hadn't even known he had.

He began attending church more regularly, not as an obligation, but as a yearning for something more profound. He participated in Bible study groups, engaging in thoughtful discussions about the teachings of Jesus. He re-read the gospels, letting the words sink into his soul, paying attention to the emphasis on service, compassion, and humility – virtues that seemed distant and almost foreign to the fiercely competitive world he had inhabited. He started reading about the lives of saints and other Christians who had found profound meaning not in material wealth but in acts of service.

His reawakening to faith wasn't a sudden epiphany but a gradual process of exploration and self-discovery. It involved grappling with his own ambition, questioning his priorities, confronting the flawed values he'd held so tightly. He realized that his pursuit of success had been fueled by a need for validation, a desire to prove himself worthy.

He began to understand that true worth wasn't measured by material possessions, but by the impact he had on the lives of others.

He started volunteering at a local homeless shelter, offering not just money, but his time and presence, listening to their stories, offering comfort and support. He found an unexpected joy in these acts of service, a sense of fulfillment far surpassing any material reward. He discovered that helping others not only enriched their lives but his own, filling the hollowness that his personal achievements couldn't touch.

He invited families from the shelter to his vineyard for picnics, sharing the bounty of his labor not only with his own family, but with those who had so little. He established a foundation dedicated to supporting local charities, using a portion of his profits to help those in need. The vineyard, initially a symbol of his individual achievement, became a platform for generosity and community engagement. His leadership in the church grew as his understanding of faith deepened, leading others to embrace similar paths.

The change wasn't just external; it was internal. He became more patient, more understanding, more forgiving, not just of others, but also of himself. He learned to embrace imperfection, to let go of the relentless pursuit of perfection that had defined his earlier years. He cultivated gratitude for the blessings in his life, focusing on what he had rather than what he lacked. The peace that followed was profound, a tranquility that extended beyond the vineyard, touching his relationships with his wife, children, and friends. He finally understood the true meaning of the parable of the talents, realizing that true fulfillment lies not in hoarding one's gifts but in sharing them generously with others.

The emptiness was replaced by a deep sense of purpose, a satisfaction that resonated from the core of his being. He'd found his purpose not in achieving his dreams, but in serving a purpose larger than himself, in aligning his life with his faith, in using his gifts to make a difference in the world. The vineyard still flourished, but it was now a symbol not just of his individual success, but of his commitment to a life lived in service to God and others. The view from the summit was breathtaking, indeed, but now, he saw not just the landscape, but the lives he touched, the differences he'd made, the love he'd shared. The true fruit of a peaceful life, he discovered, wasn't just peace itself, but the joy of giving it away. His story became a living testament to the truth that the greatest achievements are often the acts of selfless service, the quiet acts of kindness that ripple through the world, leaving a legacy of love, compassion, and enduring peace. His transformed life became an inspiration, demonstrating that the most fulfilling path isn't always the one most easily traveled, but the one that leads to a life of service, to a deeper connection with God, and to a profoundly meaningful life, exceeding even the most ambitious dreams. The aroma of success was now mingled with the sweeter fragrance of a life truly lived, a life dedicated not to personal gain but to the greater good.

The devastating hurricane had ripped through the coastal town of Seabrook like a vengeful god, leaving a trail of destruction in its wake. Homes were splintered, businesses were leveled, and the once vibrant community was reduced to a landscape of debris and despair. The salt-laced wind still howled a mournful dirge through the skeletal remains of buildings, a constant reminder of the storm's brutal power. Yet, amidst the rubble and the wreckage, a quiet strength began to emerge, a resilience born not of mere survival instinct, but of a deep-seated faith and a shared commitment to rebuilding their lives together.

Pastor Elijah, a man whose faith had been tested countless times by life's storms, walked among his parishioners, offering words of comfort and hope. He wasn't immune to the devastation; his own home had been badly damaged, yet his spirit remained unbroken. He knew that the road ahead would be long and arduous, but he also knew that their community, bound by faith and a shared history, possessed an inner strength capable of overcoming even this monumental challenge.

The initial days were a blur of chaos and emergency relief efforts. Volunteers streamed in from neighboring towns, offering assistance and support. Food, water, and medical supplies were distributed, providing a lifeline to those in desperate need. But beyond the immediate necessities, a deeper need emerged – the need for emotional healing, for spiritual sustenance, for a renewed sense of hope amidst the overwhelming despair.

Pastor Elijah organized daily prayer meetings in the town square, a makeshift sanctuary amidst the ruins. The gatherings became a source of strength and solace for the community, a testament to their unwavering faith. People shared their stories, their fears, and their hopes, finding comfort in the shared experience and the shared belief in a higher power. The prayers weren't just pleas for help; they were expressions of gratitude for survival, affirmations of resilience, and declarations of faith in a brighter future.

The rebuilding process wasn't easy. Disagreements arose, tensions flared, and the weight of the task seemed almost insurmountable. There were moments of doubt, moments of despair, when the sheer scale of the devastation threatened to overwhelm them. Yet, Pastor Elijah continued to guide them, reminding them of the biblical parable of the mustard seed – a tiny seed capable of growing into a mighty tree. He instilled in them the belief that their community, though battered and bruised, possessed the strength to grow beyond the devastation, stronger and more unified than before.

He organized work teams, assigning tasks based on individuals' skills and abilities. Some were skilled in construction, others in carpentry, and still others in providing emotional support to those struggling with the loss of loved ones and possessions. The work was back-breaking, the days were long, and the nights were filled with the sounds of the wind and the distant cries of seagulls. Yet, they persevered, driven by a shared purpose, a shared faith, and a shared vision of a restored Seabrook.

The children, who had witnessed the storm's fury and the subsequent destruction, were particularly vulnerable. Pastor Elijah organized a special program for them, providing a safe space for them to process their emotions, to express their fears, and to find comfort in the company of their peers. Through art therapy, storytelling, and play, they began to heal, to rediscover their joy, and to regain a sense of hope for the future.

The process of rebuilding was not simply about restoring physical structures but about rebuilding the community's spirit, its sense of belonging, and its faith in the future. They learned to rely on each other, to support each other, and to find strength in their shared experiences. They discovered the power of empathy, compassion, and forgiveness, virtues that strengthened their bonds and solidified their commitment to rebuilding not only their town but also their lives.

As the months passed, the town slowly began to transform. New homes rose from the rubble, businesses reopened their doors, and the streets once filled with debris were once again bustling with life. The spirit of Seabrook, though tested to its limits, had emerged stronger and more resilient than before. They had learned that the greatest storms, while destructive, could also reveal the profound strength of the human spirit, the power of faith, and the importance of community.

The experience also led to a deeper appreciation for the simple blessings in life – the warmth of a shared meal, the comfort of a friend's embrace, the beauty of a sunrise over the ocean. They had learned to live in the present moment, to appreciate the gifts they had been given, and to cultivate a profound sense of gratitude for the blessings that remained.

Their story became a beacon of hope for other communities facing similar challenges, a testament to the resilience of the human spirit and the transformative power of faith. The town of Seabrook, once ravaged by a devastating hurricane, emerged as a symbol of hope, a testament to the enduring strength of the human spirit, and a powerful example of how faith, resilience, and community can overcome even the most daunting of obstacles. The experience transformed Seabrook, not just physically, but spiritually, forging an even stronger sense of community, deepening their faith, and demonstrating that even in the face of unimaginable loss, the human spirit is capable of incredible resilience and renewal. Their story became a living parable, a testament to the power of faith to not just comfort but to empower, to inspire, and to lead to a future richer and more meaningful than before.

The rebuilding efforts continued for years, a testament to the unwavering commitment of the people of Seabrook. The town not only recovered from the hurricane but transformed, becoming a model for disaster preparedness and community resilience. Their story spread, attracting attention from disaster relief organizations and urban planners who sought to learn from their experience. Seabrook became a symbol of hope, demonstrating the profound impact of faith, perseverance, and a strong community bond in the face of adversity. The resilience of Seabrook wasn't merely a matter of physical reconstruction; it was a spiritual rebirth, a testament to the enduring strength of the human spirit and the transformative power of faith. The town's recovery became a living parable, demonstrating the ability of a community, strengthened by faith and bound by love, to not only survive but thrive after tragedy. Their story served as a constant reminder that even amidst the deepest despair, hope can bloom and resilience can triumph. The experience left an indelible mark on the lives of the individuals within Seabrook, deepening their faith, fostering stronger relationships, and instilling in them a resilience that would serve them well in the years to come. The winds of change might have ravaged their town, but they had weathered the storm, emerging stronger, more united, and more profoundly grateful for the life they had been given. The transformation wasn't merely external; it was a profound inner shift, a testament to the power of faith to nurture hope, cultivate resilience, and ultimately, lead to a more meaningful and fulfilling life. The spirit of Seabrook served as a beacon of hope, a testament to the power of collective faith, and an inspiration to communities everywhere facing trials and tribulations.

The rebuilding of Seabrook wasn't solely about bricks and mortar; it was a profound spiritual exercise, a testament to the transformative power of faith. As the physical structures rose from the rubble, so too did the spirits of its inhabitants. Pastor Elijah, ever observant, recognized a burgeoning need beyond the immediate physical necessities. He saw a hunger for purpose, a yearning for significance in the face of such overwhelming loss. He knew that merely rebuilding homes wasn't enough; they needed to rebuild their lives, imbuing them with a sense of lasting meaning and contribution.

He initiated a series of workshops, gently titled "Building a Life of Significance," a parallel construction project focused on the inner lives of the community. These weren't formal sermons, but intimate discussions, drawing on biblical parables and personal anecdotes. He spoke of the parable of the talents, reminding them that their unique gifts and abilities, however seemingly small, were precious in God's eyes and meant to be shared. He urged them to identify their strengths, to recognize their inherent worth, and to discover how those gifts could contribute to the ongoing restoration of their community and beyond.

One such individual was Sarah, a quiet woman who had lost everything in the hurricane. Initially withdrawn and grief-stricken, she found solace in helping others. Her skill lay in listening, in offering a comforting presence to those struggling with trauma and loss. She started visiting the elderly, many of whom were isolated and afraid, providing practical help and emotional support. Her quiet acts of kindness, born from her own suffering, radiated a profound sense of peace and hope. Her life, though devastated by the storm, found renewed purpose in serving others, proving that even in profound loss, significant contribution is possible.

Another was young Thomas, a talented artist whose home and studio had been destroyed. Initially despairing over the loss of his work, he slowly found solace in using his art to capture the resilience of his community. He painted murals depicting the devastation of the storm, but also the subsequent acts of kindness, resilience and unity that characterized Seabrook's recovery. His art became a powerful symbol of hope, a testament to the enduring human spirit. He started teaching art to children, helping them express their trauma and grief through creative expression. His talent, once seen as a personal expression, became a powerful tool for healing and community building, a profound source of significance in his life.

Pastor Elijah emphasized the importance of service, highlighting Jesus's teachings on loving one's neighbor and caring for the least among them. He encouraged them to view their rebuilding efforts not merely as a task, but as an act of worship, a way of honoring God through service to others. He reminded them of the biblical concept of stewardship, that their lives, talents, and resources were gifts entrusted to them, to be used wisely and generously for the benefit of all.

The workshops weren't just about identifying talents and serving others. They also focused on forgiveness, a crucial element in healing and moving forward. The hurricane had exposed deep-seated resentments and conflicts within the community, old wounds that had been reopened by the disaster. Pastor Elijah, using the wisdom of scripture, guided them towards reconciliation, urging them to forgive those who had hurt them, and to seek forgiveness from those they had wronged. This wasn't about condoning harmful behavior, but about releasing the burden of resentment that prevented them from moving forward. He explained that forgiveness, while challenging, was a liberating act, an essential step towards finding peace and significance in their lives.

The process of forgiveness was not always easy. There were tears, apologies, and difficult conversations. Yet, as they worked through their conflicts, a sense of unity and reconciliation emerged, strengthening their community bonds and creating a more harmonious environment. The shared experience of overcoming adversity, coupled with the act of forgiving and being forgiven, fostered a powerful sense of connection and mutual respect, further enhancing their sense of significance in each other's lives. The rebuilding of Seabrook became more than a physical process; it evolved into a spiritual journey of healing, reconciliation and communal growth.

As the town slowly returned to life, the focus shifted towards sustainability and long-term growth. Pastor Elijah encouraged the community to establish initiatives that would ensure their resilience in the face of future challenges. They developed a comprehensive disaster preparedness plan, creating a network of support and mutual assistance. They established a community garden, providing fresh produce and fostering a sense of shared responsibility. They started small businesses, promoting economic self-reliance and community empowerment. Every act, every initiative, was an expression of their collective faith and commitment to building a better, more resilient future.

The narrative of Seabrook's recovery became more than just a local story; it echoed the larger narrative of faith, resilience, and the pursuit of significance. The individuals who had lost so much discovered that true wealth lay not in material possessions, but in the richness of human connection, the power of faith, and the profound satisfaction that comes from living a life of service and contribution. They understood that a life of significance wasn't about accumulating achievements or possessions, but about leaving a positive impact on the world, about making a difference in the lives of others. This was the true fruit of their peaceful lives, a harvest of lasting significance, born from the ashes of devastation. The story of Seabrook became a beacon of hope, a testament to the enduring human spirit and the transformative power of faith, proving that even in the darkest of times, life can be profoundly meaningful and significant. It was a story that transcended the local context, becoming a universal parable of hope, resilience, and the enduring power of the human spirit. The people of Seabrook, once victims of a devastating storm, became beacons of hope, shining brightly for communities around the world facing their own challenges.

Their journey served as a powerful reminder that life's true significance lies not in what we accumulate, but in what we contribute. Their collective story became an inspiring testament to the enduring power of faith, compassion and unwavering dedication to building a better future.

The gentle hum of the air conditioner was the only sound in the room, a stark contrast to the tempest raging within Eleanor. Across from her sat Pastor Michael, his kind eyes reflecting the soft light filtering through the stained-glass window. He'd listened patiently as Eleanor recounted her anxieties – the crippling fear of public speaking, the constant worry about her daughter's well-being, the gnawing insecurity about her career. Now, silence hung heavy in the air, a pregnant pause before the next step in her journey towards healing.

"Eleanor," Pastor Michael began softly, his voice a calming balm, "your fears, as you've described them, are multifaceted. They're not simply isolated incidents, but rather symptoms of deeper, underlying issues. To truly overcome them, we need to identify their source."

He paused, allowing his words to settle. "The Bible speaks often of the heart, doesn't it? Not just the physical organ, but the center of our being, the wellspring of our thoughts, emotions, and actions. It's in the heart where fear often takes root."

He leaned forward, his gaze warm and encouraging. "Think back, Eleanor. Can you trace these fears back to specific events or experiences in your life?"

Eleanor closed her eyes, lost in a sea of memories. Images flickered – a childhood filled with criticism, a demanding boss, a near-accident that left her shaken. Each memory was accompanied by a visceral wave of anxiety, a tightness in her chest, a tremor in her hands.

"The criticism from my parents," she whispered, her voice barely audible, "It felt constant, relentless. I always felt like I was never good enough, never measuring up." Tears welled in her eyes, tracing paths through the carefully applied makeup.

Pastor Michael nodded sympathetically. "That's a significant starting point, Eleanor. The constant fear of disapproval can have profound and lasting effects, shaping our self-perception and fueling anxieties in various areas of our lives. It's a form of learned helplessness, a belief that our efforts are futile and that we are inherently unworthy of love and acceptance. This isn't a reflection of God's love for you, however. His love is unconditional, a bedrock of steadfast security."

He opened his Bible, turning to a passage in Romans. "Romans 8:1 tells us, 'There is therefore now no condemnation for those who are in Christ Jesus.' This verse isn't just a comforting statement, it's a powerful declaration of freedom from the condemnation that feeds our anxieties. You are loved unconditionally, Eleanor, not for your achievements or your perceived flaws, but simply because you are God's child."

Eleanor took a deep breath, trying to absorb the weight of those words. The thought of unconditional love felt almost foreign, a stark contrast to the years spent striving for validation.

"And the near-accident," she continued, her voice shaking slightly. "It left me with this constant fear of losing control, of something bad happening to my daughter."

Pastor Michael listened intently, his expression patient and understanding. “Trauma, Eleanor, can leave deep scars on our psyche. It rewires our brains, making us hyper-vigilant, always on the lookout for potential danger. This is a natural response, a survival mechanism. But it can also become a prison, trapping us in a cycle of fear and anxiety. We need to gently rewire those neural pathways, to replace fear with faith and trust.”

He spoke of the power of prayer, of surrendering anxieties to God, of trusting in His divine protection. He explained that while it’s natural to experience fear, our response to it doesn't have to be governed by anxiety. God doesn’t promise the absence of challenges, but He promises to be with us in the midst of them.

“And my job,” Eleanor added, her voice laced with frustration. “I constantly fear failure, fear of not being good enough, fear of being replaced.” She wrung her hands, a nervous habit she hadn't realized she’d developed.

Pastor Michael smiled gently. "This fear of inadequacy often stems from a lack of self-worth, a sense of being defined by our accomplishments rather than our inherent value as children of God. We often place our security in external validation, in achievements and accolades, rather than grounding it in the unwavering love and acceptance of the divine. This makes our confidence fragile and susceptible to the anxieties you described.”

He encouraged Eleanor to explore her spiritual gifts, to identify her talents and use them to serve others. He explained that when we focus on serving God and our fellow humans, our anxieties often diminish. The focus shifts from our self-perceived shortcomings to a larger purpose, leading to a greater sense of fulfillment and a more confident self-image.

"Think of the parable of the talents," he suggested. "Each servant was given a different amount of talent, reflecting their unique abilities and gifts. God doesn't expect us to all be the same, to excel in the same areas. He asks us to use what we've been given, to contribute to His kingdom in our own unique way. Your anxieties, Eleanor, might be telling you that you are trying to be someone you are not meant to be. Listen to your heart. What are you naturally drawn to? What brings you joy and fulfillment?"

Eleanor pondered this, a thoughtful expression on her face. She thought about her creative talents, her love for writing poetry and creating art. She had pushed these gifts aside, convinced they were frivolous, insignificant compared to her career ambitions.

"Maybe," she murmured, a spark of hope flickering in her eyes. "Maybe I'm trying to fit into a mold that isn't meant for me. Maybe my fears are a sign that I need to change course."

Pastor Michael smiled, his eyes filled with understanding. "Perhaps, Eleanor. Perhaps your anxieties are a gift in disguise, a wake-up call to live more authentically, to embrace your true self, the person God created you to be. It's a journey, a process of discovery and growth. But remember, you don't have to walk it alone. God is with you, every step of the way."

He continued by offering practical advice, suggesting journaling, meditation, and spending time in nature as tools for managing her anxieties. He spoke of the importance of healthy boundaries, of learning to say no, and of prioritizing self-care.

"Remember, Eleanor," he concluded, his voice filled with compassion and hope, "God's love is your refuge. It's a source of strength and peace that surpasses all understanding. Lean on Him, trust in Him, and let Him guide you towards a life free from the tyranny of fear."

The session ended, leaving Eleanor feeling a sense of peace she hadn't felt in years. The road ahead was still long, but she felt equipped with the tools and the support to face her fears, armed with faith and a newfound understanding of her own inherent worth. The journey to overcome her anxieties was far from over, but the identification of their source, the uncovering of the deep-seated wounds and insecurities that fueled them, was a crucial first step towards lasting healing and freedom. It was a journey into the heart, a pilgrimage guided by faith, and a testament to the transformative power of God's unwavering love.

The weight of his upcoming trial pressed down on David like a physical burden. He was a carpenter, a simple man of faith, but he was now facing accusations that threatened to shatter his life and reputation. He'd been falsely accused of theft, a crime he vehemently denied. The evidence, circumstantial as it was, seemed damning. The fear coiled in his gut, a cold, constricting serpent, threatening to suffocate him with its icy grip. Sleep offered no respite; his nights were filled with restless tossing and turning, haunted by visions of a prison cell, the cold, hard reality of a life overturned.

He found himself drawn to his small, worn prayer book, the pages softened by years of use, the words etched within a familiar comfort. He'd always prayed, of course, but this was different. This wasn't a casual petition for blessings or thanksgivings; this was a desperate cry for help, a plea for deliverance from a fear so profound it threatened to consume him.

He began by confessing his anxieties to God, not hiding the tremor in his voice, the desperation in his heart. He didn't try to mask his fear, to present a façade of strength he didn't possess. Instead, he laid bare his vulnerability, his raw, unfiltered emotions before his Creator. He poured out his fears, his doubts, his anxieties about his family, his livelihood, his future. He confessed his anger at the injustice, his frustration at the seemingly insurmountable odds stacked against him.

He remembered the words from Psalm 55:22: "Cast your burden on the Lord, and he will sustain you; he will never permit the righteous to be moved." These words, so often read and appreciated, now took on a new, profound significance. They were not merely comforting platitudes, but a lifeline in his storm-tossed sea of fear.

His prayers weren't eloquent or polished. They were raw, heartfelt cries from a soul grappling with overwhelming fear. He spoke of his faith, his unwavering belief in God's justice, even as doubt gnawed at the edges of his confidence. He prayed for strength, not to eliminate his fear, but to endure it, to face it with courage and resilience. He prayed for wisdom, for guidance, for the clarity to see a path through the darkness.

He began to incorporate scripture into his prayers, drawing strength and comfort from the countless promises of God's protection and guidance. He reflected on stories of individuals in the Bible who faced overwhelming odds yet emerged victorious through faith and prayer. He thought of Daniel in the lion's den, of Shadrach, Meshach, and Abednego in the fiery furnace, of David himself, facing Goliath with unwavering faith.

Each morning, before he began his day, and each evening before he lay down to sleep, he devoted time to prayer. He didn't just pray for himself; he prayed for his accusers, asking for God's mercy and forgiveness to touch their hearts. He prayed for justice, but not in a vengeful way, rather for a just and equitable resolution, regardless of the outcome.

He found himself drawn to the Psalms, their raw honesty and emotional depth resonating with his own struggles. He read them aloud, letting the words wash over him, absorbing their message of hope and solace. He found himself particularly comforted by Psalm 23, the familiar words of the Shepherd's Psalm offering a sense of peace and security amidst the turmoil.

In addition to his personal prayers, he sought the support and prayers of his community. He shared his struggles with his pastor and fellow church members, asking for their prayers and encouragement. He discovered the profound power of collective prayer, the strength found in knowing that others were standing with him in faith, lifting him up in prayer.

The support he received wasn't just about the prayers themselves, but also about the sense of community, the tangible expression of love and support. It reminded him that he wasn't alone, that he was surrounded by a network of believers who shared his faith and understood his struggles. This shared faith became a source of strength and reassurance, bolstering his courage and resilience.

As the days went by, he noticed a subtle shift within himself. The fear still lingered, but it no longer held the same paralyzing grip. He found a new strength, a sense of calm amidst the storm. His prayers, once desperate pleas, began to incorporate a growing sense of trust and hope. He wasn't sure what the outcome of the trial would be, but he found peace in knowing that whatever happened, God was with him.

He began to notice other ways God was present in his life, small blessings that he had previously overlooked. The kindness of a stranger, the unexpected help of a friend, the beauty of a sunset – these were reminders of God's constant presence, even in the midst of his trials. These small victories became significant symbols of God's unwavering support.

The trial eventually came, and it was every bit as daunting as he had feared. The accusations were presented, the evidence scrutinized. He felt the weight of the situation, the pressure to prove his innocence. Yet, even in the midst of the trial, he maintained a quiet strength, a peace that surprised even himself. He spoke with honesty and clarity, his testimony infused with the conviction of his faith.

He didn't merely recount the events; he recounted his relationship with God, the solace he found in prayer, and the strength he received from his faith. He spoke not only of his innocence but of his unwavering belief in God's justice, a belief that had sustained him through his ordeal. He didn't shy away from his vulnerability, acknowledging his fear, but emphasizing the triumph of faith over fear.

The outcome of the trial was a vindication of his innocence, but the true victory was the strength he found in God, the peace that settled in his heart through prayer. He had faced his fear, not by conquering it, but by surrendering it to a power far greater than himself. The trial had been a crucible, refining his faith, strengthening his reliance on prayer, and deepening his relationship with God.

He continued his prayer practice even after the trial, recognizing the vital role it played in his life, not just in times of crisis, but in the everyday joys and challenges of existence. Prayer was no longer just a ritual; it was a vital connection to the divine, a source of strength and guidance, a pathway to a deeper understanding of himself and his relationship with God. His experience became a testament to the power of prayer in overcoming fear, a testimony shared with others who found themselves facing similar struggles. The fear still occasionally surfaced, but now it was met not with panic, but with the unwavering assurance of God's presence and protection. The peace he found was not the absence of fear, but the presence of God within the fear itself.

The acquittal was a relief, a weight lifted, but the echoes of the trial, the chilling whispers of doubt and accusation, still lingered. David found himself wrestling not just with the aftermath of the legal battle, but with the lingering wounds inflicted upon his self-esteem. He had faced the trial with courage, yes, but the experience had shaken him to his core. He realized that alongside his faith in God's justice, he needed to cultivate a deeper wellspring of self-compassion.

He began to understand that true strength wasn't the absence of fear, but the ability to navigate it with kindness toward himself. He had been so focused on proving his innocence to others that he'd neglected the crucial task of proving his innocence to himself. The self-doubt, the gnawing fear that perhaps there was something he'd overlooked, something he'd done wrong, persisted even after the court's verdict. This self-criticism, he realized, was a far more insidious threat than the false accusations themselves.

He started small. Each morning, after his prayers, he would sit quietly, reflecting not on the events of the trial, but on his own inner landscape. He'd ask himself, "David, how are you truly feeling today?" He didn't seek to repress or ignore his emotions; he acknowledged them, validated them, and treated them with the same gentle understanding he would extend to a dear friend in distress.

He recalled a passage from the book of Proverbs: "A gentle answer turns away wrath, but a harsh word stirs up anger." He began to apply this principle to his inner dialogue. Instead of berating himself for his anxieties, he spoke to himself with soothing words, offering encouragement and reassurance. He practiced self-soothing techniques, like deep breathing exercises and mindful meditation, to calm his racing thoughts and soothe his anxious heart.

One particularly difficult evening, as the memories of the trial threatened to overwhelm him, he found himself reciting Psalm 139:14, "I praise you because I am fearfully and wonderfully made; your works are wonderful, I know that full well." He repeated the verse again and again, allowing its truth to sink into his weary soul. He began to focus not on his perceived flaws and shortcomings, but on the inherent goodness and value within him, a value instilled by his Creator.

He also began to examine his past with a new lens of self-compassion. He confessed to God, and to himself, the mistakes he'd made in the past, not with self-recrimination, but with a humble desire to learn and grow. He understood that his past mistakes didn't define him; they were merely part of his journey, lessons learned along the way.

He remembered a parable Jesus told, about the prodigal son. The son had squandered his inheritance, lived recklessly, and ultimately returned home in shame and remorse. Yet, his father embraced him without judgment, celebrating his return with open arms. David reflected on this parable, recognizing that God's love, like the father's love, was unconditional and unwavering, even in the face of our mistakes. This realization instilled in him a sense of grace, not just for his past actions, but for his present struggles.

He recognized that self-compassion wasn't about self-indulgence or complacency; it wasn't about avoiding responsibility or ignoring the consequences of his actions. Rather, it was about treating himself with the same kindness and understanding he would offer to someone he loved. It was about acknowledging his struggles without judgment, validating his emotions, and offering himself the same grace and forgiveness that he sought from God.

He started to journal, writing down his thoughts and feelings without censorship. This allowed him to process his emotions, to understand their origins, and to gradually disarm their power. He wrote about his fears, his doubts, his self-criticism, acknowledging them as normal parts of the human experience. He wrote about his triumphs, too, celebrating his small victories and acknowledging his strengths. He viewed his journal as a sacred space, a place where he could be honest with himself, without judgment or fear of condemnation.

He also sought the support of his pastor and his close friends in the church community, sharing his struggles with self-compassion and seeking their encouragement and prayers. He found comfort and strength in their understanding, in the knowledge that he wasn't alone in his struggles. They reminded him of his worth, validating his feelings, and reaffirming his inherent goodness. They shared their own experiences of self-doubt and struggle, creating a sense of shared humanity that lessened the burden of his own internal conflict.

One evening, while reading the writings of St. Augustine, he came across a quote that profoundly resonated with him: "Love yourself first, and then love others as yourself." He realized that the commandment to love thy neighbor was inextricably linked to the ability to love oneself. He couldn't truly love others until he learned to love and accept himself, flaws and all. Self-compassion, therefore, became a vital aspect of his spiritual journey, a pathway to a deeper, more fulfilling relationship with himself and with God.

David's journey towards self-compassion wasn't a linear path; it was a gradual process, a journey marked by both setbacks and breakthroughs. There were days when self-doubt threatened to engulf him, days when the old patterns of self-criticism resurfaced. But each time, he would gently redirect himself, reminding himself of the progress he'd made, the lessons he'd learned, and the unwavering love of God that surrounded him.

He discovered the power of forgiveness, not only for others but also for himself. He understood that holding onto resentment and self-condemnation was a form of self-inflicted suffering. He forgave himself for his past mistakes, recognizing that they were part of his growth, opportunities for learning and self-discovery. He acknowledged that he was a work in progress, a vessel still being shaped and molded by God's grace.

He also learned to celebrate his strengths and accomplishments, acknowledging his talents and abilities without arrogance or self-aggrandizement. He recognized that self-compassion wasn't about self-deprecation; it was about striking a balance between humility and self-acceptance. He focused on nurturing his self-worth, building up his confidence, and recognizing his inherent value as a child of God.

He integrated self-compassion into his daily life, practicing mindfulness, gratitude, and self-care. He paid attention to his physical and emotional needs, ensuring he got enough rest, exercise, and healthy food. He indulged in activities that brought him joy and peace, like spending time in nature, listening to music, or engaging in creative pursuits. He recognized that taking care of himself was an act of self-love, an essential part of cultivating self-compassion.

As time went on, David's self-compassion deepened. His self-perception shifted, and the fear and anxiety that had once plagued him began to lose their grip. He found a new sense of inner peace, a quiet strength that emanated from a place of self-acceptance and love. He realized that true freedom came not from the absence of fear, but from the embrace of self-compassion, a love that allowed him to face his imperfections with grace and understanding. His journey became a testament to the power of self-compassion, a powerful tool in navigating the complexities of life, and a testament to the transformative power of God's unwavering love. The scars of the trial remained, but they were now reminders of his resilience, of his journey towards a deeper understanding of himself, and of the profound love that had sustained him throughout his ordeal. His experience became a beacon of hope, a testament to the transformative power of faith, self-compassion, and unwavering belief in the enduring love of God.

The quiet strength David had found wasn't a sudden arrival, but the culmination of deliberate choices, small acts of self-kindness woven into the fabric of his days. He understood that true self-esteem wasn't a destination, but a journey, a continuous process of self-discovery and self-acceptance. His journey had led him to a newfound appreciation for the power of positive affirmations. He started small, whispering words of encouragement to himself throughout the day. "I am worthy," he'd murmur during a stressful moment at work. "I am capable," he'd remind himself before tackling a challenging task. These affirmations, initially hesitant and uncertain, gradually gained strength and conviction.

He discovered the transformative power of gratitude. Each evening, he took a few moments to reflect on the day's events, focusing not on what went wrong, but on what went right, no matter how insignificant it seemed. He expressed gratitude for his health, his family, his friends, his job – even for the small blessings, like a sunny day or a kind word from a stranger. This practice shifted his perspective, helping him to focus on the positive aspects of his life, strengthening his sense of self-worth.

He began attending a small support group at his church, a gathering of individuals facing similar challenges. The group wasn't about dwelling on negativity or comparing struggles; it was a space for mutual encouragement, a place where vulnerability was embraced and celebrated. He shared his journey, his struggles with self-doubt and fear, and was surprised by the outpouring of support and understanding from the other members. He heard similar stories, each unique yet universally relatable, tales of overcoming adversity and rebuilding self-esteem. The shared experience created a powerful sense of community, a comforting reminder that he was not alone.

Within this group, David learned the importance of celebrating achievements, no matter how small. What might seem insignificant to one person could be a significant milestone for another. He witnessed individuals praising each other for the smallest victories – completing a challenging workout, finishing a difficult project, simply getting out of bed on a particularly dark day. This emphasis on celebrating even the smallest of wins created a ripple effect of encouragement and positivity. David began to celebrate his own achievements, no matter how trivial they may have initially seemed. Finishing a book, preparing a healthy meal, completing a household chore – each accomplishment was an opportunity for self-affirmation, a small step in the ongoing process of building his self-esteem.

He realized that self-esteem wasn't simply about ignoring imperfections or pretending they didn't exist; it was about acknowledging them, accepting them, and focusing on his strengths. He started to list his positive attributes, his talents, and his accomplishments. He focused on the good things about himself – his kindness, his compassion, his resilience. This wasn't a boastful exercise; it was a mindful acknowledgement of his value, a recognition of the inherent worth he possessed as a child of God.

He incorporated affirmations into his daily routine. He created a vision board, filled with images and words that represented his goals, his aspirations, and his ideal self. He looked at it every morning, allowing the positive messages to sink into his subconscious. He started to speak positively about himself, not just to himself but also to others. He found himself engaging in self-care activities, nurturing both his physical and emotional well-being. He prioritized sleep, exercised regularly, ate nutritious meals, and spent time in nature. He engaged in activities that brought him joy and relaxation, hobbies that nurtured his creativity and fostered a sense of accomplishment. He found solace in painting, sketching and spending time in his garden, activities that engaged his mind and soothed his spirit.

The support group continued to be a source of strength. He found solace in the shared stories of resilience and healing, a testament to the transformative power of faith and community. He was amazed by the courage and vulnerability of his fellow members, each sharing their experiences with such honesty and openness. He witnessed the impact of genuine support and encouragement, seeing how others blossomed through the process of self-acceptance and self-compassion.

One member of the group, Sarah, shared her story of overcoming chronic self-doubt. She had struggled with feelings of inadequacy for many years, often comparing herself to others and feeling a deep sense of unworthiness. But through persistent self-affirmations, mindful practices, and the unwavering support of the group, she had made significant progress. She spoke about her journey with humility and honesty, acknowledging the setbacks along the way while celebrating her hard-won victories.

Another member, Michael, spoke about the importance of forgiving himself for past mistakes. He had harbored deep feelings of guilt and self-recrimination for years, hindering his self-esteem and hindering his progress. He discovered that forgiving himself, accepting his past, and focusing on his future potential, liberated him from the weight of his self-condemnation. His newfound freedom empowered him to engage in life with enthusiasm and self-belief.

Through their shared experiences and mutual support, the members of the group developed a stronger sense of self-esteem and resilience. They learned to recognize and challenge negative thoughts, replace self-criticism with self-compassion, and celebrate even the smallest of achievements. The group became a safe space where vulnerability was embraced, support was freely given, and progress was celebrated.

David's personal journey wasn't always easy. There were days when self-doubt resurfaced, when the old patterns of negative self-talk crept back in. But he had learned coping mechanisms, strategies he employed to gently redirect his thoughts and re-affirm his self-worth. He would engage in mindfulness practices, focusing on his breath, his body, and his present surroundings. He would reach for his journal, writing down his thoughts and feelings, processing his emotions without judgment. He would turn to his support group, sharing his struggles and seeking the encouragement and understanding of his fellow members. He would revisit his vision board, reminding himself of his goals and his inherent worth. He would repeat his affirmations, whispering them to himself as reminders of his strength and resilience.

His understanding of self-esteem became increasingly nuanced. He realized it wasn't about arrogance or inflated ego, but about a balanced and honest view of himself, acknowledging both his strengths and his weaknesses. He understood the importance of self-acceptance, the ability to embrace his imperfections while still striving for growth and self-improvement. It was a journey of ongoing self-discovery, a continuous process of self-compassion and self-acceptance, guided by his unwavering faith and the love and support of his community.

He came to understand that self-esteem is a vital aspect of spiritual well-being, a cornerstone of a healthy and fulfilling relationship with God and others. It's a recognition of the inherent dignity and worth that each person possesses as a child of God. By nurturing his self-esteem, David opened himself to a deeper connection with his faith, experiencing a profound sense of peace and contentment. His journey had transformed him, not just in his understanding of self-worth but in his ability to extend that compassion and understanding to others. He discovered that his own journey of self-discovery had become a source of inspiration and hope for others, a testament to the transformative power of faith, self-compassion, and unwavering belief in the enduring love of God. His newfound self-esteem wasn't merely a personal victory; it was a gift he could share with others, offering hope and encouragement along their paths to self-discovery and healing.

David's newfound self-esteem, however, didn't erase the underlying anxieties that had plagued him for years. He still found himself wrestling with moments of fear, moments where the shadow of doubt lingered, despite his progress. It was in these moments, when his carefully constructed sense of self-worth felt fragile, that he turned to a deeper wellspring of strength: his faith in God's unwavering protection.

He remembered a passage from Psalm 91: "He who dwells in the secret place of the Most High shall abide under the shadow of the Almighty. I will say of the Lord, "He is my refuge and my fortress; my God, in Him I will trust."" These words resonated deeply within him, offering a solace that went beyond self-help strategies and affirmations. It was a promise, a divine assurance of safety and security, not just from external threats, but from the internal turmoil of fear and anxiety.

He began to actively engage with this promise, not simply as a comforting verse, but as a living truth. He started his days with prayer, seeking God's guidance and protection, consciously placing himself under His care. He visualized himself dwelling in God's secret place, feeling enveloped by His love and power. This wasn't a passive act; it was a conscious decision to surrender his fears to a higher power, trusting in God's ability to navigate him through the storms of life.

One day, while walking home from work, a situation arose that tested his newly found faith. He was walking down a dimly lit street when he heard footsteps behind him, quick and heavy. A wave of apprehension washed over him; the old familiar fear threatened to consume him. He instinctively quickened his pace, his heart pounding in his chest. But then, he remembered the promises of Psalm 91. He took a deep breath, and instead of panicking, he whispered a silent prayer: "Lord, I trust in your protection."

As he continued to walk, a sense of calm descended upon him. The fear didn't entirely disappear, but it lost its paralyzing grip. He felt a strange sense of peace, an inner assurance that he was not alone, that God was with him. He continued walking, his pace steady, his heart still beating quickly, but no longer filled with terror.

As he turned the corner onto a more brightly lit street, he saw that the footsteps had stopped. Looking back, he saw nothing. He wasn't sure if the footsteps had been a real threat or just a product of his own anxiety, but the experience solidified his belief in God's protective presence. The fact that he had faced his fear without succumbing to panic, and had emerged unscathed, felt like a direct answer to his prayer, a tangible manifestation of God's loving care.

This experience became a pivotal moment in David's journey. It wasn't a miracle in the grand, spectacular sense, but it was a profound personal revelation. He learned that God's protection isn't always about avoiding difficult situations, but about navigating them with courage, faith, and peace. It's about experiencing God's presence in the midst of fear, finding strength in vulnerability, and emerging stronger on the other side.

He understood that trusting in God's protection wasn't a passive resignation to fate, but an active engagement with faith. It required conscious effort, regular prayer, and a deep understanding of God's character, His love, and His unwavering commitment to His children. He delved deeper into scripture, studying passages that spoke of God's protection and guidance, finding comfort and encouragement in the stories of others who had experienced God's faithfulness in times of adversity.

He reflected on the lives of biblical figures who had faced seemingly insurmountable challenges yet found solace and safety in God's unwavering love. He thought of Daniel in the lion's den, protected by divine intervention. He pondered the story of Shadrach, Meshach, and Abednego, spared from the fiery furnace because of their unwavering faith. He considered the countless examples throughout scripture of individuals who found protection and deliverance through their trust in God.

He understood that God's protection may manifest in different ways. It might involve a miraculous escape from danger, as in the cases of Daniel and the three Hebrew men. But it could also manifest as inner peace during challenging times, a sense of calm amidst the storm, the strength to persevere even when facing overwhelming odds. God's protection can be a subtle whisper guiding our steps, a gentle hand leading us through the darkness, a constant companion providing unwavering support and strength.

David realized that his faith in God's protection wasn't a shield against all hardship, but a source of strength and resilience in the face of it. It wasn't a guarantee of a life free from trouble, but a promise of God's unwavering presence and guidance through whatever challenges life may bring. His understanding of God's protection was not a magical formula for avoiding adversity, but a spiritual anchor in the midst of the storm. It was a relationship of trust, built on prayer, faith, and a deep understanding of God's character.

He continued to attend his support group, sharing his experiences and encouraging others to explore their faith as a source of strength and comfort. He found that sharing his journey helped him process his own emotions and deepened his understanding of God's grace. He witnessed how faith, combined with practical coping mechanisms, could transform lives, bringing peace and healing to those struggling with fear and anxiety.

His personal journey became a testament to the power of faith in mitigating fear and anxiety. He discovered that true security wasn't found in avoiding all potential threats, but in cultivating a deep and abiding trust in God's protective presence. His life became a living example of the profound truth expressed in Psalm 23: "The Lord is my shepherd, I shall not want. He makes me lie down in green pastures; He leads me beside quiet waters. He restores my soul; He leads me in paths of righteousness for His name's sake."

His transformation wasn't merely a personal triumph; it was a demonstration of the transformative power of faith, a beacon of hope for those grappling with their own fears. His experience highlighted the importance of combining practical coping strategies with spiritual practices, creating a holistic approach to overcoming fear and anxiety. He understood that true peace and security are not found in the absence of challenges, but in the unwavering presence of God, a refuge and a fortress in the midst of the storm. His journey, marked by both personal growth and spiritual deepening, became a source of inspiration and encouragement to others, a testament to the life-changing power of faith, self-compassion, and unwavering trust in the love and protection of God. He learned that the journey of faith, like the journey of self-discovery, is a lifelong process, a continuous unfolding of God's love and grace in his life. And in the heart of that unfolding, he found not only peace but purpose, a life lived in faith, courage, and unwavering trust in his Heavenly Father. The fear was still there at times, a whisper in the background, but it no longer held the power to control him. He had found a strength far greater than his own, a strength that came from surrendering to God's will and resting in His loving embrace. This profound understanding became the foundation of his ongoing spiritual journey, a source of comfort and guidance throughout his life. He knew, deep in his heart, that even in the darkest hours, God's protection was his, a constant, unwavering presence that would see him through any storm.

David's journey of faith had led him to a place of profound peace, but he knew that this newfound tranquility was not solely a personal achievement. He realized that his growth was inextricably linked to the supportive community he had found within his church. This wasn't merely a social gathering; it was a spiritual family, a haven of encouragement and shared faith that nurtured his spiritual development and bolstered his resilience. He had discovered that faith, though deeply personal, thrived in the fertile ground of community.

He remembered his first hesitant steps into the church. He had felt apprehensive, a stranger in a seemingly unfamiliar land. He'd been greeted with open arms, not judgmental stares. A warm smile, a welcoming handshake, a genuine interest in his life—these small acts of kindness had disarmed his initial anxieties, creating space for him to breathe and belong.

Elder Thomas, a man with a gentle heart and wise eyes, had taken him under his wing. He wasn't overly solicitous, but his presence was a comforting anchor in the sea of new faces and unfamiliar hymns. Elder Thomas listened patiently as David shared his struggles, offering words of wisdom gleaned from years of navigating life's complexities. He didn't offer easy answers, but guided David towards finding his own answers within the scriptures. He showed him how to apply the timeless wisdom of the Bible to the very real challenges of his modern life, bridging the gap between ancient truths and contemporary anxieties.

The other members of the congregation had been equally welcoming. They weren't perfect, of course; they were a community of flawed, imperfect people striving towards perfection in Christ. But their imperfections felt endearing, a testament to the inclusivity of God's love. There were lively discussions during Bible studies, debates that were never harsh but always rooted in respect and a shared yearning for spiritual understanding. There were moments of laughter and fellowship, shared meals that tasted all the sweeter because of the bonds that were forged around the table.

David found himself becoming increasingly involved in the life of the church. He joined a small group Bible study, sharing his experiences, both his struggles and his triumphs, with a small, intimate group of fellow believers. The vulnerability felt liberating, creating an environment of trust and understanding where everyone felt safe to be themselves. The group's collective wisdom and shared experiences provided a rich tapestry of support, encouragement, and divine guidance.

He volunteered to help with the church's outreach program, finding purpose in serving others. This wasn't a duty; it was a privilege, an opportunity to live out his faith in tangible ways. The simple act of helping others shift his focus from his own worries to the needs of those around him, bringing a profound sense of fulfillment and spiritual growth.

The regular worship services provided a consistent source of comfort and inspiration. He found solace in the familiar rituals, the shared prayers, and the collective praise. The music uplifted his spirit, the sermons challenged his thinking, and the communal singing bonded him to a larger spiritual body, reminding him that he was not alone on his journey. The hymns, filled with centuries of faith, offered him a sense of continuity and hope, strengthening his resolve to endure whatever trials lay ahead.

David learned that finding a spiritual community wasn't merely about finding a place of worship; it was about finding a family, a group of individuals who shared his values, supported his growth, and challenged him to become a better version of himself. It was about finding people who would walk alongside him through the joys and sorrows of life, offering unconditional love and unwavering support. He realized that the church was more than just a building; it was a living organism, a vibrant body of believers, growing together in faith and love.

He began to see the church as a microcosm of the kingdom of God, a place where different personalities, backgrounds, and experiences coalesced into a harmonious whole. He witnessed people from all walks of life—doctors and laborers, students and retirees, individuals from diverse cultural backgrounds—all united by their shared faith and commitment to serving Christ. The diversity was a testament to God's universal love and acceptance, fostering an environment of understanding, tolerance, and mutual respect.

He learned from the older members, whose life experiences provided a deep reservoir of wisdom and guidance. He was inspired by the youthful energy and enthusiasm of the younger members, reminding him of the vitality and hope that pervaded the community. The various ministries within the church—from music to outreach to youth groups—offered multiple avenues for participation, allowing him to find his niche and contribute his unique gifts and talents.

David discovered that the sense of belonging extended beyond the church walls. He began to form deeper relationships with some members, extending his fellowship beyond Sunday services and Bible studies. He found himself sharing meals, engaging in friendly conversations, and offering support during times of need. These connections strengthened his spiritual foundation, providing a comforting sense of community and shared purpose. These friendships were built on shared faith, mutual respect, and genuine care, fostering a profound sense of belonging and spiritual growth.

He found that the community served as a mirror reflecting his own progress, a constant reminder of his strengths and areas where he needed to grow. The encouragement he received from others helped him overcome self-doubt, and the accountability provided by the community kept him on the path towards spiritual maturity. The community offered a safe space for him to confess his weaknesses, seek forgiveness, and receive the grace and unconditional love of Christ.

His newfound spiritual community became an essential component of his overall well-being. It provided a powerful support system that nurtured his emotional, mental, and spiritual health. He felt less alone in his struggles, empowered by the collective strength of the community and the unwavering love of his fellow believers. He discovered that the community wasn't just a source of support; it was a catalyst for his own spiritual growth, a fertile ground for him to blossom into the person God intended him to be.

The sense of belonging extended beyond the individual connections; it fostered a sense of shared purpose. The community worked together on projects that extended beyond the church walls—serving the homeless, providing food to the needy, and offering support to those in crisis. These acts of service not only benefited those in need, but also deepened the bonds within the community, solidifying their sense of shared identity and purpose.

He found that this shared purpose transcended the individual struggles and fostered a sense of collective identity, a feeling of being part of something larger than himself. This identity wasn't based on personal accomplishments or social status; it was grounded in the shared belief in Christ, and the shared commitment to serving others. This sense of belonging was invaluable, providing a sense of grounding, purpose, and unwavering support.

David's journey emphasized the importance of not just seeking faith, but fostering it within a nurturing spiritual community. It was in the context of this community that his faith flourished, becoming a source of strength, comfort, and unwavering hope. The community didn't erase his struggles, but it provided a supportive environment where he could face those struggles with courage, resilience, and the unwavering support of fellow believers. His faith became a beacon of hope, not only for himself, but also for others in the community. It was in the heart of this community that he discovered the transformative power of faith, a power that extended far beyond his personal growth to touch the lives of countless others. And as his faith continued to grow, so too did his commitment to his community, creating a virtuous cycle of spiritual growth and shared purpose. He understood that his spiritual journey was a lifelong process, and the community was an essential part of that ongoing journey, a constant source of support, encouragement, and unwavering love.

The warmth of the small group Bible study enveloped David like a comforting blanket. He'd initially hesitated to join, fearing vulnerability, fearing judgment. But the gentle encouragement of Sarah, a woman whose life story was a testament to God's unwavering grace, had persuaded him. He sat amongst five others, each with their unique stories etched onto their faces, each carrying the weight of their own burdens, yet radiating an unshakeable faith.

That evening, the topic was forgiveness. Not just forgiving others, but the often-more-difficult task of forgiving oneself. Mark, a retired teacher with a kind smile that belied the deep sorrow in his eyes, shared his struggle with a past mistake that continued to haunt him. He spoke of the shame, the self-recrimination, the relentless cycle of guilt that threatened to consume him. His voice trembled as he spoke, but his honesty was breathtaking. There was no pretense, no attempt to portray himself as anything other than a flawed human being, seeking redemption.

The others listened intently, their faces etched with empathy. No one interrupted, no one offered platitudes. They simply listened, offering a silent affirmation of his pain, a shared understanding of the human condition. Then, quietly, carefully, they began to share their own struggles with self-forgiveness. Maria, a vibrant young woman working as a nurse, spoke of her battles with self-doubt, her constant fear of making mistakes. John, a successful businessman, admitted his struggles with pride and ambition, confessing how he'd allowed his career to eclipse his faith at times. Each confession was a testament to the power of vulnerability, a powerful act of faith within the safe confines of their shared fellowship.

David, witnessing their courage, felt emboldened to share his own story. He spoke of his past resentment, his bitterness towards those who had hurt him. He confessed his difficulty in letting go of those negative emotions, in truly forgiving those who had caused him pain. As he spoke, a weight lifted from his shoulders. The words themselves were cathartic, but the acceptance he received from the group was even more profound.

Sarah, with her gentle wisdom, spoke of the transformative power of God's grace. She reminded them that forgiveness wasn't about condoning wrongdoing, but about releasing the burden of resentment that weighed heavily on the soul. She explained how clinging to anger and bitterness only served to poison the heart, preventing spiritual growth and hindering the experience of true peace. She spoke of the liberating power of letting go, of surrendering those painful memories to God, trusting in His ability to heal and restore.

The conversation flowed naturally, seamlessly weaving together scripture, personal experiences, and insightful reflections. They discussed the parable of the unforgiving servant, exploring its implications for their own lives. They pondered the profound love and forgiveness offered by Christ, a love that surpasses human comprehension. They prayed together, a collective plea for strength, healing, and the grace to forgive themselves and others.

The evening ended with a sense of profound peace. The shared vulnerabilities had created an unbreakable bond, a sense of community that transcended their individual struggles. They had not only offered each other support but had also witnessed the transforming power of God's grace, a grace that flowed freely within the safe embrace of their fellowship. The strength they gained wasn't solely from their individual faith, but from the collective power of their united faith, their shared journey.

This experience highlighted for David the crucial role of accountability within fellowship. Knowing that he would be sharing his struggles and triumphs with a group of supportive friends held him accountable for his actions, his thoughts, and his spiritual growth. The gentle nudges, the encouraging words, and the shared prayers helped him to stay focused on his spiritual journey. He realized that the community was not only a source of comfort but also a vital element in his spiritual discipline. The fear of disappointing his friends, the desire to live up to their expectations, spurred him to persevere in his faith. He knew that he wasn't alone in his struggles; he had a team of fellow believers holding him up, encouraging him, and celebrating his progress.

The sense of belonging that David experienced within his small group extended throughout the entire congregation. He found himself increasingly involved in various church activities, fostering deeper relationships with other members. He participated in community service projects, helping to organize food drives and visit the elderly. He played a key role in the church's annual Christmas outreach program. He discovered a talent for organizing and delegating, leading him to take on a greater leadership role within the church. This sense of purpose and contribution further strengthened his connection to the community and enriched his spiritual journey.

He found friendship with families who welcomed him into their homes, sharing meals, celebrations, and everyday life. He discovered that this sense of community wasn't limited to church walls. He connected with others through shared interests, mutual support and shared hobbies outside of church functions. The support network expanded beyond the confines of scheduled events, creating genuine and lasting relationships.

These relationships weren't just social connections; they were profound spiritual bonds, forged in the fires of shared faith, mutual respect, and unwavering support. He found comfort in knowing that he was surrounded by people who loved him unconditionally, people who would celebrate his joys and share his sorrows. He knew that there were others who would pray for him, who would lift him up in times of need, and who would offer a listening ear and a compassionate heart. These connections provided him with the emotional, mental, and spiritual support he needed to navigate life's challenges. The church wasn't just a place to attend; it became a vibrant, supportive community that enriched every aspect of his life.

The benefits of fellowship extended far beyond the personal. David witnessed the power of collective prayer, the shared strength that came from united voices. He saw the impact of their combined efforts in the community outreach programs, the tangible differences they were making in the lives of others. This sense of shared purpose and collective achievement strengthened the bonds within the community, creating a sense of shared identity and mutual support. This collaborative work highlighted the power of community action, fostering a deeper sense of connection and purpose among members.

His faith wasn't confined to personal experiences; it became a force for good in the world, radiating outward from the church to the wider community. This outward expression of faith fueled his own spiritual growth, creating a virtuous cycle of giving and receiving. The community became a microcosm of God's love, a place where individuals could grow, share, and serve, creating a lasting impact on the world. He discovered that the most profound benefits of fellowship were not just personal, but extended to the world around him. His journey in faith was made richer and more meaningful through the unwavering support, shared experiences, and collective purpose of his Christian community. The fellowship was more than a network; it was a family, a tapestry woven with threads of faith, hope, and love, providing him with a sense of belonging and purpose that continues to shape his spiritual growth.

The rhythmic clang of metal on metal, the sizzle of onions in a vast pan, the low hum of conversation—these were the sounds that greeted David as he stepped into the bustling kitchen of the city's largest soup kitchen. He'd initially felt a twinge of apprehension. He wasn't a culinary expert, far from it. His cooking skills peaked at boiling water, a fact he'd confessed to Sarah with a self-deprecating chuckle. But Sarah, ever the encourager, had simply smiled and said, "It's not about culinary skills, David. It's about serving."

And serve he did. He found himself surprisingly adept at peeling potatoes, a task that seemed deceptively simple yet required a steady hand and a surprising amount of patience. He learned to chop vegetables with surprising efficiency, his movements becoming smoother and more precise with each passing hour. He discovered a rhythm to the work, a meditative quality in the repetitive tasks, a counterpoint to the frenetic energy of the kitchen.

He wasn't alone. Around him, a diverse group of volunteers worked with a quiet efficiency, their hands moving in a synchronized dance of service. There was Mrs. Henderson, a retired schoolteacher with a twinkle in her eye, who seemed to know every volunteer's name and their favorite pie recipe. There was young Michael, a college student struggling to balance his studies with his desire to make a difference. And there was Father Thomas, a quiet man of faith whose gentle presence radiated peace.

The soup kitchen wasn't just a place to hand out meals; it was a microcosm of the community, a place where people from all walks of life came together, united by a common purpose: to serve those in need. David watched as Mrs. Henderson engaged in conversation with a homeless man, listening patiently to his stories, offering a word of encouragement and a warm smile. He saw Michael patiently assist an elderly woman with her meal, his kindness evident in his every gesture. He observed Father Thomas offering a prayer of blessing over the food, his voice filled with compassion and sincerity.

One afternoon, a young woman named Emily approached David. She was clearly struggling, her eyes red and swollen, her shoulders slumped with fatigue. She spoke in a low, hesitant voice, sharing her story of job loss, eviction, and the crushing weight of despair. David listened, offering not platitudes but genuine empathy. He didn't offer solutions, not at first. He simply listened, letting her share her burden, acknowledging her pain.

As Emily spoke, David remembered his own struggles with self-doubt and the overwhelming nature of life's challenges. He recalled the comfort and support he'd received from his small group, the unwavering faith of his fellow believers. He realized that his own journey of faith had prepared him for this moment, had given him the empathy, the patience, the listening ear to offer Emily.

He offered her a warm cup of tea and a plate of freshly baked bread. He sat with her, offering a quiet presence, a silent affirmation of her inherent worth. He shared a simple prayer, asking for God's grace and comfort to envelop her. In that shared silence, a connection formed, a bond forged not in words but in shared humanity. As Emily's tears subsided, a faint smile touched her lips. She thanked David, her voice choked with emotion.

This encounter, more than any culinary skill, solidified for David the true meaning of service. It wasn't merely about handing out food; it was about offering a listening ear, a compassionate heart, a tangible expression of God's love. He realized that the act of serving others wasn't just a way to help others; it was a profound act of spiritual growth for himself. In serving others, he served God.

The soup kitchen became more than a place of work; it became a classroom, a sanctuary, a place of profound spiritual learning. He learned about patience from Mrs. Henderson's unwavering calm amidst the chaos. He learned about empathy from Michael's gentle interactions with the elderly. He learned about the power of prayer from Father Thomas's quiet faith. He learned about resilience from Emily's quiet strength in the face of adversity.

The experience extended beyond the confines of the kitchen. He found himself reaching out to others in his community, finding new ways to serve. He volunteered at a local homeless shelter, spending time with the residents, playing games and simply talking. He participated in a neighborhood cleanup initiative, beautifying a neglected park. He visited elderly members of his church, offering companionship and assistance with everyday tasks.

He learned that serving others wasn't always about grand gestures; it was often about the small acts of kindness, the quiet moments of connection, the unassuming expressions of compassion. He learned to see the face of Christ in every person he encountered, whether in the bustling kitchen of the soup kitchen or on the streets of his community.

The act of service fostered deeper connections within his own community. The shared experience of working together at the soup kitchen created a sense of camaraderie, a feeling of shared purpose. He found himself bonding with fellow volunteers, sharing stories, laughter, and moments of quiet reflection. The friendships he forged were not just casual acquaintanceships but profound relationships built on shared values and a commitment to serving others.

His service work also challenged him to confront his own preconceptions and biases. He learned to see beyond the surface, to recognize the dignity and worth of every individual, regardless of their circumstances. He learned to appreciate the diversity of his community, to celebrate its richness and its complexity.

His faith deepened through this active engagement in his community. He found that serving others was not just a religious duty; it was a deeply satisfying and enriching experience. It brought him joy, purpose, and a sense of profound connection to something larger than himself. He learned that the true measure of a life well-lived wasn't material success or personal achievement, but the impact one had on the lives of others. His life became a testament to the transformative power of faith in action.

As the weeks turned into months, David's involvement in community service evolved. He found himself not just participating but leading. He helped organize fundraising events for the soup kitchen, leveraging his newfound organizational skills. He became a mentor to younger volunteers, sharing his experiences and offering guidance. He discovered a leadership style rooted in humility and service, reflecting his growing faith and understanding of God's grace.

The impact of his service wasn't limited to the individuals he served; it extended to his own spiritual growth. He discovered that the most profound blessings came not from receiving but from giving. The joy he felt in serving others surpassed any personal reward. His faith became less of a theoretical belief and more of a lived experience, a tangible force for good in the world.

His experiences in the soup kitchen, in the homeless shelter, and throughout his community challenged his faith, strengthened it, and molded it into a vibrant, dynamic expression of love and compassion. He understood more profoundly that being a Christian wasn't just about attending church services or reciting prayers. It was about living a life of service, extending God's love to all, and becoming a tangible expression of His grace in the world. His journey of faith continued, enriched by the profound experience of serving others and finding in that service, a deeper connection to God and to the community He had called him to serve. His life, once defined by personal struggles, was now illuminated by the radiant light of service, a testament to the transformative power of faith in action.

The aroma of freshly brewed coffee hung heavy in the air, a comforting scent that usually signified peace and fellowship within the walls of Bethany Chapel. Today, however, the atmosphere felt thick with unspoken tension. The recent conflict between the long-standing choir director, Mrs. Eleanor Ainsworth, and the newly appointed youth pastor, Rev. Samuel Jones, had cast a long shadow over the congregation. The division wasn't just a disagreement over musical styles or youth group activities; it had fractured the very fabric of their community.

The root of the problem, as David discovered during his quiet conversations with various members, went far deeper than mere personality clashes. It stemmed from a long-held resentment Mrs. Ainsworth harbored towards the church leadership, a feeling amplified by the perceived preferential treatment given to Rev. Jones's youth initiatives. She felt overlooked, undervalued, her years of dedicated service seemingly disregarded. Meanwhile, Rev. Jones, fresh from seminary with a vibrant energy, inadvertently stepped on several toes, his enthusiasm sometimes misconstrued as arrogance. The clash was a perfect storm of miscommunication, hurt feelings, and long-simmering grievances.

David, having witnessed the transformative power of forgiveness in his own life and in his service work, saw an opportunity for reconciliation. He wasn't a conflict mediator by profession, but his heart ached for the fractured unity of Bethany Chapel. He recalled a sermon Father Thomas had once preached about the liberating power of forgiveness, not just for the recipient but for the one extending it. He remembered the weight of his own past mistakes and the immense relief that came with seeking and offering forgiveness.

His approach wasn't to force a resolution, but to gently guide the community toward healing. He started with small gestures, initiating conversations with both Mrs. Ainsworth and Rev. Jones individually. He listened patiently to their perspectives, validating their feelings without taking sides. He emphasized the importance of understanding the other person's point of view, even if it didn't resonate with his own.

With Mrs. Ainsworth, he spent hours listening to her story, her voice sometimes choked with emotion as she recounted years of feeling overlooked and unappreciated. He validated her feelings, acknowledging the hurt she experienced and the legitimacy of her concerns. He gently reminded her of the biblical accounts of forgiveness, citing instances where God extended undeserved grace and mercy. He shared personal anecdotes about his own struggles with forgiveness, emphasizing its transformative power. He helped her reframe her perspective, not to condone the actions that caused her pain, but to shift the focus from resentment to healing.

His conversations with Rev. Jones were different but equally crucial. He helped him understand the importance of humility, recognizing that even well-intentioned actions can cause unintentional harm. He encouraged Rev. Jones to reflect on his approach, suggesting ways to better communicate his vision and to be more sensitive to the feelings of long-standing members. He emphasized the importance of collaboration and shared leadership, acknowledging Mrs. Ainsworth's invaluable contributions.

He then organized a small, informal gathering—a potluck dinner, a familiar setting to break down barriers. He invited Mrs. Ainsworth, Rev. Jones, and a few key members of the congregation—individuals known for their wisdom and their ability to bridge divides. The atmosphere was initially tense, punctuated by strained silences. David initiated a prayer, asking for God's grace and guidance.

He then facilitated a guided conversation, encouraging open communication, empathy, and active listening. He created a space where both Mrs. Ainsworth and Rev. Jones could express their feelings honestly and respectfully. He helped them identify the misunderstandings that had fueled the conflict and to find common ground.

The breakthrough came unexpectedly, when Mrs. Ainsworth, tearful but resolute, expressed her regret for allowing resentment to cloud her judgment. She acknowledged her own part in the conflict and extended an apology to Rev. Jones and the church leadership. Rev. Jones, in turn, apologized for his insensitivity and expressed his appreciation for Mrs. Ainsworth's years of dedicated service. The apology wasn't just a recitation of words; it was a heartfelt expression of remorse and a sincere commitment to reconciliation.

The potluck, initially a symbol of strained fellowship, became a celebration of reconciliation. The shared meal, punctuated by laughter and heartfelt conversations, served as a powerful symbol of the restored unity. The communal act of eating together, sharing stories and breaking bread, fostered a renewed sense of belonging and shared purpose.

The reconciliation wasn't instantaneous or complete. There were still moments of tension, occasional reminders of past hurts. But the spirit of forgiveness had taken root, creating a fertile ground for healing and growth. The process fostered deeper relationships within the community, transforming conflicts into opportunities for understanding and empathy. The experience strengthened the bonds of community, reminding them of the importance of forgiveness, not just as a religious ideal, but as a crucial element of healthy human relationships.

David's role was not as a judge, but as a facilitator, guiding the community towards a path of healing and restorative justice. His work wasn't simply about resolving a dispute; it was about fostering a culture of forgiveness, empathy, and understanding within Bethany Chapel. The experience underscored the vital role of community in spiritual growth, demonstrating how shared struggles and triumphs can deepen faith and strengthen bonds. The healing of Bethany Chapel served as a powerful testament to the transformative power of forgiveness and the importance of community in fostering spiritual growth. The lessons learned extended far beyond the confines of the church, offering a model for resolving conflict and rebuilding relationships in any community.

The following Sunday service, the atmosphere was palpable different. The usual quiet murmur of the congregation was replaced with a sense of joyful anticipation. Mrs. Ainsworth and Rev. Jones sat side-by-side, a visible sign of their reconciliation. Their combined performance of a hymn, their voices blending harmoniously, symbolized the healing that had taken place. The church, once fractured, was whole again, stronger and more unified because of the experience. The spirit of forgiveness, once a fragile seed, had blossomed into a vibrant flower, enriching the lives of the members of Bethany Chapel and serving as a beacon of hope for other communities struggling with division and conflict. The experience served as a profound reminder that forgiveness isn't a sign of weakness, but a powerful act of strength, a testament to the enduring power of faith and the resilience of the human spirit. It was a testament to the transformative power of God's grace, working through the hearts and lives of a community striving for reconciliation. David's role, he realized, was not to solve every problem, but to facilitate the process of healing, offering guidance, support, and a listening ear—a living embodiment of the love and forgiveness he had learned to embrace. His journey of service continued, enriched by the knowledge that even the deepest wounds can be healed through the power of forgiveness and the strength of community.

The rhythmic thud of hammers against wood echoed through the crisp autumn air, a counterpoint to the cheerful chatter of the Bethany Chapel youth group. They weren't just building a new playground for the local elementary school; they were building something far more profound – a stronger sense of community, a tangible expression of their shared faith. David, observing from a slight distance, smiled. The recent reconciliation between Mrs. Ainsworth and Rev. Jones had created a ripple effect, a renewed sense of unity that permeated every aspect of the church's activities. This youth group project, born from a desire to serve others, was a powerful testament to that transformation.

Sarah, a shy teenager who had previously kept to herself, was now laughing as she worked alongside Michael, a boisterous young man known for his infectious enthusiasm. Their collaboration, a testament to the growing sense of inclusivity, was a far cry from the fractured atmosphere of just a few weeks ago. The shared purpose, the common goal of serving the community, had broken down barriers and fostered unexpected friendships. David watched as they struggled together, celebrating small victories, learning from mistakes – all while embodying the spirit of teamwork and mutual support that he had been striving to cultivate within Bethany Chapel.

He approached the group, offering a helping hand and engaging in lighthearted conversation. He observed how they were not just building a playground; they were building relationships, forging bonds of friendship that extended beyond the confines of their shared project. The laughter, the shared jokes, the mutual encouragement – these were the building blocks of a thriving community, a community that extended its reach far beyond the walls of Bethany Chapel. Their service project became a metaphor for their faith journey, a reminder that even the simplest acts of kindness can have a profound impact.

As the day progressed, David noticed a pattern emerging. Those who had previously been on the periphery, often overlooked or marginalized, found themselves at the heart of the activity. Emily, a young woman with a history of personal struggles, discovered a newfound confidence as she directed the placement of the playground's safety surfacing. Her newfound leadership was both inspiring and deeply moving. It was a testament to the power of community to empower and uplift its members.

The project wasn't without its challenges. There were disagreements, moments of frustration, and the occasional clash of personalities. But instead of escalating into conflict, these disagreements were addressed with a surprising maturity and grace. Members listened to one another, offering constructive criticism and seeking compromise. David's previous work on conflict resolution and fostering forgiveness had paid off. The youth group members, witnessing his example, learned to navigate disagreements with empathy and understanding, turning potential problems into opportunities for growth and strengthening their bonds.

In the evenings, after a long day of work, the youth group gathered for shared meals. These weren't just meals; they were sacred spaces, a time for fellowship and spiritual reflection. The sharing of stories, both joyful and challenging, fostered a sense of vulnerability and trust. David noticed a shift in the group dynamic. Conversations became more open and heartfelt. Young people, who once hesitated to share their struggles, were now finding comfort and support within the group.

The community service project wasn't merely a charitable endeavor; it was a catalyst for spiritual growth. The shared experiences, the challenges overcome, the successes celebrated – these forged an unbreakable bond between the youth and strengthened their faith. They learned the importance of selflessness, the rewards of serving others, and the deep satisfaction that came from making a positive impact on their community.

David observed that the project's success wasn't simply measured in terms of the physical structure they built. The real measure of success was the transformation that took place within the hearts and lives of the young people involved. They were learning invaluable life lessons – about teamwork, perseverance, problem-solving, and the power of community to uplift and transform. Their service to others became a form of self-discovery, a path toward spiritual maturity and a deeper understanding of their faith.

As the playground neared completion, a sense of anticipation filled the air. This wasn't just the completion of a project; it was a celebration of their collective efforts, their shared commitment to serving others. The final day was a culmination of their hard work, a testament to the transformative power of community and the bonds they had forged. The playground, a testament to their dedication, became a symbol of their spiritual growth, a reminder of the profound impact they had made on their community and on each other.

The official opening ceremony was a joyous occasion. Children from the elementary school squealed with delight as they explored the newly built playground. The youth group members, beaming with pride, watched them play, their hearts filled with a sense of accomplishment. David joined them, offering words of encouragement and heartfelt gratitude. He praised not only their hard work but also the spirit of unity and mutual support that had characterized their efforts.

The playground wasn't just a place for children to play; it was a living testament to the power of faith in action, a tangible representation of the supportive community they had cultivated. It stood as a beacon of hope, a symbol of their shared commitment to serve others, and a reminder of the transformative power of community service in fostering spiritual growth.

The experience also served as a powerful reminder to David of the importance of creating safe and supportive spaces within the church. He saw how the youth group's shared experiences had fostered a sense of belonging, creating a welcoming environment where young people felt comfortable sharing their struggles and celebrating their successes. This, he realized, was the essence of a healthy and vibrant Christian community.

Building a supportive community wasn't merely a matter of organizing events or implementing programs. It was about creating a culture of love, acceptance, and mutual support – a culture where every member felt valued, respected, and empowered. This required ongoing effort, a consistent commitment to fostering relationships, addressing conflicts constructively, and celebrating the unique gifts and talents of each individual.

David realized that his role wasn't just to preach sermons or lead services, but to actively nurture the community, to create space for authentic relationships, and to encourage individuals to engage in acts of service. He understood that a thriving community wasn't simply a collection of individuals; it was a tapestry of interconnected lives, bound together by shared faith and a commitment to mutual support. The experience of building the playground served as a powerful reminder that the greatest acts of faith are often found in the simplest acts of service and in the nurturing of genuine community. The building of the playground was not just about wood and hammers; it was about building a stronger, more vibrant community, a community grounded in faith, love, and a shared commitment to serving others. And that, David realized, was the truest measure of success. It was a journey, not a destination, a continuous process of growth and transformation, a testament to the enduring power of community and the transformative grace of God.

The rhythmic hammering faded into the quiet of the evening as David sat on his porch, the scent of woodsmoke and damp earth filling the air. The successful playground project had left him feeling a profound sense of peace, but he knew that the journey to lasting inner tranquility required more than just community service. He had long understood the power of prayer, but now he felt drawn to explore other spiritual disciplines, specifically mindfulness and meditation.

He remembered a conversation with Sister Agnes, a wise elderly woman from his congregation, who had spoken of the transformative power of meditation. She had described it not as an escape from life, but as a way to engage with life more fully, more consciously. He had dismissed it initially, viewing it as something esoteric and perhaps even a bit "new age," but the peace he witnessed in Sister Agnes had piqued his curiosity. Now, sitting on his porch, he felt ready to delve deeper.

He started simply, with mindful breathing. He found a comfortable position, sitting upright in his chair, his back straight but not rigid. He closed his eyes gently, focusing his attention on the sensation of his breath entering and leaving his body. At first, his mind raced, a whirlwind of thoughts and anxieties about upcoming sermons, church budgets, and the needs of his parishioners. But slowly, patiently, he brought his attention back to his breath, each inhale and exhale a gentle anchor in the present moment.

The simple act of focusing on his breath felt surprisingly challenging. His mind wandered repeatedly, drawn to the anxieties and distractions of his daily life. He didn't judge himself for these distractions; Sister Agnes had warned him about this. She had said that the wandering mind is a natural part of the process, like a playful puppy that needs to be gently guided back to its master. Each time his mind wandered, he simply acknowledged it without judgment, and gently redirected his focus back to his breath.

Over the next few weeks, he made mindful breathing a regular part of his day, incorporating it into his morning routine and using it as a brief respite during moments of stress. He found that even these short periods of focused attention had a noticeable calming effect. He felt less reactive, more centered, and better equipped to handle the challenges of his day. His interactions with parishioners became more thoughtful and empathetic; his sermons gained a new depth and resonance.

He then progressed to guided meditations, using online resources and audio recordings. These guided meditations often involved visualizing peaceful scenes – a serene forest, a tranquil ocean, a sun-drenched meadow. He found these visualizations incredibly helpful in quieting the chatter of his mind and cultivating a sense of inner calm. He imagined himself walking along a sandy beach, the gentle rhythm of the waves washing away his worries. He pictured himself sitting beneath a towering redwood, feeling grounded and connected to the earth.

He also experimented with walking meditations, paying close attention to the sensations of his feet on the ground, the rhythm of his steps, the movement of his body. He found this particularly grounding, a way to connect with his physical body and the present moment. He walked in nature, feeling the sun on his skin, the wind in his hair, the earthy scent of the forest floor. He found that these moments were not just calming, but deeply spiritual, a way to connect with God's creation.

The process wasn't always easy. There were days when his mind felt like a tempest, his thoughts swirling and churning, resistant to any attempts at stillness. But he persevered, recognizing that meditation wasn't about achieving perfect stillness, but about cultivating a consistent practice of attention and awareness. He learned that the very act of trying to quiet the mind was itself a form of meditation.

As his practice deepened, he began to notice subtle changes within himself. He became more aware of his thoughts and emotions, less prone to impulsive reactions. He developed a greater capacity for compassion, not just for others but also for himself. He began to see his anxieties and fears not as insurmountable obstacles, but as transient states of mind, fleeting clouds that eventually pass across the sky.

He started incorporating mindfulness into his everyday activities. He ate more slowly, savoring the taste and texture of his food. He listened more attentively during conversations, truly hearing what others were saying. He engaged in simple tasks like washing dishes or gardening with a heightened sense of awareness, appreciating the beauty and simplicity of these mundane activities.

Mindfulness and meditation weren't quick fixes, he realized; they were practices, habits to be cultivated over time, with patience and persistence. It wasn't about escaping the challenges of life, but about facing them with greater clarity, calmness, and compassion. He continued to build on his practice, sometimes meditating in the quiet of his study, other times during his morning walk, even incorporating brief moments of mindfulness throughout his busy day.

He found that integrating these practices into his life enriched not only his spiritual life but also his relationships with others. He was a better husband, a better pastor, a better friend. He was able to respond to challenges with greater wisdom and grace. He found that the peace he had cultivated within himself radiated outward, touching the lives of those around him.

The benefits extended beyond the personal. He started incorporating mindfulness techniques into his sermons and pastoral counseling sessions. He found that the principles of mindful breathing and attentive listening were incredibly helpful in helping others navigate difficult emotions and find inner peace. He shared his newfound knowledge with his congregation, encouraging them to explore these techniques for themselves.

He discovered that the spiritual journey, like the building of the playground, was a collaborative effort. Sharing his experiences and offering guidance to others deepened his own practice. The act of teaching became an act of learning, a mutual exchange of wisdom and support. He witnessed firsthand the transformative power of mindfulness and meditation, not only in his own life, but in the lives of others he served. It became a cornerstone of his ministry, a powerful tool for fostering inner peace, spiritual growth, and a deeper connection with God and with community. His understanding of faith had expanded; it was no longer simply belief but a way of being, a conscious engagement with the world, a mindful participation in the divine dance of life. The journey to inner peace was an ongoing process, a continuous unfolding, a testament to the enduring power of faith and the transformative grace of God. And he knew, with a deep and abiding certainty, that this journey was worth every step.

Sarah clutched the worn leather journal, its pages filled with the messy scribbles of her thoughts and feelings. The quiet hum of the evening settled around her as she sat by the window, the city lights painting a shimmering tapestry against the night sky. The playground project, a whirlwind of community effort and shared purpose, had left her with a sense of accomplishment, yet a quiet unease lingered. The peace she'd sought, the tranquility she'd glimpsed through David's journey with mindfulness, felt elusive, a shimmering mirage just out of reach.

David's story had resonated deeply. His exploration of mindfulness and meditation had sparked something within her, a desire to delve deeper into her own spiritual life, to unearth the buried anxieties and unresolved emotions that clouded her inner peace. She'd attempted meditation, following online guides and using calming nature sounds, but the persistent chatter of her mind proved a formidable opponent. Her thoughts, like restless children, clamored for attention, demanding to be heard, leaving her feeling more frustrated than serene.

Then, during a women's Bible study group, a member mentioned journaling as a tool for self-reflection. At first, Sarah was skeptical. Writing felt like a chore, a tedious task reserved for official documents and grocery lists. But the group leader, a kind woman named Esther, had shared her own journaling experience, describing it not as a rigid exercise but as a free-flowing conversation with her own soul. Esther's words planted a seed of curiosity in Sarah's heart. That night, she picked up the leather journal, a gift from her grandmother, and began to write.

The first entry was hesitant, filled with self-consciousness and a reluctance to confront her inner turmoil. She wrote about the superficial aspects of her day, the mundane tasks and routine events, avoiding the deeper emotions that simmered beneath the surface. But as she continued to write, a subtle shift occurred. The act of putting pen to paper, of transforming her swirling thoughts into tangible words, felt strangely cathartic. It was as if the act itself was easing the pressure.

She started to explore her feelings more openly, acknowledging her anxieties, her frustrations, her fears. She wrote about the constant pressure she felt to meet the expectations of others, the nagging sense of inadequacy that often accompanied her. She wrote about her struggles with perfectionism, the relentless pursuit of an unattainable ideal that left her perpetually exhausted and dissatisfied. She poured out her heart onto the pages, allowing her emotions to flow freely without judgment.

Over time, her journal entries became more intimate and revealing. She wrote about her relationship with her husband, Mark, acknowledging the communication breakdowns and unresolved conflicts. She wrote about her strained relationship with her mother, a complex tapestry of love, resentment, and unspoken hurts. She wrote about her struggles with guilt and self-doubt, the internal critic that relentlessly questioned her worth and her capabilities. She even wrote about her doubts about her faith, the moments of spiritual dryness and the lingering questions that challenged her belief system.

The act of writing became a form of prayer, a conversation with God in which she laid bare her vulnerabilities and sought His guidance. She found solace in expressing her fears and anxieties, realizing that God's love transcended her imperfections and accepted her exactly as she was. Through journaling, she discovered a deeper connection to her faith, a more profound understanding of God's grace and mercy.

One particularly challenging entry detailed a conflict she had with a member of her congregation. The disagreement had left her feeling hurt and betrayed, fueling a simmering resentment that poisoned her thoughts and actions. As she wrote about the situation, she began to see things from the other person's perspective, acknowledging the underlying fears and insecurities that may have driven their behavior. This newfound empathy didn't erase her hurt feelings, but it softened the edges of her anger and resentment, creating space for forgiveness and reconciliation.

Another entry explored her feelings about her career. She'd always felt a pull towards creative writing, but she had chosen a more stable, albeit less fulfilling, career path. Through journaling, she examined the reasons behind her choice, acknowledging the fear of failure and the pressure to provide for her family. As she wrote, she realized that her fear was holding her back from pursuing her true passion. The journal became a catalyst for change, prompting her to explore new possibilities and pursue her dream of writing.

Journaling became a ritual, a sacred space where she could explore her emotions, confront her vulnerabilities, and seek God's guidance. It was a journey of self-discovery, a process of peeling back the layers of her self-deception and uncovering her authentic self. The messy scribbles in her journal weren't just words on paper; they were a roadmap to her heart, a testament to her spiritual journey. She realized that true peace wasn't the absence of conflict or challenge, but the ability to navigate life's storms with grace, resilience, and a deeper understanding of herself and her relationship with God.

Sarah discovered that journaling was more than just emotional catharsis; it was a powerful tool for self-understanding and personal growth. By meticulously documenting her thoughts and feelings, she began to identify patterns in her behavior, recognizing triggers and responses. She became more aware of her strengths and weaknesses, her tendencies and habits. She could trace the roots of her anxieties and insecurities, understanding the origins of her emotional pain. This awareness became a stepping stone towards healing and personal transformation.

The journal also helped her to track her spiritual growth. By recording her prayers and reflections, she could see the progress she had made in her faith journey. She noticed shifts in her perspective, changes in her attitude, and an increasing sense of peace and contentment. The journal became a chronicle of her spiritual transformation, a tangible record of God's work in her life.

It wasn't always easy. There were days when the words wouldn't flow, when the emotions felt too raw and overwhelming. On those days, she simply sat with her journal, allowing herself to feel the pain and sadness without forcing herself to write. She learned that the act of acknowledging her feelings was just as important as expressing them. She discovered that silence could be just as powerful as words, that the space between the lines could hold as much meaning as the words themselves.

Sarah also learned the importance of consistency. She set aside a specific time each day for journaling, even if it was just for a few minutes. She treated it as a sacred appointment, a time dedicated to self-reflection and spiritual growth. She found that regular journaling helped her to maintain a sense of balance and perspective, to stay grounded amidst the chaos and uncertainties of life.

And as she continued to write, she realized the power of gratitude. She began each entry with a list of things she was thankful for, no matter how small or insignificant they may seem. This practice helped her to shift her focus from her problems to her blessings, fostering a sense of contentment and appreciation for the good things in her life. This gratitude journal became a source of strength and resilience, reminding her of God's abundant provision and unfailing love.

The journey of self-reflection through journaling wasn't a quick fix; it was an ongoing process, a continuous unfolding of her soul. It was a journey of self-discovery, healing, and spiritual growth. And as she looked back over the pages of her journal, she saw not just a collection of words, but a testament to the power of self-reflection, the grace of God, and the transformative journey towards inner peace. The peace she'd sought wasn't a destination but a continuous process of understanding and accepting oneself, with all the complexities, imperfections, and beauty that entails. And Sarah knew, with a certainty that warmed her heart, that the journey was well worth the effort.

The worn leather of Sarah's journal felt comforting beneath her fingertips. The city lights outside cast long shadows across her desk, but the soft glow of her lamp illuminated the page where she'd begun a new entry. Journaling had become her sanctuary, a space where the chaos of her life could quieten, allowing her to connect with God and herself on a deeper level. But even in this sacred space, a nagging unease remained. The peace she craved, the tranquility she'd glimpsed through her exploration of her faith and her own emotions, still felt somewhat elusive. David's journey with mindfulness had shown her a path, but the practical application felt...difficult.

Then, during a quiet moment of reflection, a simple idea emerged: gratitude. It wasn't a grand revelation, not a sudden flash of insight, but a gentle whisper, a quiet nudge from the Holy Spirit. She remembered hearing sermons on thankfulness, reading passages in Psalms about giving thanks to God in all circumstances, and the countless times she'd heard her grandmother express gratitude for the smallest blessings. Yet, she hadn't truly

practiced gratitude in a consistent, intentional way.

That night, she added a new element to her journaling routine. At the beginning of each entry, before she delved into the complexities of her day, she started a list. A simple list of things she was grateful for. At first, it felt forced, almost artificial. Her mind, accustomed to focusing on anxieties and worries, resisted the shift in perspective. She found herself listing the obvious: her health, her family, a roof over her head. These were essential, yes, but they lacked the depth, the genuine emotion she felt she needed to fully embrace this new practice.

But as days turned into weeks, and weeks into months, something remarkable happened. The act of consciously seeking out things to be grateful for became a habit. And with that habit came a subtle but significant change in her perspective. She began to notice the small things, the often-overlooked blessings that surrounded her. The warmth of the sun on her skin on a crisp autumn morning, the laughter of her children as they played in the park, the kindness of a stranger offering help. These small moments, once unnoticed or taken for granted, suddenly became vibrant sources of joy and appreciation.

One morning, she wrote about the aroma of freshly brewed coffee, a simple pleasure that had become a daily ritual. Another entry documented the beauty of a sunrise, the colors painting the sky in breathtaking hues. She expressed thanks for the ability to walk, to breathe, to feel the beating of her heart, things she had previously overlooked. She even found herself thankful for the challenges she faced, recognizing them as opportunities for growth and spiritual deepening.

This wasn't simply a matter of listing things; it was a transformation of her mindset. She started to approach her day with a different lens, actively seeking out the positive aspects, searching for reasons to be thankful. The small acts of kindness from others, previously dismissed as insignificant gestures, now became powerful reminders of God's love working through people's lives.

The gratitude journal became a mirror reflecting her growing awareness of God's grace. She documented moments of unexpected support, like a timely phone call from a friend who offered exactly the encouragement she needed, or the serendipitous meeting with someone who offered invaluable advice. These were not mere coincidences; she saw them as God's divine interventions, reminders of His constant presence and guidance.

Moreover, the practice of gratitude didn't simply benefit her spiritual life. It had a tangible, positive impact on her mental and emotional well-being. She found herself less prone to anxiety and stress. Her outlook on life became significantly brighter, more positive, and less clouded by negativity. Problems, previously insurmountable obstacles, now seemed more manageable, less daunting, even opportunities for growth.

She started expressing her gratitude to others more openly and sincerely. Simple words of thanks, spoken with genuine feeling, transformed her relationships. A heartfelt "thank you" to her husband for his support, to her children for their love, to her colleagues for their collaboration – these small gestures created a ripple effect of positivity, strengthening the bonds that held her life together. She found herself engaging more deeply in her community, connecting with others on a level beyond superficial pleasantries.

However, the journey wasn't without its moments of struggle. There were days when negativity crept in, when the weight of her responsibilities felt overwhelming, when she struggled to find something to be grateful for. On those days, she didn't force herself. Instead, she acknowledged her feelings, allowed herself to feel the frustration and disappointment, but then gently redirected her thoughts towards even the smallest blessings. She might focus on the comfort of her bed, the warmth of her home, or the love of her pet. Even in the darkest moments, she found pockets of light, tiny sparks of gratitude that kept her hope alive.

She realized that gratitude wasn't about ignoring the challenges of life, but about finding the strength and resilience to navigate them with a more positive perspective. It wasn't about pretending that everything was perfect, but about acknowledging the good, even amidst the bad. It was about recognizing God's hand in both the joys and the sorrows, understanding that even in difficult times, He is always present, always working for her good.

One day, she stumbled upon a quote from the Psalms: "Give thanks in all circumstances; for this is God's will for you in Christ Jesus." This verse became her mantra, a constant reminder of the importance of cultivating gratitude, even during the most trying times. It wasn't always easy, but it became a practice she deeply cherished, recognizing the transformative power it held.

As she continued to journal, she noticed a pattern emerging. The more she focused on gratitude, the less space there was for negativity and anxiety. It was a gentle, yet powerful shift, a transformation of her heart and mind. The practice of gratitude became a spiritual discipline, a daily act of faith, an acknowledgment of God's unwavering love and boundless provision. She discovered that true peace wasn't the absence of problems, but the ability to find joy and thankfulness even amidst life's storms. It was a journey of cultivating a grateful heart, a heart that recognized the beauty of God's creation and the immeasurable grace He showered upon her every day. And it was a journey that had profoundly changed her life. The worn leather of her journal held not just words, but a testament to the transformative power of gratitude, a tangible reminder of God's unwavering love, and a source of continuous inner peace.

Sarah closed her journal, the faint scent of old paper and ink lingering in the air. The quiet contentment she felt was a stark contrast to the turmoil that had once consumed her. Gratitude, she realized, had been a crucial stepping stone, but it wasn't the entire path to peace. A new challenge loomed: learning to set healthy boundaries. The concept felt foreign, even rebellious. She had always strived to please everyone, to be accommodating, to put others' needs before her own. This selfless nature, while rooted in her faith, had often left her feeling depleted, resentful, and overwhelmed.

The next morning, she started a new entry in her journal, this time focusing on the concept of boundaries. She reflected on her relationships, both personal and professional. At work, she'd often found herself taking on extra tasks, working late, and agreeing to projects beyond her capacity. Her colleagues appreciated her dedication, but she felt the pressure mounting, her sense of self-worth dwindling under the weight of expectation. She'd often said "yes" when she really meant "no," fearing rejection or seeming uncooperative. This pattern repeated itself in her personal life as well, leaving her feeling stretched thin and emotionally exhausted.

She recalled a sermon about stewardship, not just of finances and time, but also of oneself. God had entrusted her with her talents, her energy, her very being. To neglect those gifts, to constantly overextend herself, was a form of disrespect to the divine design. Setting boundaries, she realized, wasn't selfish; it was an act of self-preservation, a way of honoring the sacred gift of her own life. It was a way of actively caring for her soul.

The first step, she decided, was to identify her limits. She spent time in prayer, seeking God's guidance, asking for wisdom and discernment. She reflected on her energy levels, her time commitments, and her emotional capacity. What could she realistically handle without feeling overwhelmed or depleted? She started to make a list, a simple inventory of her resources and limitations. This helped her to see her boundaries not as rigid walls but as flexible lines, capable of shifting depending on circumstances and priorities.

Next, she began practicing saying "no." It felt awkward at first, almost painful. The fear of disappointing others, of being perceived as selfish or unhelpful, was strong. But she started small. She politely declined invitations she didn't have the energy for, she refused extra tasks at work that would compromise her existing commitments, and she gently but firmly asserted her limits in conversations with family and friends.

One particular instance at work stands out. A new project emerged, demanding extra hours and significant dedication from the team. Her colleagues, knowing her history of overcommitment, looked to her to take the lead. This time, however, something felt different. She paused, taking a deep breath before responding. She explained that she admired the project, but due to her existing workload, she wouldn't be able to take on additional responsibilities without compromising the quality of her current commitments. She expressed a willingness to assist where possible, offering support and advice without personally leading the project.

The initial reaction wasn't what she had expected. There was a slight hesitation, a moment of surprise. But her colleagues, after a brief discussion, understood. They appreciated her honesty and her willingness to help, even if she couldn't take on the full responsibility. They didn't perceive her refusal as a lack of teamwork but rather as a sign of responsible self-management. In fact, her clear boundaries actually improved team dynamics, encouraging a more realistic distribution of workload and preventing burnout amongst her peers. This experience empowered her, confirming that setting boundaries wasn't about isolating herself but about fostering healthier, more sustainable relationships.

Sarah began incorporating regular self-care practices into her routine. This wasn't about indulging in luxury but about prioritizing activities that nourished her body, mind, and spirit. She scheduled time for prayer and meditation, ensuring at least 30 minutes daily for quiet reflection and connection with God. She resumed her daily walks in nature, finding solace and rejuvenation in the beauty of God's creation. She made a conscious effort to get enough sleep, a simple yet powerful way to restore her energy levels. And she sought support from her faith community, sharing her journey with trusted friends and mentors who understood and encouraged her efforts.

The journey of setting boundaries wasn't linear. There were setbacks, moments of doubt, times when she felt guilty or overwhelmed. Sometimes, she stumbled, and occasionally she fell back into old patterns. But each time she found herself slipping, she gently reminded herself of the importance of her commitment to self-care and honoring God's gift of her life. She returned to her journal, documenting her progress, her struggles, and her victories. The journal became a safe space for self-reflection, a place where she could honestly assess her actions and make adjustments along the way. She continued to seek guidance through prayer and scripture, reminding herself of God's grace and unconditional love.

Over time, she developed greater discernment. She learned to differentiate between genuine requests for help and manipulative demands. She began to recognize situations where her boundaries needed to be firm and those where a degree of flexibility was appropriate. She discovered that setting boundaries didn't mean being unkind or uncaring; it was about prioritizing her own well-being while maintaining healthy, respectful relationships.

Furthermore, Sarah realized that setting boundaries wasn't just a personal matter; it had a ripple effect on her entire life. As she prioritized her own needs, she found she had more energy and capacity to truly invest in her relationships. She was able to give more authentically, less from a place of obligation and more from a place of genuine love and care. Her relationships deepened, becoming stronger and more meaningful. The resentment she'd once felt diminished, replaced by a sense of self-respect and empowerment.

She found herself communicating more clearly and directly, learning to express her needs and preferences without feeling apologetic or hesitant. This improved communication led to healthier dynamics in all her relationships, fostering mutual respect and understanding. She was able to navigate conflict more constructively, addressing issues with clarity and grace. She discovered that setting boundaries didn't create distance; it fostered intimacy, creating space for genuine connection.

The changes weren't drastic or immediate; they were subtle shifts in perspective, small adjustments in behavior, and gradual but significant alterations in her overall approach to life. The peace she sought, once elusive, became a more consistent presence, a deep-seated feeling of serenity and contentment. It wasn't the absence of challenges, but a different way of relating to them, a new capacity to navigate difficulties with resilience, and a renewed understanding of her own strength and worth. The gratitude journal, now accompanied by reflections on setting healthy boundaries, became a testament to her journey, a chronicle of growth and transformation, a tangible record of her increasing peace. The worn pages held not just words, but a narrative of faith, resilience, and the profound transformation that came with learning to love and honor herself, mirroring the immeasurable love of God. It was a journey that confirmed her belief that true peace is not merely the absence of struggle but a state of being, cultivated through intention, nurtured through faith, and manifested through the wisdom of setting healthy boundaries.

The quiet strength Sarah felt was a new sensation, a quiet hum beneath the surface of her daily life. Setting boundaries, she discovered, wasn't a single act but a continuous process, a muscle that needed to be flexed and strengthened. Saying "no" felt less like a rejection and more like an affirmation of her own well-being. It was an act of self-love, a reflection of the divine love she received.

One evening, while volunteering at the local soup kitchen, a familiar feeling of overwhelm crept in. It was the end of a long week, and she was physically and emotionally drained. A new volunteer, enthusiastic and well-meaning, approached her, eager to assist. He proposed taking over Sarah's usual task, which involved preparing a large batch of vegetable stew. In the past, Sarah would have gladly accepted the offer, seeing it as a sign of his commitment and a chance for her to take a break. But this time, something felt different.

She paused, taking a deep breath before responding. "Thank you so much for the offer," she said, her voice calm and steady, "I truly appreciate your willingness to help. However, I think I'll finish preparing the stew tonight. I want to make sure it's done to my usual standard." The young man, slightly taken aback, nodded respectfully. There was no anger, no resentment, only understanding. He chose another task, and Sarah felt a sense of calm wash over her. It wasn't just about the task; it was about protecting her mental space. She recognized the subtle manipulation, the unspoken pressure to always say yes. Learning to identify those pressures, she realized, was a crucial part of setting healthy boundaries.

Another challenge emerged when her sister, Martha, called, her voice filled with urgency. Martha, a single mother of three, was struggling to balance work and family responsibilities. She was always on the verge of a crisis, and she frequently called on Sarah for help—babysitting, errands, emotional support—often with little notice. While Sarah loved her sister dearly, she was beginning to feel exploited. Her own needs were consistently overshadowed by Martha's seemingly endless demands.

This time, when Martha requested Sarah to babysit her children for the entire weekend, Sarah hesitated. It was a significant commitment, one that would completely disrupt her plans for rest and rejuvenation. In the past, she would have automatically agreed, fueled by guilt and a sense of obligation. This time, she took a moment to gather her thoughts.

When she finally responded, her voice was firm, yet laced with compassion. "Martha," she began, "I love you, and I want to support you. However, I'm not able to babysit this weekend. I have prior commitments that I need to attend to." The silence on the other end of the line was palpable. She anticipated a cascade of guilt-inducing comments, but instead, Martha's reply surprised her. "I understand," she said, her voice subdued but composed. "I'll figure something out."

The conversation, devoid of the usual drama and conflict, left Sarah feeling empowered. She had asserted her boundaries without causing a rift in their relationship. The fear of disappointing Martha had been replaced by the quiet confidence of self-respect. She knew that it would take multiple attempts, numerous conversations, to re-establish this healthier balance in their relationship. She realized setting boundaries isn't a one-time fix but a continual process of refining communication, establishing expectations, and advocating for her own wellbeing.

At her church, Sarah faced another test. The church was planning a major fundraising event, and the committee, aware of Sarah's organizational skills, approached her to take on the leading role. She was tempted; the event was important, and it offered a chance to showcase her abilities and contribute to the church's growth. But, she had to consider her current workload, her energy levels, and her personal commitments.

This time, instead of automatically agreeing, Sarah spent time in prayer, seeking God's guidance. She reflected on her capabilities and limitations, acknowledging that her desire to serve shouldn't come at the expense of her well-being. When she met with the committee, she expressed her admiration for the event and her willingness to assist, but she firmly stated that she wouldn't be able to take on the leading role. She offered to support the chosen leader in any way she could, offering her organizational skills in a less demanding capacity.

The committee members, initially surprised by her refusal, quickly understood. They respected her honesty and appreciated her willingness to help without overextending herself. Sarah's example prompted a more equitable distribution of tasks, ensuring that everyone contributed without feeling overwhelmed. The event ultimately became a testament to collaborative work rather than reliance on one individual, demonstrating that true service stems from healthy boundaries and respect for personal limitations.

Sarah began documenting her "no's" in her journal, along with her reflections on how each instance affected her, her relationships, and her peace of mind. She found patterns emerging; certain types of requests triggered stronger feelings of guilt or obligation. Through this self-reflection, she developed greater self-awareness and honed her ability to identify potentially problematic situations. She started to see her "no's" not as acts of selfishness, but as acts of self-preservation, a crucial part of her spiritual journey.

Moreover, Sarah discovered that learning to say "no" wasn't solely about protecting her time and energy; it was also about protecting her spiritual well-being. She found that by setting boundaries, she was able to create space for more meaningful engagement with her faith. The quiet moments of prayer and meditation, once disrupted by constant demands, became sanctuaries of peace and rejuvenation. Her relationship with God deepened, as she learned to prioritize her spiritual life without guilt or apology.

Over time, the act of saying "no" transformed from a source of anxiety into a source of strength and empowerment. Sarah learned to express her limits with grace and clarity, fostering healthier relationships based on mutual respect and understanding. She discovered that true connection wasn't about sacrificing oneself, but about creating space for authentic and balanced interaction. The journey of learning to say "no" wasn't easy, but it was profoundly transformative, leading her to a deeper sense of peace, self-respect, and spiritual well-being, a peace that emanated from a heart grounded in faith and fortified by healthy boundaries. It was a testament to the power of self-care, not as a selfish pursuit, but as an act of divine stewardship, honoring the sacred gift of her life, a life entrusted to her care by a loving God. The pages of her journal, filled with reflections on gratitude and boundaries, bore witness to her transformation, a tangible representation of her growing peace, a peace that flowed not from the absence of challenges, but from her ability to navigate them with grace, wisdom, and the quiet confidence of a soul deeply connected to its source.

Sarah's newfound ability to set boundaries wasn't just about managing her time; it was about protecting her spiritual well-being. She began to notice a subtle shift in her internal landscape. The constant pressure to please everyone, to say "yes" even when she felt overwhelmed, had left her spiritually depleted. It was as if a constant low hum of negativity was present, a subtle drain on her energy and faith. She started to recognize this as a form of spiritual warfare—a subtle but persistent assault on her peace and connection with God.

This wasn't the dramatic, fiery warfare often depicted in apocalyptic visions. Instead, it was a quiet, insidious attack, manifesting as persistent self-doubt, nagging anxieties, and a general sense of unease. It was the insidious whisper of the enemy, trying to undermine her confidence and distract her from her spiritual journey. The enemy didn't roar; it hissed, its voice disguised as self-criticism, as the anxieties of others, as the pressure to conform.

One morning, while engaging in her daily devotional, Sarah felt a wave of discouragement wash over her. The familiar verses she had found comfort in now felt stale, devoid of their usual spiritual resonance. A voice, not external but internal, whispered doubts about her faith, questioning her worthiness, suggesting that her efforts were futile. It was a familiar feeling, one she had experienced before, but this time, she recognized it for what it was: a spiritual attack. She understood that this was not a sign of waning faith, but rather a test, a challenge designed to derail her spiritual progress.

Instead of succumbing to despair, Sarah consciously chose to engage in spiritual combat. She didn't fight with anger or resentment, but with prayer and affirmation. She spoke aloud scriptures of protection and faith, declaring God's promises over her life. She reminded herself of her inherent worth in Christ, of her identity as a beloved child of God. She visualized a shield of faith surrounding her, deflecting the darts of negativity.

The battle wasn't instantaneous; it was a process. The doubts didn't vanish overnight. But with each affirmation, each prayer, each act of faith, the negativity's grip loosened. The stale verses slowly regained their vibrancy, their words resonating with renewed spiritual power. The quiet hum of negativity diminished, replaced by a growing sense of peace and inner strength.

Sarah realized that spiritual warfare is not a passive experience. It requires active participation, a conscious decision to resist the enemy's influence. This involved not just prayer but also self-care – prioritizing rest, healthy eating, and meaningful connections with supportive individuals. It was a holistic approach, recognizing that the spirit, mind, and body are interconnected. Neglecting one area weakened her overall spiritual defense.

She began to see the importance of discernment—the ability to distinguish between God's voice and the enemy's whispers. She learned to recognize the subtle signs of spiritual attack—persistent negativity, unexplained anxiety, sudden discouragement, and a feeling of being overwhelmed. She knew that these weren't simply signs of human weakness, but rather attempts by the enemy to disrupt her spiritual growth. She started to keep a spiritual journal, recording her observations of these subtle attacks, noting the circumstances surrounding them and how she responded. This helped her develop a deeper understanding of her spiritual vulnerabilities and to refine her strategies for spiritual defense.

Sarah also realized that spiritual warfare was not a solitary battle. She relied heavily on the support of her faith community, sharing her struggles with her pastor and trusted friends. Their prayers, encouragement, and accountability were invaluable in her fight against negativity. The shared experience of spiritual struggle created a powerful bond, reminding her that she wasn't alone in her fight.

Over time, Sarah's ability to discern and resist spiritual attacks grew stronger. The subtle whispers of negativity still came, but their impact diminished. She had learned to recognize them as the enemy's tactics, not as reflections of her own worth or faith. She learned to approach these attacks with a spirit of resilience, fortified by prayer, self-care, and the support of her faith community.

She developed a routine of spiritual disciplines—daily prayer, Bible study, meditation, and regular fellowship with other Christians. These practices became her spiritual armor, strengthening her resistance to negative influences. She understood that spiritual warfare is an ongoing battle, but it's a battle she could win through faith, perseverance, and a commitment to spiritual growth.

One particularly challenging week, when a series of unexpected setbacks left her feeling overwhelmed, Sarah found herself tempted to give up. The familiar voice of self-doubt whispered suggestions of hopelessness and despair. However, she remembered the lessons she had learned. Instead of succumbing to negativity, she engaged in a fervent prayer session, confessing her struggles and claiming God's promises of strength and peace. She then engaged in a period of meditation, focusing on God's love and presence. She recalled a specific verse from scripture that had brought her comfort in the past: "For I am the Lord your God, who takes hold of your right hand and says to you, Do not fear; I will help you" (Isaiah 41:13).

The act of recalling and meditating on this verse brought a wave of calm over her. The feeling of being overwhelmed subsided, replaced by a sense of quiet confidence. The enemy's whispers grew faint, drowned out by the powerful voice of God's promises. She felt a renewed sense of purpose, a strengthened resolve to continue her journey of faith.

Sarah's experience underscored the importance of spiritual vigilance. She realized that spiritual warfare is a constant reality for all believers. It is not a matter of

if we will face spiritual attacks, but *when*. The key is to be prepared, to develop strategies for resistance, and to cultivate a strong spiritual foundation built on prayer, faith, and community. She shared her insights with others in her church, encouraging them to remain vigilant, to recognize the subtle attacks of the enemy, and to engage in spiritual warfare with courage and faith. Her story became a powerful testament to the resilience of the human spirit, fortified by the unwavering love and grace of God.

Through it all, Sarah discovered that spiritual warfare was not a battle against flesh and blood, but against spiritual forces of evil (Ephesians 6:12). Understanding this clarified her approach. She focused less on fighting directly against the negativity and more on strengthening her relationship with God, reinforcing her spiritual armor, and relying on the power of prayer and the Holy Spirit for guidance and strength. This shift in perspective freed her from the burden of constant combat, allowing her to focus on spiritual growth and nurturing her connection with God. She realized that spiritual victories often come not through direct confrontation, but through building a stronger and more resilient spiritual life.

Moreover, Sarah understood that spiritual warfare also involved cultivating a thankful heart. Gratitude, she found, was a powerful antidote to negativity. By focusing on God's blessings and goodness, she redirected her thoughts away from the enemy's whispers and toward the positive affirmations of faith. She started a gratitude journal, recording daily instances of God's love and provision. This simple practice became a powerful weapon in her spiritual arsenal, strengthening her resilience and bolstering her faith.

Her understanding of spiritual warfare was continually evolving. She realized that it's not just about repelling negativity but also about actively pursuing spiritual growth and development. This involved engaging in regular spiritual disciplines, strengthening her relationship with God through prayer and Bible study, and nurturing her connection with her faith community. She understood that spiritual growth provided her with the spiritual strength and resilience to overcome any challenges she faced. The more she grew spiritually, the more equipped she became to face and overcome spiritual attacks. It became a cycle of growth and resilience. Each victory strengthened her faith, leading to further growth and an even stronger defense against future attacks.

Finally, Sarah learned that spiritual warfare is a marathon, not a sprint. There will be times of intense spiritual battle and times of relative peace. The key is to remain steadfast in her faith, continually growing spiritually, and always relying on God for strength and guidance. She understood that her spiritual journey is not just a personal one; it's a participation in God's ongoing work in the world.

And in this participation, she found a deeper purpose, a renewed sense of strength, and a peace that surpassed all understanding. The quiet hum beneath the surface of her life was no longer just a sense of inner strength; it was a profound connection with the divine, a source of unwavering peace and resilience in the face of spiritual battles. This was her victory.

Sarah's journey of spiritual growth had led her to a deeper understanding of the unseen battles waged around her. She'd learned that spiritual warfare wasn't simply a matter of overcoming negative thoughts, but a genuine fight against spiritual forces of darkness. This understanding prompted her to delve deeper into scripture, particularly the passage in Ephesians 6:10-18, which speaks of the "armor of God." This passage, she realized, wasn't just a metaphorical description; it offered a practical framework for spiritual protection and engagement.

The first piece of armor, she pondered, was the "belt of truth." This wasn't simply about adhering to moral principles, but about aligning her life with God's unwavering truth. It meant constantly seeking to understand God's will and living in accordance with His word. For Sarah, this involved regular Bible study, prayerful meditation, and a commitment to discerning truth from falsehood in all areas of her life. She found herself becoming increasingly discerning, able to identify lies, both internal and external, that sought to undermine her faith. One such example came in the form of a tempting career opportunity that, while seemingly beneficial on the surface, would have required her to compromise her values. By firmly grounding herself in the truth of God's word, she was able to resist the allure of this opportunity, choosing instead to trust in God's provision for her life. This choice, while challenging, reinforced the importance of the "belt of truth" and the protection it offered. It was a truth-based decision, a shield against the deceptive whispers of compromise.

The "breastplate of righteousness" was another crucial element. For Sarah, this wasn't simply about avoiding sin; it was about living a life of integrity, fueled by God's grace. She realized that righteousness wasn't a performance-based achievement, but a gift received through faith in Christ. This understanding freed her from the constant pressure to be perfect, allowing her to approach her spiritual journey with grace and humility. She started focusing less on her shortcomings and more on God's love and forgiveness. This shift in perspective transformed her internal landscape; the self-criticism that once plagued her began to subside, replaced by a growing sense of self-acceptance and peace. She found that this inner peace acted as a strong defense against the enemy's attacks, which often targeted her self-worth and identity. It was a vital armor against the constant barrage of self-doubt and insecurity that characterized spiritual warfare. Righteousness, in its truest sense, was a fortress against her internal foes.

Next came the "shoes of the gospel of peace." For Sarah, this meant walking in peace and spreading the message of peace to others. This wasn't merely about avoiding conflict, but actively pursuing reconciliation and extending grace to those around her, even to those who had wronged her. She started actively practicing forgiveness, a practice that proved to be immensely powerful in breaking the cycle of negativity and bitterness that often accompanied spiritual attacks. This involved letting go of grudges, refusing to harbor resentment, and extending empathy and compassion to others. One instance where this was particularly challenging involved a difficult relationship with a family member. Through prayer and conscious effort, she began to let go of the hurt and anger, choosing instead to focus on extending forgiveness. The ensuing peace that she experienced was transformative, bolstering her spiritual strength and resilience. The act of walking in peace became an active defense, a powerful countermeasure to the negativity that surrounded her. It was a shield forged not in resistance, but in grace.

The "shield of faith" was perhaps the most visually striking piece of armor. Sarah interpreted this as a constant reliance on God's promises, a shield against the fiery darts of doubt and discouragement. She realized that faith wasn't merely believing in God's existence, but trusting in His unwavering love and provision, even in the face of adversity. It was using faith as a weapon, not a passive belief. She actively sought to reinforce her faith through regular prayer, Bible study, and fellowship with other Christians. She found comfort in recalling specific verses that spoke of God's protection and love, using them as affirmations during moments of doubt. During a period of financial hardship, she actively claimed God's promise of provision, trusting that He would meet her needs. The peace and confidence that came from this unwavering faith served as an impenetrable shield against the darts of anxiety and fear. This faith was an active defense, a powerful weapon against uncertainty.

The "helmet of salvation" represented the protection of her mind and thoughts from the insidious attacks of the enemy. Sarah realized that her thoughts greatly influenced her feelings and actions. Consequently, she cultivated a habit of guarding her mind by filling it with positive and uplifting content. This included engaging in positive affirmations, listening to inspiring sermons and music, and surrounding herself with uplifting friends and family. She consciously avoided negative news cycles and social media that often induced feelings of anxiety and fear. This practice was a conscious effort to keep her mind shielded from the enemy's attempts to influence her thoughts and emotions. The helmet was a constant protection, securing the fortress of her mind against negativity.

Finally, the "sword of the Spirit, which is the word of God" was the weapon of offense, a powerful tool for spiritual warfare. Sarah realized that the Bible wasn't simply a book of history and moral instruction; it was a living word filled with power and authority. She practiced engaging with scripture daily, allowing it to shape her thoughts, guide her actions, and provide strength during moments of weakness. This involved not just reading but meditating on verses, allowing their meaning to penetrate her heart and mind. She utilized scripture as a weapon to rebuke negative thoughts and resist temptation, claiming God's promises over her life and situations. The sword of the Spirit was not a passive defense; it was an active weapon, a tool for spiritual conquest.

Sarah's life became a testament to the power of the armor of God. It wasn't a static protection but a dynamic process of daily engagement. She understood that spiritual warfare is a constant, ongoing battle, but with the armor of God, she was equipped to stand firm against the enemy's attacks, confident in the unwavering love and protection of her Heavenly Father. Her story served as an inspiration to others in her community, encouraging them to take up their own armor and engage in the fight with unwavering faith and courage. The armor, she found, wasn't just a protective shield but a source of strength and confidence, a constant reminder of God's presence and power in her life. It was a powerful tool not only for defense but also for offense, for advancing God's kingdom and spreading His love and peace to the world around her. Her life was a living example of the efficacy of God's armor, a powerful testimony to the reality and power of spiritual warfare and the victory that could be won through faith and reliance on God. The quiet hum beneath the surface of her life was now a symphony of resilience and faith, a testament to the power of God's armor and the ongoing victory that it provided. Her transformed life, changed by the armor and her reliance on God, helped her transform the lives of others around her, spreading hope and the strength only found in a relationship with God. The journey, she discovered, was a lifelong commitment, requiring vigilance, but yielding a harvest of peace and spiritual strength far greater than any earthly triumph.

Sarah's newfound understanding of spiritual warfare, solidified by her diligent application of the armor of God, led her to explore another critical element: prayer. She had always prayed, of course, but now she viewed prayer not simply as a personal devotion, but as a powerful weapon in her spiritual arsenal. Ephesians 6:18, she realized, wasn't just a concluding verse; it was a call to action, a command to engage in constant prayer, a battle cry against the unseen forces at work.

This realization shifted her prayer life dramatically. It wasn't enough to murmur requests before meals or whisper thanks before bed. Prayer, she learned, was a constant communion with God, a vital lifeline connecting her to His strength and protection. She began to pray more consistently, weaving prayer into the fabric of her daily life – in the morning, during her commute, during work breaks, and before bed. These weren't necessarily lengthy sessions; they were short, focused bursts of communication, a constant conversation with her Heavenly Father. She'd whisper prayers of protection for herself and her loved ones, prayers of gratitude for His blessings, and prayers for strength to face the challenges ahead. These moments of connection, often seemingly insignificant, became powerful shields against the subtle attacks of the enemy.

One day, while facing a particularly stressful situation at work, she found herself overwhelmed by anxiety and doubt. The pressure felt immense, the task insurmountable. Instead of succumbing to panic, Sarah paused, closed her eyes, and began to pray. It wasn't a formulated prayer; it was a heartfelt cry to God, a desperate plea for help and guidance. As she prayed, a sense of calm washed over her, replacing the anxiety with a quiet confidence. The situation didn't magically disappear, but her perspective shifted. She found clarity, insight, and the strength to navigate the challenge with grace and resilience. This experience became a turning point, solidifying her conviction about the power of prayer in spiritual warfare.

But Sarah's understanding of prayer went beyond personal devotion. She began to delve into the biblical accounts of collective prayer, understanding its amplified power. She recalled the stories of early Christians, united in prayer, facing persecution and hardship yet unwavering in their faith. Their combined faith, their united voices raised to God, created a force field of protection and strength, enabling them to overcome incredible odds. This understanding led her to actively seek opportunities for collective prayer.

She started attending prayer meetings at her church with increased fervor, finding strength and encouragement in the shared faith of her fellow believers. The collective prayers, she discovered, were significantly more potent than her individual prayers. The combined voices, the unified faith, created a synergy that seemed to pierce the veil between heaven and earth, bringing down God's power in a tangible way. There was a palpable sense of the Holy Spirit moving amongst them, filling the space with a tangible presence of God's power.

During one particularly challenging period in her community, marked by rising crime and societal unrest, Sarah spearheaded a community-wide prayer initiative. She organized a series of prayer walks, inviting people of all faiths to join in a united plea for peace, protection, and healing. Hundreds gathered, their voices rising in unison, invoking God's intervention. The impact was remarkable. Not only did the event bring the community together, fostering a sense of unity and hope, but it also seemed to usher in a period of relative calm. Crime rates declined, tensions eased, and a sense of peace settled over the community. Sarah witnessed firsthand the tangible power of collective prayer, a potent force for good in the midst of spiritual warfare.

This experience further reinforced the importance of prayer as a vital weapon in spiritual warfare. Prayer, she realized, wasn't just a passive act of supplication; it was an active engagement with the divine, a powerful force that could overcome spiritual opposition. She saw it as a strategic offensive, a way to penetrate the enemy's strongholds and disrupt their plans. Through prayer, she could command God's angels to protect her and her loved ones, to bring divine intervention into difficult situations, to bind the forces of darkness and release the power of God's love and grace.

Sarah began to incorporate specific biblical prayers into her routine, using scripture as a guide for intercession. She'd recite verses from Psalms, invoking God's protection and strength, quoting passages from Ephesians, calling upon the armor of God, and reciting the Lord's Prayer, aligning her will with God's. These weren't rote recitations; they were expressions of faith, powerful declarations of her trust in God's power and provision. She found herself reciting the 23rd Psalm during moments of fear, finding solace and comfort in its promises of God's unwavering presence. The words, imbued with faith, served as a shield against anxiety and doubt.

Furthermore, Sarah discovered the importance of intercessory prayer. She began to pray not only for herself but also for others—for friends, family, and even strangers in need. She learned to pray for those who were struggling spiritually, those who were caught in the grip of addiction or despair, those who were facing difficult circumstances. Through intercession, she found a deeper connection to God's compassion and a renewed sense of purpose in her own spiritual journey. Intercession extended her spiritual warfare beyond the personal realm, creating a ripple effect of healing and transformation. She prayed for her community, for her nation, and for the world, understanding that spiritual warfare isn't limited to individual battles; it's a cosmic struggle requiring widespread intercession.

Sarah's commitment to prayer was not without its challenges. There were times when she felt discouraged, when her prayers seemed unanswered, when the battles seemed insurmountable. But even in these moments, she persevered, clinging to the unwavering belief in God's power and faithfulness. She learned that prayer wasn't about receiving immediate answers or seeing immediate results; it was about maintaining a constant connection with God, trusting in His perfect timing and His sovereign plan. She found strength in the assurance that God hears her prayers, even when she doesn't understand His response.

The change in Sarah's life was profound. The constant hum of spiritual warfare that had once filled her with fear and anxiety was now accompanied by a deeper sense of peace and resilience. She learned to wield prayer not just as a weapon of defense but as a tool of offense, actively engaging in spiritual combat, disrupting the enemy's plans and advancing God's kingdom. The power of prayer, coupled with the armor of God, transformed her life into a beacon of faith, a living testament to the victory that can be achieved through unwavering faith and persistent prayer. Her journey became a source of inspiration for others, a testament to the power of prayer in spiritual warfare and a compelling narrative demonstrating the potent combination of faith, spiritual armor, and unwavering prayer. The once quiet hum beneath the surface of her life now resonated with a powerful symphony of faith, a testament to the transformative power of prayer and the ongoing victory won through persistent communion with God. Her life served as a guiding light, showing others the path to unwavering faith and spiritual strength, a testament to the power of prayer in the midst of spiritual conflict. It was a journey not of passive resistance, but of active engagement with the divine, a testament to the unwavering power of prayer in a world constantly engaged in spiritual warfare.

Beyond the consistent prayer that had become a cornerstone of Sarah's spiritual life, she discovered the power of other spiritual disciplines in bolstering her defenses against spiritual attacks. Fasting, a practice often overlooked in modern Christianity, became a significant part of her spiritual arsenal. Initially hesitant, she began with short periods of abstinence from food, viewing it not as a self-punishment, but as a deliberate act of seeking God's face. These periods weren't about deprivation; rather, they were about prioritizing spiritual communion, creating space for focused prayer and deeper reflection on scripture.

The first time Sarah fasted, she felt a surprising clarity. The physical hunger seemed to heighten her spiritual sensitivity, allowing her to perceive God's presence more acutely. The distractions of daily life faded into the background, allowing her inner voice, the quiet whispers of the Holy Spirit, to rise to the forefront. She felt a heightened awareness of her reliance on God, a humbling dependence that deepened her relationship with her Heavenly Father. During these periods of fasting, she found herself praying with a fervor and intensity she hadn't experienced before, her requests imbued with a depth and sincerity born out of intentional spiritual focus.

She wasn't alone in this experience. She began reading the accounts of biblical figures who had employed fasting as a spiritual discipline, recognizing its transformative power. Moses, Elijah, and Daniel, amongst others, had used fasting to seek God's guidance, to receive revelation, and to strengthen their spiritual resolve during times of crisis. These biblical examples served as encouragement, reminding her that fasting wasn't a novelty but a tried and tested spiritual practice with a rich heritage in the faith.

As Sarah's practice of fasting matured, she found herself using it strategically, employing it during times of spiritual warfare, petitioning God for intervention in specific situations. She would fast before important decisions, seeking God's wisdom and guidance. She fasted when facing particularly challenging circumstances, seeking strength and resilience. She even organized corporate fasting periods with her church community, joining her fellow believers in united prayer and seeking God's blessing upon their community. These collective fasts were powerful experiences, filled with a palpable sense of God's presence and a renewed commitment to His will. The combined spiritual focus amplified their prayers, creating a synergy that transcended individual effort.

But Sarah understood that fasting, like prayer, wasn't a magic formula. It was a discipline that required intentionality, humility, and perseverance. There were times when the physical hunger was intense, when her willpower wavered. But she persevered, driven by a desire to deepen her relationship with God and to strengthen her spiritual defenses. She realized that the true benefit of fasting wasn't solely the physical abstinence, but the spiritual transformation it fostered—a deepening of faith, an increased dependence on God, and a heightened awareness of His presence in her life.

In addition to prayer and fasting, Sarah embraced the discipline of regular Bible study as an essential part of her spiritual warfare strategy. She moved beyond casual readings, dedicating specific times for focused study, prayerfully seeking God's guidance and understanding as she delved into scripture. She utilized study Bibles, commentaries, and other resources to deepen her comprehension of the text, recognizing that a thorough understanding of God's word was crucial in equipping herself for spiritual battle. She didn't just read; she meditated on the scriptures, allowing the words to penetrate her heart and transform her mind. She found herself recalling verses during moments of spiritual attack, drawing strength and comfort from God's promises.

Sarah's Bible study went beyond personal edification. She began to understand scripture as a strategic manual for spiritual warfare, equipping her with the knowledge and understanding necessary to discern spiritual realities and engage in effective spiritual combat. She studied passages detailing the battles of faith found throughout the Old and New Testaments, recognizing recurring patterns of spiritual attack and divine intervention. She learned to identify the enemy's tactics, to understand his strategies, and to recognize his attempts to deceive and discourage her. This knowledge empowered her, providing her with a framework for understanding and resisting spiritual oppression.

She learned to discern the subtle whispers of doubt and fear, recognizing them as the enemy's attempts to undermine her faith. She learned to replace these negative thoughts with the truths found in scripture, wielding verses as weapons against the lies of the adversary. She would memorize key passages, reciting them during moments of spiritual attack, declaring God's promises and invoking His protection over herself and her loved ones. These weren't mere recitations; they were powerful declarations of faith, potent affirmations of her reliance on God's strength and provision.

Furthermore, Sarah explored the rich tradition of spiritual warfare found within the scriptures. She studied accounts of exorcisms, deliverance, and spiritual battles fought by biblical figures, learning from their experiences and applying their strategies to her own life.

She discovered the importance of spiritual discernment, learning to distinguish between the promptings of the Holy Spirit and the subtle manipulations of the enemy. She sought guidance from mature Christians, gaining wisdom and understanding from their experience in spiritual warfare. She realized that spiritual growth was a continuous journey, a lifelong process of learning and applying biblical principles to every aspect of her life.

The combination of consistent prayer, strategic fasting, and diligent Bible study transformed Sarah's spiritual life. She became a warrior of faith, equipped to engage in spiritual combat and to stand firm against the assaults of the enemy. The anxieties and fears that had once plagued her were replaced by a quiet confidence, a deep-seated assurance in God's unwavering love and protection. The spiritual disciplines she embraced weren't merely religious practices; they were vital strategies for strengthening her spiritual defenses, empowering her to overcome spiritual challenges and to advance God's kingdom in her life and in the lives of others.

Her newfound spiritual strength wasn't merely a personal accomplishment; it extended to her relationships and her community. She became a source of strength and encouragement for others, sharing her experiences and guiding others in their own spiritual journeys. She actively sought opportunities to mentor and disciple others, passing on the knowledge and wisdom she had gained through her own struggles and triumphs. Her transformed life was a testament to the transformative power of spiritual disciplines, a living embodiment of faith in action.

Moreover, Sarah's experience taught her the importance of perseverance in spiritual warfare. There were times when she felt discouraged, when the battles seemed overwhelming, when her prayers felt unanswered. But she persisted, clinging to her faith and trusting in God's timing. She understood that spiritual warfare wasn't a sprint but a marathon, requiring continuous vigilance, unwavering faith, and persistent reliance on God's strength and guidance. The very act of maintaining these spiritual disciplines, even amidst discouragement, became a declaration of her unwavering faith, a refusal to surrender to the enemy's attacks. She became a beacon of hope for others, demonstrating that even in the midst of spiritual conflict, victory is possible through persistent faith and unwavering commitment to spiritual disciplines. Her journey served as a powerful example, a testament to the enduring strength that is born out of a life lived in close communion with God. Her story, filled with the triumphs and struggles of spiritual warfare, became a powerful message of hope and resilience, a testament to the transforming power of faith when combined with intentional spiritual disciplines. It became a story of not just survival but thriving in the midst of spiritual conflict, a beacon of light illuminating the path towards a life of victory and spiritual maturity.

Sarah's journey of spiritual growth hadn't ended with her mastery of prayer, fasting, and Bible study. A new layer of understanding unfolded as she delved deeper into the promises of God concerning protection. She began to see that spiritual warfare wasn't just about repelling attacks; it was also about proactively claiming the shield of faith offered by God's unwavering promises.

This realization wasn't a sudden epiphany but a gradual unfolding, a deepening of her understanding of God's character and His covenant relationship with His people. She started by meticulously studying passages that spoke of God's protective hand, verses that resonated with the overwhelming assurance of His presence in the midst of danger. Psalms 91 became a favorite, its verses a balm to her soul, a constant reminder of God's sheltering presence. She memorized key phrases, repeating them like mantras during moments of vulnerability or fear. "He who dwells in the shelter of the Most High will rest in the shadow of the Almighty," she would whisper, finding strength and comfort in the imagery of divine protection.

Her understanding deepened as she explored the narratives of biblical figures who had experienced God's miraculous interventions. The story of Daniel in the lion's den became a powerful symbol of unwavering faith and divine protection. The unwavering belief of Daniel, combined with God's miraculous intervention, became a tangible example of claiming God's promises in the face of seemingly insurmountable odds. Sarah reflected on how Daniel's faith wasn't passive; it was an active claiming of God's power and protection. He didn't merely hope for deliverance; he expected it, based on his understanding of God's character and His covenant promises.

She meticulously examined the accounts of the Israelites' journey through the wilderness, noting God's provision and protection despite their constant trials and tribulations. The pillar of cloud and fire that guided and protected them became a powerful image of God's constant presence and unwavering care. She began to view her own life as a pilgrimage, a journey guided and protected by God's unwavering love and grace. The challenges and difficulties she faced were not random occurrences but opportunities to trust in God's provision and to claim His promises of protection.

This proactive approach to spiritual warfare transformed Sarah's perspective. She moved from a reactive stance, merely fending off attacks, to a proactive one, actively claiming God's promises as her shield and weapon. She learned to speak God's word over herself and her loved ones, declaring His promises of protection, health, and provision. These weren't empty pronouncements; they were acts of faith, powerful declarations that released God's power into her circumstances.

One particular incident vividly illustrated this transformation. Sarah's elderly mother, Martha, fell ill unexpectedly. The diagnosis was grave, and the doctors offered little hope. Sarah was overwhelmed with fear and anxiety, but she refused to succumb to despair. Instead, she immediately began praying, not only for Martha's healing but for God's supernatural protection over her. She recalled the numerous verses she had memorized, speaking them over her mother, claiming the promises of healing and restoration found in the scriptures. She fasted and prayed with renewed fervor, drawing strength from her deeper understanding of spiritual warfare and God's promises.

Her church community rallied around her, joining her in prayer and fasting. The collective faith and intercession created a powerful atmosphere of spiritual protection. Days turned into weeks, and while Martha's condition remained critical, Sarah remained resolute in her faith. She continued to claim God's promises, believing that God's power could transcend medical limitations.

Then, unexpectedly, Martha's condition began to improve. The doctors were amazed at the swift and dramatic turnaround. While they couldn't explain it medically, Sarah knew it was a direct answer to prayer, a powerful demonstration of God's protective hand. Martha's recovery wasn't just physical; it was a spiritual victory, a testament to the power of claiming God's promises amidst adversity. This experience solidified Sarah's conviction that claiming God's promises wasn't a passive act; it was a powerful weapon in spiritual warfare, a declaration of faith that released God's power to intervene and protect.

This newfound confidence extended beyond personal circumstances. Sarah began to mentor others in claiming God's promises for protection. She taught them the importance of studying scripture, identifying God's promises, and speaking those promises over their lives. She emphasized the need to move beyond merely reading the Bible and instead to actively engage with its promises, incorporating them into daily prayers, affirmations, and declarations of faith.

She shared stories of God's protection with her community, reminding them that God's promises weren't limited to specific individuals or situations. They were universal truths applicable to everyone who believed and claimed them. She encouraged them to develop a deeper relationship with God through prayer, fasting, and Bible study, recognizing these disciplines as essential tools for engaging in spiritual warfare and claiming God's protection.

Sarah recognized that spiritual protection wasn't a guarantee against all harm or suffering, but it was a promise of God's presence and guidance in the midst of any storm. She emphasized that claiming God's promises didn't eliminate difficulties; instead, it empowered individuals to face challenges with courage, faith, and the unwavering assurance of God's protective hand. It offered them a peace that surpasses all understanding, a strength that comes from knowing that they are not alone in their battles, but are surrounded by the unwavering love and protection of the Almighty.

She also taught the importance of discernment in claiming God's promises. She warned against manipulating scripture to fit personal desires or expectations. Instead, she encouraged individuals to seek God's wisdom and guidance in understanding and applying His promises. She stressed that claiming God's protection involves a humble dependence on His sovereignty, an understanding that His will, not our own, ultimately prevails.

Through her teaching and mentoring, Sarah became a beacon of hope and encouragement, helping others navigate the complexities of spiritual warfare and claim the power of God's promises. Her journey was a testament to the transformative power of faith, a living example of how claiming God's promises can lead to a life filled with peace, protection, and unwavering confidence in the face of any adversity. Her life became a powerful illustration of the truth that those who dwell in the shelter of the Most High will indeed find refuge and rest in the shadow of the Almighty. Her story, etched with both struggle and triumph, became a living testament to the enduring power of faith in the face of adversity and a clear demonstration of how to actively claim the promises of divine protection. It was a narrative filled with the vibrant colors of faith, hope, and the undeniable power of God's unwavering love. The legacy she left behind was not just one of personal victory but of empowering countless others to claim the very same promises that had transformed her life.

The sweet fragrance of lilies filled the air in Martha's sun-drenched room, a stark contrast to the bitterness that had taken root in Sarah's heart. Martha, miraculously recovered, now sat knitting, a serene smile playing on her lips. Yet, Sarah felt a persistent knot of resentment tightening within her. It wasn't directed at Martha or even the doctors who had initially offered so little hope. The bitterness was far deeper, a tangled vine grown from the neglected soil of her past.

Martha's recovery had been a breathtaking miracle, a resounding testament to the power of prayer and unwavering faith. Yet, amidst the joy, Sarah found herself battling a shadow self, a lurking resentment that refused to yield to gratitude. The seeds of this bitterness had been sown long ago, in the fertile ground of childhood wounds.

It started subtly, a small pebble of hurt that grew into a boulder over time. A casual remark from a schoolmate, a hurtful snub from a friend, a sense of being overlooked by her own parents—each seemingly insignificant incident had chipped away at her self-worth. She had learned to bury these wounds, to plaster over them with a smile and a forced acceptance. But now, like a festering wound finally breaking the surface, the bitterness had erupted, casting a long shadow over her newfound spiritual strength.

Recognizing this internal struggle was the first step. She understood, through years of dedicated study and prayer, that spiritual growth wasn't merely about achieving a blissful state of constant happiness, but rather about confronting and overcoming the shadows within. The Bible spoke repeatedly about the importance of forgiveness, not just for others, but also for oneself. She recalled the parable of the unforgiving servant, where the harshness of unforgiveness was portrayed as a direct impediment to spiritual freedom.

Sarah began a process of introspection, a careful excavation of her emotional landscape. She started journaling, pouring out her heart onto the pages, naming the hurts, the injustices, the betrayals both large and small, that had contributed to her bitterness. The words flowed freely, a cathartic release of pent-up emotions that had been long suppressed.

She found solace in the Psalms, the ancient cries of a people grappling with their own pain and suffering. David's lamentations, his raw honesty, his pleas for God's mercy and justice, resonated deeply within her. She found kinship in his struggles, recognizing that even a man after God's own heart had experienced profound disappointment and heartache. His words became a mirror reflecting her own internal turmoil, a validation of her emotions, and a comfort in knowing that she wasn't alone in her struggle.

As she wrote, a pattern emerged. The bitterness wasn't simply a reaction to individual events; it was a manifestation of deeper, unresolved issues. She realized that much of her resentment stemmed from a pervasive sense of inadequacy, a feeling of not being good enough, of constantly falling short of expectations, both self-imposed and externally imposed. This sense of inadequacy was fueled by a deep-seated fear of rejection, a fear that had its roots in early childhood experiences. The hurtful words and actions of others had affirmed this fear, creating a cycle of self-doubt and resentment.

One particular entry in her journal stood out: "I always felt like I had to be perfect to earn love. If I wasn't perfect, I wasn't worthy." This statement revealed the core of her bitterness – a desperate need for validation, a longing for unconditional love that had never been fully met. She had subconsciously equated love with performance, believing that she had to constantly prove her worth to be loved and accepted.

The realization was both painful and liberating. Painful because it exposed a deep-seated wound that had festered for years. Liberating because it allowed her to understand the root cause of her bitterness. It was not about the individual events themselves; it was about the underlying belief system that had shaped her perception of herself and her relationships.

With this newfound understanding, Sarah began to challenge her negative beliefs. She started by actively replacing negative self-talk with affirmations of God's love and acceptance. She repeated verses like Psalm 139:14, "I praise you because I am fearfully and wonderfully made; your works are wonderful, I know that full well," reminding herself of her inherent worth in God's eyes.

She also sought guidance from her pastor, a wise and compassionate man who listened patiently to her struggles and offered biblical counsel. He reminded her of God's unconditional love, a love that was not contingent on performance or perfection. He helped her understand that forgiveness wasn't about condoning the actions of others but about releasing the burden of resentment from her own heart.

This process of identifying and addressing the root causes of her bitterness wasn't quick or easy. It required consistent effort, persistent prayer, and a willingness to confront her own vulnerabilities. There were days when the bitterness returned, a tenacious weed stubbornly refusing to be uprooted. But with each act of forgiveness, each affirmation of God's love, each prayer for healing, Sarah found herself gaining ground.

She realized that overcoming bitterness was not merely an emotional exercise; it was a spiritual battle. It required engaging in spiritual warfare, wielding the weapons of faith, prayer, and the Word of God. She started to view her struggle not as a failure but as an opportunity for growth, a chance to demonstrate the transformative power of God's grace.

As she diligently worked through this process, a remarkable transformation began. The heavy weight of resentment lifted, replaced by a sense of peace and freedom. The joy of Martha's recovery became truly unburdened, a source of genuine happiness rather than a bittersweet victory. Her relationship with God deepened, moving beyond a transactional exchange of prayers and blessings to a profound relationship of trust, vulnerability, and unwavering love.

Sarah's journey became a powerful reminder that overcoming bitterness is a process, not a destination. It requires honesty, courage, and a willingness to confront the painful realities of the past. But with God's help, the healing is possible. The bitterness can be replaced with grace, resentment with forgiveness, and a wounded spirit with a renewed sense of peace and purpose. Her story served as a beacon, a testament to the power of self-reflection, spiritual guidance, and the transformative love of God, offering hope and healing to those bound by the chains of bitterness and resentment. The lilies in Martha's room continued to bloom, a fragrant symbol of the healing that was blossoming in Sarah's heart, a testament to the enduring power of God's grace. And in the quiet moments, Sarah finally felt the peace that surpasses all understanding, a peace that had been long elusive but was now firmly rooted in the fertile ground of a forgiven heart.

The pastor, a kind-faced man with eyes that held the wisdom of years spent guiding souls, gently placed his hand on Sarah's arm. "Sarah, forgiveness isn't about condoning wrongdoing; it's about releasing yourself from the prison of resentment. It's about choosing freedom over bitterness." His words resonated deeply, echoing the sentiments she had been wrestling with. He continued, "Think of it like this: resentment is a heavy cloak, weighing you down, hindering your ability to move forward, to embrace the joy that God offers."

He spoke of the parable of the unforgiving servant, a story that had always felt distant, theoretical. Now, it felt achingly personal. The servant, forgiven a massive debt, refused to show mercy to a fellow servant who owed him a far smaller sum. The harshness of his unforgiveness mirrored Sarah's own struggle. She had been granted a miracle – Martha's recovery – yet she clung to the bitterness of the past, refusing to grant herself the same grace she had witnessed in her sister's healing.

"Forgiveness," the pastor explained, "is an act of releasing, not forgetting. You don't have to pretend the hurtful events never happened. But you can choose to release the power they have over you. You can choose to stop letting them dictate your emotions, your relationships, your very life." He paused, allowing his words to sink in. "This is a process, Sarah, a journey, not a destination. There will be setbacks, moments when the bitterness threatens to resurface. But with God's grace, you will find the strength to overcome."

He suggested a practical exercise, a form of spiritual accounting. He urged Sarah to write a letter to each person who had caused her pain, expressing her hurt, her anger, her disappointment. These weren't letters intended for mailing; they were letters to release her emotions, to pour out her heart without fear of judgment or reprisal. He emphasized that the purpose wasn't to accuse or condemn, but to articulate her feelings honestly, to confront the pain without holding onto it. After writing each letter, she was to symbolically release it—burning it, burying it, or simply letting it go into the wind, a physical act to represent the emotional release.

He also stressed the importance of self-forgiveness. Sarah's sense of inadequacy had been a major contributor to her bitterness. She had carried a heavy burden of self-criticism, judging herself harshly for perceived failures and shortcomings. The pastor gently reminded her of God's unconditional love, a love that wasn't earned through performance but freely given. He encouraged her to replace negative self-talk with affirmations of God's grace and acceptance. He suggested she repeat verses like Psalm 103:12-14: "As far as the east is from the west, so far has he removed our transgressions from us. As a father has compassion on his children, so the Lord has compassion on those who fear him; for he knows how we are formed, he remembers that we are dust."

This practice of self-compassion was crucial, he emphasized. It was about acknowledging her mistakes and imperfections without dwelling on them, accepting her humanity without condemning herself. It was about embracing the grace that God freely offers, extending that same grace to herself.

The following weeks were a crucible of emotions. Sarah diligently followed the pastor's advice. She wrote letters, pouring out her heart onto the pages, confronting the pain, the betrayal, the disappointment that had accumulated over the years. Some letters were filled with accusations, others with tears, others with a quiet acceptance. The act of writing itself was a cathartic release, a way to acknowledge and process the emotions that had long been suppressed.

The physical act of releasing the letters was surprisingly powerful. The flames consumed the paper, the smoke carrying away the residue of her pain. Burying the letters felt like burying the past, a conscious act of letting go. The wind carried the weight of her unspoken words, releasing the burden she had carried for so long.

She also focused on self-forgiveness, a difficult but essential part of the process. It wasn't easy to let go of the self-criticism, the harsh judgment that had become ingrained over the years. But as she repeated affirmations of God's love and acceptance, as she focused on her inherent worth in His eyes, a gradual shift began to take place. The relentless self-criticism lessened, replaced by a growing sense of self-acceptance and self-compassion.

She found solace in prayer, spending extended periods in communion with God, pouring out her heart, seeking His strength and guidance. In those quiet moments, she felt a presence of peace, a sense of being held and loved unconditionally. It was a profound experience, a deepening of her relationship with God, moving beyond a transactional exchange to a genuine connection of trust, vulnerability, and love.

The transformation wasn't instantaneous. There were days when the bitterness threatened to resurface, when old wounds ached, when the weight of the past seemed too heavy to bear. But each time, she returned to the practices the pastor had suggested – writing, releasing, praying, affirming. She learned to view these setbacks not as failures but as opportunities for growth, chances to demonstrate the transformative power of God's grace.

Over time, the heavy cloak of resentment began to lift. The joy of Martha's recovery became unburdened, a source of genuine happiness rather than a bittersweet victory. Sarah found herself embracing life with a renewed sense of purpose, a sense of freedom she hadn't known before. The bitterness had been replaced by grace, resentment by forgiveness, a wounded spirit by a renewed sense of peace and purpose. The lilies in Martha's room continued to bloom, a symbol of the healing that was blossoming within Sarah's heart – a testament to the enduring power of God's grace, the transformative power of forgiveness, and the profound peace that comes from releasing the weight of the past. The fragrance of those lilies became a constant reminder of the healing that had taken root in her soul, a healing that extended beyond herself, touching those around her, and offering a powerful testament to the restorative power of faith, forgiveness, and the unwavering love of God.

The pastor leaned forward, his gaze gentle but firm. "Sarah, we've talked about forgiving others, about releasing the grip of resentment. But true freedom lies also in forgiving yourself. Many of us carry burdens of self-reproach, a relentless inner critic that whispers doubts and insecurities. This self-criticism, this relentless self-judgment, often fuels bitterness. It keeps us trapped in the past, unable to embrace the present, or look forward to the future God has planned."

He paused, allowing his words to settle. "Think of the times you've been hardest on yourself, Sarah. The mistakes you've made, the opportunities you feel you've missed. Can you bring some of those memories to mind?"

Sarah hesitated, then confessed, her voice barely above a whisper, "I still replay the argument I had with Martha before her illness. I was so harsh, so unforgiving. I said things I can never take back. I could have been kinder, more patient...more loving. If I had been, perhaps things would have turned out differently."

The pastor nodded understandingly. "Self-reproach often stems from a mistaken belief that our worth is dependent on our performance. We believe we must be perfect, flawless, to be worthy of love. But that's a lie, Sarah. A lie whispered by the enemy to steal our joy and keep us bound. God's love is unconditional. It isn't earned; it's freely given."

He opened his Bible, reading aloud from Psalm 139:14: "I praise you because I am fearfully and wonderfully made; your works are wonderful, I know that full well." He looked at Sarah, his eyes twinkling. "God doesn't look at you through the lens of your mistakes. He sees you as His beloved child, created in His image, wonderfully and fearfully made. Every single one of us falls short of perfection. That's part of being human. It's what makes us need grace, God's undeserved and boundless love."

He continued, "Forgiveness, especially self-forgiveness, is a process, not a single event. It's like slowly untangling a knotted rope. It takes time, patience, and persistent effort. It's not about ignoring your mistakes or pretending they didn't happen. It's about acknowledging them, accepting them as part of your story, without letting them define your identity or dictate your future."

He suggested a new exercise: a daily practice of self-compassion. "Each morning," he instructed, "take a few moments to reflect on God's love for you. Read a scripture that speaks of His grace and mercy. Speak affirmations to yourself, reminding yourself of your inherent worth. Focus on your strengths and accomplishments, big or small. Celebrate your resilience, your perseverance, your capacity for love and compassion. Acknowledge your mistakes, but don't dwell on them."

He provided examples: "Instead of saying, 'I'm such a failure,' say, 'I made a mistake, but I am learning and growing from it.' Instead of 'I'm not good enough,' say, 'I am loved unconditionally by God, and that's all that matters.' Instead of 'I'm a terrible sister,' say, 'I am learning to be a better sister, and God is with me in this journey.'"

He emphasized the importance of self-care as a critical component of self-forgiveness. "When we neglect our physical and emotional well-being, we make it harder to forgive ourselves," he explained. "Adequate sleep, healthy eating, regular exercise—these are not luxuries; they are essential components of healing and self-compassion."

He also suggested journaling as a tool to process her emotions, to explore the roots of her self-criticism, and to challenge negative self-talk. "Write down your thoughts and feelings without judgment," he advised. "Ask yourself questions: What beliefs are fueling my self-criticism? Where did these beliefs originate? Are they true? What evidence contradicts these beliefs? What would I tell a friend who was experiencing these same thoughts?"

Sarah started small, writing a few sentences each day. Initially, the entries were filled with self-recrimination, but gradually, a shift began to take place. As she examined her beliefs with a more compassionate lens, she started to identify the distorted thinking patterns that underpinned her self-criticism.

She also started to notice a pattern: her self-judgment was often triggered by comparisons to others. This insight led to a deeper understanding of her need for self-acceptance. She realized that true worth wasn't about measuring up to external standards, but about embracing her unique identity as a beloved child of God.

The pastor encouraged her to engage in activities that brought her joy, that nourished her soul. He urged her to spend time in nature, to listen to uplifting music, to read inspiring books, to connect with friends and family who supported her. These were not trivial distractions; they were acts of self-nurturing, essential elements of the healing process.

Weeks turned into months. The process wasn't always easy. Sarah still experienced moments of self-doubt and self-recrimination. But she learned to treat these moments with kindness and understanding, to acknowledge them without allowing them to overwhelm her. She learned to approach self-criticism with the same compassion she would offer a friend struggling with similar thoughts.

Through consistent practice of self-compassion, prayer, and journaling, Sarah's perspective shifted. The relentless inner critic grew quieter, replaced by a growing sense of self-acceptance. She discovered a reservoir of strength and resilience she hadn't known she possessed. The weight of the past gradually lessened, replaced by a lighter, more hopeful outlook. The joy in her life was no longer shadowed by the bitterness of self-recrimination. The lilies in Martha's room continued to bloom, a silent testament to the healing that was unfolding within her heart, a healing that extended to every aspect of her life, renewing her capacity for love, for forgiveness, and for the boundless grace of God. She had broken free from the prison of her past, emerging into the radiant light of God's unwavering love, a love that embraced her imperfections, celebrated her strengths, and empowered her to live a life of purpose, peace, and joy. The fragrance of those lilies was a constant reminder of her journey, a fragrance that spoke of forgiveness, healing, and the unwavering love of God, a love that had transformed her from a heart burdened by bitterness to one overflowing with grace.

The pastor smiled gently. “Sarah, we've explored forgiving yourself, releasing the grip of self-recrimination. But true healing extends beyond personal forgiveness; it encompasses extending compassion to those who have caused us pain. This isn't condoning their actions, but rather recognizing their humanity, their own struggles, their own wounds that may have driven their behavior.”

He paused, allowing the weight of his words to settle. “Think about Martha's actions, the things she did that you found hurtful. Before we condemn, let's try to understand. Perhaps she acted out of fear, insecurity, or unresolved pain of her own. Can you imagine what might have been happening in her life, what struggles she might have been facing that led her to behave as she did?”

Sarah furrowed her brow, a thoughtful expression replacing her earlier sadness. "It's difficult," she admitted. "I always saw her actions as deliberate, as a personal attack. I focused so much on the hurt she caused me that I never really considered what might have been driving her."

The pastor nodded. "That's understandable. Bitterness often blinds us to the complexities of other people's lives. It's easy to focus on our own pain and forget that everyone carries their own burdens, their own stories of hurt and struggle. Compassion isn't about excusing wrongdoing; it's about recognizing the human condition, the fact that we all make mistakes, that we all fall short, that we all carry pain."

He picked up a small, smooth stone from his desk, turning it over in his hands. "Imagine this stone, Sarah. It might seem smooth and unblemished on the surface, but if you were to examine it closely, you would likely find imperfections, scratches, perhaps even cracks. Those imperfections are part of its history, shaping its unique form. In the same way, the people who have hurt us carry their own imperfections, their own histories of pain and struggle. These shape their actions and behaviours. Recognising this doesn't justify their actions, but it can help us to approach them with more understanding, more compassion."

He continued, "Consider the parable of the Good Samaritan. The priest and the Levite saw the injured man and passed by, their minds perhaps occupied with their own concerns, their own prejudices. But the Samaritan, someone considered an outsider, an enemy, saw the man's suffering and acted with compassion. He didn't judge the man; he didn't ask why he was injured. He simply responded to his need. That, my dear, is the essence of compassion: responding to another's suffering with empathy and kindness, regardless of their background, their actions, or our personal feelings towards them."

He suggested an exercise: "Try to imagine Martha's perspective. Write a letter from her point of view, describing her feelings, her struggles, the motivations behind her actions. Don't worry about whether this is 'accurate'; it's an exercise in empathy. It's about stepping into her shoes, trying to understand her world from her perspective."

Sarah initially resisted, her voice laced with skepticism. "But that's so difficult. I don't know what she was thinking or feeling."

“Exactly,” the pastor replied, "and that's why this exercise is so valuable. It forces you to move beyond judgment and engage with the possibility of different perspectives, the possibility of understanding the underlying causes of her hurtful actions. Focus on the potential pain and vulnerabilities fueling her behaviours. This isn’t about excusing her, but about broadening your understanding of the situation.”

Sarah reluctantly agreed, committing to the exercise. She began to write, initially finding it excruciatingly difficult. Her words were filled with anger and resentment, but slowly, as she forced herself to consider Martha's possible feelings, her perspective began to shift.

She imagined Martha’s fear of losing her independence, the anxieties that plagued her as her illness progressed, the frustration that stemmed from her declining physical capabilities. She pictured the pain she must have been enduring, both physical and emotional, the desperation that might have fueled her outbursts and cutting words. She contemplated Martha's fear of being a burden, her anxieties about her future, the insecurity that simmered beneath her outward strength.

As Sarah wrote, a wave of empathy washed over her. It wasn't easy; the hurt she had experienced was still raw. But she began to see Martha not as a villain, but as a human being, a person struggling with her own demons, her own deep-seated fears. The anger began to recede, replaced by a growing sense of understanding, a dawning compassion. She found herself shedding tears of pity, of sadness for Martha's suffering, rather than tears of anger over her own pain.

The pastor also encouraged Sarah to engage in acts of compassion towards others. "Volunteer at a local charity," he suggested. "Visit someone who is sick or lonely. Offer a helping hand to a neighbor in need. These acts of kindness extend beyond Martha; they nurture your own capacity for compassion and help to heal the wounds of your heart."

Sarah began volunteering at a local soup kitchen, finding solace and purpose in serving those less fortunate. She befriended an elderly woman living alone, offering companionship and emotional support. Through these acts of service, she not only helped others but also found a profound sense of healing within herself. The bitterness that had once consumed her began to dissipate, replaced by a growing sense of empathy, understanding and inner peace.

Her compassion wasn't a sudden switch; it was a gradual, transformative process. It involved confronting her anger, challenging her judgment, and cultivating a greater understanding of the human condition. It was about acknowledging her pain without allowing it to define her, while at the same time acknowledging Martha's struggles, even if those struggles were never explicitly revealed. It was about recognising that even those who have wronged us are complex human beings, burdened by their own wounds, often acting out of fear, insecurity or pain.

Through consistent practice of self-compassion, prayer, and acts of kindness, Sarah found herself transformed. The lilies in Martha's room continued to bloom, a symbol of the healing that had taken place not only within Sarah's heart, but in her ability to extend compassion, understanding and even forgiveness, towards those who have caused her pain. Her heart, once burdened by bitterness and resentment, now overflowed with a quiet joy born of inner peace and the expanding capacity for love and understanding. The fragrance of those lilies was a reminder of a journey of healing that extended beyond herself, a journey that transformed bitterness into compassion, and resentment into empathy, and ultimately, helped her to find true and lasting freedom. The transformative power of compassion had opened doors to a richer, more meaningful life, a testament to the boundless grace of God.

Sarah's journey, though arduous, had yielded a harvest beyond her initial expectations. The weight of bitterness, once a crushing burden, had begun to lift, replaced by a lightness she hadn't felt in years. This wasn't a magical overnight transformation, but a slow, deliberate unfurling of her heart, a blossoming of emotional freedom that surprised even her. The pastor's words, the exercise of writing from Martha's perspective, and her acts of service had all played a crucial role in this profound shift.

The peace that settled over her was palpable, a tranquil stillness within the storm that had raged inside her for so long. It wasn't the absence of feeling, but rather a deep, abiding sense of calm amidst the waves of life. She could still feel the sting of Martha's words, the memory of the hurt, but these were no longer the dominant forces shaping her emotions. They were now just shadows, receding into the background as the light of emotional freedom illuminated her path.

This newfound peace also brought with it an unexpected joy. It wasn't the boisterous, ecstatic joy of a celebration, but a quiet, gentle joy that permeated her being, a constant hum of contentment. It manifested in simple pleasures: the warmth of the sun on her skin, the laughter of children playing in the park, the comforting aroma of freshly brewed coffee. Things she had once taken for granted, or had been too consumed by bitterness to fully appreciate, now filled her with a deep sense of gratitude.

Her relationships, once strained by resentment, began to heal. She found herself reaching out to others, not with an expectation of reciprocation, but with a genuine desire to connect, to offer understanding and support. Her interactions with her family members, once tense and fraught with unspoken resentments, became more relaxed and open. Conversations flowed more easily, and a sense of warmth and connection began to permeate their interactions. She found herself more patient, more forgiving, more willing to see the best in others, even when they fell short of her expectations.

The transformation extended beyond her immediate circle. Her work relationships improved. She approached conflicts with more empathy, seeking understanding rather than confrontation. She was less likely to take things personally, and more willing to see situations from multiple perspectives. This new approach not only reduced workplace tension, but also fostered a more collaborative and positive work environment. Her colleagues seemed to sense her shift in attitude, responding with greater respect and cooperation.

Even her relationship with Martha, though still fragile, had taken on a new dimension. While they hadn't directly addressed the past hurts, a subtle change in their dynamic was undeniable. Their interactions were less charged, less burdened by the unspoken resentments that had once defined their relationship. There was a tentative peace, a fragile truce, that held the promise of future reconciliation. Sarah found herself praying for Martha, not with resentment or anger but with heartfelt concern for her well-being, recognizing the complexities of human suffering and fallibility.

One Sunday, after church service, Sarah encountered Martha in the church hall. Martha, frail and stooped, was struggling with her walking aid. Without hesitation, Sarah rushed to her side, offering her support and a warm smile. For the first time in a long time, Martha's eyes met Sarah's with a glimmer of gratitude and perhaps even, a touch of contrition. There was a shared moment of quiet understanding, a silent acknowledgment of the healing that had transpired, unspoken yet profoundly felt.

Sarah realised that emotional freedom wasn't about erasing the past; it was about choosing not to be defined by it. It was about freeing herself from the chains of bitterness and resentment, allowing herself to embrace the present and to look forward to the future with hope and optimism. The past remained, but its power to control her emotions had been significantly diminished. She had reclaimed her emotional sovereignty, choosing to respond to life's challenges with grace, empathy, and forgiveness.

The pastor's guidance had been invaluable, providing her with a framework for understanding her own emotions and developing strategies for coping with past hurts. He had helped her to see that forgiveness wasn't about condoning wrongdoing, but about releasing the burden of resentment that weighed heavily on her soul. It was about choosing love over hate, compassion over judgment.

She had learned to practice self-compassion, recognizing that she, too, was flawed, that she, too, had made mistakes and caused pain. This self-acceptance had been crucial in her ability to extend compassion to others. She understood that we are all broken vessels, in need of grace and understanding. This understanding had helped her to move beyond the blame game, recognizing that Martha, like herself, was a product of her own experiences and circumstances.

The journey to emotional freedom was ongoing, a continual process of self-discovery and growth. There would be times when old wounds might resurface, when the temptation to revert to bitterness might arise. But she had the tools, the strength, and the faith to navigate these challenges with renewed confidence. She knew now that forgiveness wasn't a destination, but a journey, a continuous practice of choosing love, compassion, and understanding in the face of adversity.

The joy she experienced wasn't a fleeting emotion, but a deep-seated sense of inner peace that emanated from a heart that had been healed, a heart that had learned to forgive, to let go, and to embrace the transformative power of compassion. This joy was a testament to the transformative power of God's love, a tangible manifestation of the grace that had sustained her throughout her difficult journey. It was a radiant glow that illuminated her path, guiding her toward a brighter, more meaningful future, a future free from the shackles of bitterness, resentment and self-recrimination. The lilies in Martha's room were a beautiful metaphor; reminders of the quiet strength, the quiet resilience and the extraordinary power of love and forgiveness.

The journey of healing had shown Sarah the importance of self-care. She had learned to prioritize her physical, emotional, and spiritual well-being, recognizing that taking care of herself was not selfish, but essential for her emotional and spiritual growth. She engaged in regular exercise, practiced mindfulness, and sought spiritual guidance through prayer and meditation. These practices helped her to manage stress, to regulate her emotions, and to maintain a healthy perspective. She discovered the importance of setting healthy boundaries, of protecting her emotional well-being by limiting exposure to toxic relationships or situations. She learned to say "no" to things that drained her energy or compromised her values. This self-advocacy strengthened her resilience and self-esteem.

Her newfound emotional freedom wasn't merely an absence of negative emotions; it was the presence of something infinitely more powerful: love, compassion, and a profound sense of inner peace. It was a freedom that allowed her to experience the fullness of life, to savor the simple joys, and to connect with others in meaningful ways. It was a freedom born of forgiveness, not for the sake of others, but for her own soul's sake. It was a freedom that set her spirit free, opening her heart to a future brimming with hope, purpose, and the boundless love of God. The lilies continued to bloom, a constant reminder of the transformative power of letting go and allowing the love of God to heal the deepest wounds of the heart. The fragrance of forgiveness had permeated her soul, creating a sanctuary of peace and joy, a testament to the enduring power of love and grace.

Sarah's journey of emotional healing had brought her to a place of unexpected peace, but the quiet joy she felt was subtly tinged with an underlying exhaustion. The intensity of confronting her past, processing her emotions, and rebuilding her relationships had taken its toll. She found herself increasingly irritable, her sleep disrupted by restless nights filled with fragmented dreams and anxieties. Simple tasks that once came easily now felt overwhelming, and a persistent weariness settled upon her like a heavy cloak. This wasn't the vibrant energy she'd felt blossoming within her just weeks before. This was something different, a subtle yet insistent warning sign that her body and spirit were crying out for respite.

One evening, as she sat alone in her quiet apartment, the weight of her exhaustion finally hit her with full force. The silence, once a source of comfort, now felt oppressive. Her usually vibrant spirit felt dimmed, her heart heavy with a fatigue that went beyond physical tiredness. It was a deep-seated weariness, a hollowness that touched the very core of her being. She realized with a start that she had been neglecting the vital need for rest and renewal. In her zeal to heal and to move forward, she had pushed herself relentlessly, neglecting the essential elements of self-care that were crucial for sustaining her journey.

The pastor's teachings, while profoundly impactful, hadn't explicitly addressed the importance of rest. She now understood that true healing wasn't solely about confronting the past and letting go of bitterness; it was also about nurturing her whole self – her physical, emotional, and spiritual well-being. She had been so focused on the destination – emotional freedom – that she'd forgotten to attend to the journey itself. She realized that she had equated rest with laziness, a misguided belief that had prevented her from prioritizing the essential need for rejuvenation.

The concept of Sabbath rest, a central theme in the pastor's teachings, suddenly resonated with her in a new and profound way. It wasn't merely a day of inactivity, but a conscious setting aside of time for reflection, renewal, and reconnection with God. It was a time to replenish her spiritual reservoirs, to allow her soul to be refreshed and renewed. She had been so busy trying to fix herself that she'd failed to notice that her very attempt to heal was causing her further harm.

That night, Sarah made a conscious decision to prioritize rest. She started with small, manageable changes. She went to bed earlier, avoiding the late-night scrolling through social media that had become a habit. She incorporated short periods of mindfulness meditation into her daily routine, finding solace in the quiet stillness. She took longer walks in nature, allowing the beauty of the natural world to soothe her frayed nerves. She reconnected with old hobbies, finding joy in simple activities that once brought her pleasure, like reading and painting. She consciously chose activities that nourished her soul and brought her a sense of calm.

She also learned to say "no" to additional commitments, realizing that setting boundaries was essential for her well-being. She politely declined invitations to events that felt draining or overwhelming, prioritizing her need for rest and solitude. This wasn't about selfishness; it was about self-preservation, a recognition that she couldn't pour from an empty cup.

The changes, though gradual, had a profound impact. Her sleep improved, her energy levels rose, and the persistent weariness began to lift. She discovered the restorative power of silence, finding peace in the quiet moments of solitude. The quiet spaces allowed her to connect with her inner self, to listen to her intuition, and to hear the gentle whisper of God's guidance.

In addition to physical and emotional rest, Sarah focused on spiritual renewal. She dedicated more time to prayer and meditation, seeking God's comfort and guidance in her journey. She actively engaged with her church community, finding support and encouragement in the fellowship of believers. She volunteered at a local soup kitchen, finding fulfillment in acts of service that connected her to a larger purpose. These spiritual practices nurtured her soul, replenishing her inner wellspring of strength and resilience.

Her relationship with her pastor deepened during this time. She sought his counsel, sharing her struggles with exhaustion and the realization of her need for rest. He offered words of encouragement and understanding, reminding her that rest is not a sign of weakness but a testament to wisdom and self-awareness. He reaffirmed that God's grace is sufficient, and that rest is an integral part of receiving that grace.

The pastor suggested that she try a spiritual retreat, a time of dedicated reflection and renewal away from the demands of daily life. Sarah, initially hesitant, eventually agreed. The retreat provided her with a space for quiet contemplation, allowing her to connect with her inner self and with God in a deeper and more profound way. The solitude allowed her to process her emotions, to reflect on her journey of healing, and to receive God's restorative power. She engaged in activities like journaling, prayer walks, and silent meditation, each providing a different pathway to reconnect with herself and her faith.

The retreat wasn't just about escaping the pressures of life; it was about actively engaging in a process of spiritual renewal. It was a time to replenish her spiritual reserves, to reconnect with her faith, and to receive God's grace and love. Through this spiritual replenishment, she rediscovered the joy and purpose that had been dimmed by her exhaustion. Returning home, she felt renewed, refreshed, and invigorated.

The experience taught Sarah that rest isn't a luxury; it's a necessity. It's not an indulgence, but a vital component of a healthy and balanced life. Just as her body needed physical rest, her soul needed spiritual rest. Learning to rest wasn't passive; it was an active choice, a deliberate commitment to self-care that empowered her to continue her journey of healing with renewed energy and vitality. She realized that true strength lies not in relentless striving, but in the wise integration of work, rest, and spiritual renewal. The fragrance of the lilies in Martha's room, once a potent symbol of her past pain, now became a symbol of quiet strength and resilience, a testament to the healing power of rest and God's unwavering grace. The lilies, like her own spirit, were now thriving, nourished by the gentle rain of God's love and the peaceful sunshine of her newly discovered wisdom. The journey had taught her that true growth isn't linear, but rather a cyclical process of work, rest, and renewal, a dance between exertion and replenishment, a harmonious blend of action and stillness, reflecting the rhythmic ebb and flow of life itself. Her renewed spirit, strengthened and refreshed, was ready to face whatever challenges lay ahead, knowing that she possessed the resilience and wisdom to navigate them with grace and courage. The lilies continued to bloom, a silent testament to her journey, a promise of peace and resilience in the seasons to come.

Sarah's newfound understanding of rest extended beyond simple physical rejuvenation. The pastor's teachings on the Sabbath, initially a peripheral element in her healing journey, now took center stage. He had often spoken of the Sabbath not as a mere day off, but as a sacred appointment with God, a time for spiritual renewal and reflection, mirroring God's own rest after creation. This wasn't about idleness, he emphasized, but about intentional stillness, a deliberate withdrawal from the relentless demands of daily life to cultivate a deeper connection with the divine.

The concept resonated deeply with Sarah. She realized that her relentless pursuit of healing, while commendable, had been driven by a frantic energy that left her depleted. The Sabbath, she understood now, offered a counterpoint to this frenetic pace, a sanctuary where she could find respite and reconnect with the source of her strength.

She began by experimenting with a simple, modified version of Sabbath observance, starting with a half-day on Sundays. She chose not to completely cut off all activities, understanding that a sudden, drastic change might feel overwhelming. Instead, she focused on minimizing distractions and maximizing opportunities for quiet contemplation and spiritual nourishment. She turned off her phone notifications for a few hours, intentionally disconnecting from the constant influx of information and demands. She engaged in simple activities that brought her joy and peace – reading a devotional, listening to calming music, spending time in nature, or simply enjoying a quiet cup of tea.

The difference was subtle at first, but gradually, she noticed a shift in her perspective. The quiet stillness allowed her to process her emotions more effectively, to hear the gentle whisper of God's guidance more clearly. It was in those moments of silence that she truly felt her connection to the divine, experiencing a sense of peace and serenity she had not felt before. The Sabbath became her refuge, a safe haven from the relentless storms of daily life.

One Sunday, as Sarah was strolling through a nearby park, she encountered an elderly woman sitting on a bench, her face etched with lines of worry and weariness. As she approached, she learned the woman's name was Mrs. Evans, and she was grieving the recent loss of her husband. Sarah sat beside her, offering a listening ear and a comforting presence. The two spent the afternoon sharing stories, finding solace in their shared humanity and their mutual faith. Mrs. Evans confessed she had been neglecting her spiritual practices since her husband's passing, allowing grief to consume her. Sarah shared her own journey of healing, emphasizing the importance of rest and the power of God's grace. The conversation brought them both unexpected comfort, a testament to the unexpected blessings found in Sabbath observance.

The following week, Sarah decided to extend her Sabbath observance to a full day. She prepared in advance, organizing her tasks and delegating responsibilities where possible. She prepared a simple meal for her family, explaining the purpose of their day of rest. This was a significant step, as it involved encouraging her family to join her in this practice of intentional stillness and spiritual rejuvenation. Her family wasn't initially enthusiastic about the idea of limiting their usual activities, but Sarah gently explained the importance of Sabbath rest not just for herself but for them as well.

The first full Sabbath was challenging. Old habits of busyness and distraction surfaced, testing Sarah's resolve. However, she persevered, choosing to focus on the intention behind the practice rather than the perfection of its execution. She learned to be kind to herself, accepting that there would be times when the distractions would win, and that was okay.

The family spent the day engaging in simple activities together – going for a walk in the park, playing board games, reading aloud from the Bible, and praying together. They even attempted to bake a cake, which resulted in a lot of laughter and a somewhat lopsided but delicious dessert. The important thing was not the perfection of the cake but the shared experience of creating something together, in a spirit of peace and tranquility.

The impact of the Sabbath on Sarah's family was remarkable. The children, usually restless and constantly on the go, were unusually calm and content. Her husband, initially skeptical, also found himself benefiting from the respite. He confessed that he had been feeling overwhelmed by work pressures and that the Sabbath provided a much-needed break from the relentless demands of his career.

Their shared Sabbath experience fostered a deeper sense of connection within their family. They learned to communicate better, to listen more attentively, and to appreciate the simple joys of being together without the distractions of technology or external pressures. The Sabbath became a time for intentional connection, for strengthening family bonds, and for nurturing their shared faith.

As the weeks and months passed, Sarah became increasingly proficient at incorporating the Sabbath into her daily routine. She realized it wasn't just about taking a day off; it was about creating a rhythm of life that balanced rest and activity, work and worship, stress and serenity. It was about intentionally crafting spaces for spiritual nourishment, for quiet reflection, and for deep connection with God and her loved ones.

The Sabbath became a cornerstone of her healing journey, a testament to the wisdom of prioritizing rest and renewal. It was a powerful reminder that true strength lies not in relentless striving, but in the wise integration of work and rest, action and stillness, exertion and replenishment. The Sabbath was a sacred space, a haven of peace, a time for reconnection and renewal, a rhythmic pulse that beat in harmony with the rhythm of God's own loving heart. It was a profound testament to the restorative power of faith, a symbol of hope, and a beacon of peace in the often tumultuous currents of life's journey. It was a living testament to the profound truth that God's grace is sufficient, and that rest is an integral part of receiving that grace, a gift freely given, a blessing to be embraced. The lilies in Martha's room, now vibrant and full of life, became a poignant reminder of this vital truth: that rest, like the gentle rain nurturing the earth, brings forth the most beautiful blossoms of resilience and peace.

The crisp morning air, scented with pine and damp earth, invigorated Sarah as she stepped onto the veranda of the Serenity Springs Spa. This wasn't just a vacation; it was a deliberate act of self-care, a retreat recommended by her pastor as a crucial complement to her Sabbath observance. He'd emphasized that spiritual renewal couldn't exist in isolation; it needed to be nurtured by a holistic approach to well-being, encompassing mind, body, and spirit.

The spa, nestled in the heart of a tranquil forest, was a haven of peace. The gentle murmur of a nearby stream, the rustling of leaves in the breeze, and the soft chirping of birds created a symphony of serenity, a stark contrast to the frenetic energy of her life before her journey of healing. She'd arrived feeling weary, not just physically, but emotionally and spiritually depleted. The relentless demands of life, even amidst the newfound peace of her Sabbath observance, had left their mark. This retreat was her chance to replenish her reserves, to pour into herself the same loving care she so readily extended to others.

Her first appointment was a gentle yoga session overlooking the valley. As she moved through the poses, her body uncoiling and stretching, she felt a release of tension she hadn't realized she was holding. The instructor, a calm and reassuring woman named Evelyn, emphasized the connection between physical and spiritual well-being. She spoke of the importance of mindful movement, of paying attention to the breath, and of finding a rhythm that harmonized with the body's natural flow. Sarah found herself reflecting on the pastor's teachings on the Sabbath, recognizing the parallel between the intentional stillness of yoga and the deliberate quietude of her Sabbath rest. Both were acts of surrender, of allowing oneself to be guided by a higher power, a surrender not of weakness but of trust.

After yoga, Sarah indulged in a rejuvenating massage. The therapist's skillful hands worked out knots of tension she hadn't even been aware of, releasing years of accumulated stress. As she lay there, enveloped in warmth and tranquility, a sense of deep relaxation washed over her. It was as if her body, finally given permission to rest, was sighing with relief. This physical release mirrored the spiritual release she experienced during her Sabbath observances, a release from the burden of striving and the weight of expectation.

The spa offered a variety of other self-care options, and Sarah chose to explore them all. She participated in a guided meditation session, where she learned to focus her mind and quiet the incessant chatter of her thoughts. She spent time in the sauna, allowing the heat to cleanse her body and soothe her soul. She also indulged in a luxurious facial, feeling pampered and cherished. Each of these experiences was a small act of self-love, a conscious decision to prioritize her own well-being.

Throughout the retreat, Sarah took time for mindful eating. She savored each bite of the healthy, nutritious meals, paying attention to the flavors and textures. She consciously avoided processed foods and sugary drinks, opting for fresh fruits, vegetables, and whole grains. She understood that nourishment was not just about fueling her body but also about nurturing her soul. The meals became a form of prayer, a thankfulness for the gifts of nature and the provision of God. This echoed the way she was learning to view the Sabbath as a gift, not a burden, a time of celebration rather than constraint.

In between her spa treatments, Sarah spent time walking in the forest, immersing herself in the beauty of nature. The trees, the flowers, the birds – all spoke of God's creation, reminding her of His boundless love and unwavering care. She found herself praying more easily amidst the trees, feeling a deep connection with the divine. The silence of the woods was a different kind of silence from the Sabbath's quiet, more of a natural stillness that invited contemplation of the majesty of creation.

One evening, she attended a workshop on stress management techniques. The facilitator introduced various methods for managing stress, including deep breathing exercises, progressive muscle relaxation, and mindfulness meditation. Sarah learned to identify her stress triggers and to develop coping mechanisms to deal with them effectively. She realized that stress management wasn't about eliminating stress entirely – that was unrealistic – but about developing healthy strategies for navigating its challenges. This skill complemented her Sabbath practices, offering a way to address stress before it overwhelmed her and jeopardized her spiritual equilibrium.

The retreat was a journey of self-discovery, a time for Sarah to reconnect with her body, her mind, and her spirit. It was a chance to practice self-compassion, to acknowledge her limitations, and to celebrate her strengths. She realized that self-care wasn't selfish; it was an essential part of her spiritual journey, an act of obedience to God's command to love herself as He loved her. Just as she took time to nurture her spiritual life through Sabbath observance, she now understood the importance of nurturing her physical and emotional well-being.

One of the most significant lessons Sarah learned during her retreat was the importance of setting boundaries. She realized that saying "no" to certain commitments didn't mean she was rejecting people; it meant she was protecting her own well-being. It was an act of self-preservation, allowing her to prioritize the things that truly mattered. This newfound ability to set boundaries extended beyond her personal life to her spiritual practice. She learned to discern between activities that genuinely nourished her faith and those that simply consumed her time and energy, allowing her to prioritize genuine spiritual growth. This discerning application of boundaries made her Sabbath practice even more effective.

As she prepared to leave Serenity Springs, Sarah felt a profound sense of peace and renewal. She was not only physically rejuvenated but also emotionally and spiritually refreshed. The retreat had been a powerful complement to her Sabbath observance, reinforcing the importance of a holistic approach to well-being. She realized that true rest and renewal required more than just a day off; it demanded a conscious effort to integrate self-care into the fabric of her daily life. The retreat was a reminder that she was not an inexhaustible resource, but a precious vessel created in God's image, deserving of his care and her own.

Returning home, Sarah incorporated the self-care practices she'd learned at the spa into her daily routine. She continued her yoga practice, making time for mindful movement and meditation each day. She made conscious choices about her diet, prioritizing healthy, nutritious foods. She continued to set boundaries, protecting her time and energy for the things that were truly important. And most significantly, she continued to observe her Sabbath, understanding it as a crucial component of her holistic well-being, a sacred time for spiritual renewal and connection with God. The lilies in her room, now vibrant and thriving, continued to serve as a constant, silent reminder of the power of rest and renewal, a testament to the harmonious balance between her spiritual journey and the cultivation of her own well-being. She was no longer merely surviving; she was thriving, a testament to God's grace and the transformative power of genuine self-care. The journey, she realized, was not about achieving perfection, but about embracing the ongoing process of growth and renewal, guided by the wisdom of the scriptures and empowered by the boundless love of her Creator. Her life, once a chaotic whirlwind of activity, was now a more tranquil current, flowing gently towards the shores of peace and fulfillment.

The scent of woodsmoke and damp earth hung heavy in the air as Sarah stepped onto the porch of the secluded cabin. Serenity Springs Spa was a haven, but this was different. This was a deeper immersion, a retreat focused specifically on spiritual renewal, a concept her pastor had carefully explained as the essential counterpoint to the physical and emotional replenishment she'd experienced at the spa. He'd spoken of the well, deep within the soul, that needed tending, not just the surface waters of physical and mental health.

The cabin was small, rustic, and undeniably peaceful. A single window framed a breathtaking view of the valley, awash in the golden light of the setting sun. Inside, a simple fireplace crackled merrily, casting dancing shadows on the rough-hewn wooden walls. It was starkly different from the luxurious amenities of the spa, yet it held a unique kind of comfort, a quiet invitation to introspection. This wasn't about pampering; this was about pilgrimage.

Sarah had brought her Bible, a journal, and a comfortable blanket. She'd been instructed to disconnect from all technology, a daunting but ultimately liberating prospect. The silence, at first unsettling, gradually became a companion, a gentle nudge toward the inner sanctuary of her soul.

Her first evening began with a simple act of prayer. She knelt by the fireplace, the warmth radiating through her as she poured out her heart to God. It wasn't a formal, rehearsed prayer, but a spontaneous conversation, filled with gratitude, confession, and a yearning for deeper connection. She thanked God for the gift of this time, for the opportunity to withdraw from the clamor of daily life and to focus solely on her relationship with Him. She confessed her struggles, her shortcomings, her anxieties, laying them bare before the one who understood her better than she understood herself. And she expressed her longing for spiritual renewal, a deeper intimacy with God, a stronger sense of His presence in her life.

The following days unfolded in a rhythm of prayer, Bible study, and communion with nature. Each morning, Sarah began with a time of quiet meditation, allowing the stillness to settle over her like a gentle blanket. She read passages of scripture, allowing God's word to seep into her heart and mind. She sought not just intellectual understanding, but spiritual nourishment, reflecting on the passages' relevance to her life and seeking God's guidance in her daily walk. She discovered the beauty of "lectio divina," the ancient practice of slow, contemplative reading, savoring each word, each phrase, each sentence.

Her Bible study wasn't confined to the cabin. One crisp morning, she ventured onto a wooded trail, a worn path winding through the heart of the forest. She found a secluded spot beside a rushing stream, the sound of the water a constant, soothing murmur as she immersed herself in the Scriptures. The sun dappled through the leaves, creating an ethereal glow that bathed everything in a sense of peace. She felt a profound connection with God in that natural setting, realizing that creation itself was a testament to His power and majesty.

Evenings were set aside for worship. Without instruments or a congregation, Sarah simply sang hymns and worship songs, her voice a quiet offering to God, her heart overflowing with praise and adoration. The songs were familiar and comforting, each note a prayer, each word a testimony to her love for God and her dependence upon Him. These simple acts of worship became deeply personal and profound, far exceeding the experience of corporate worship she was used to.

Sarah spent hours exploring the surrounding woods. The trail she walked was a tapestry of vibrant colors and textures. The vibrant hues of autumn foliage, the intricate patterns of the bark on ancient trees, and the soft moss clinging to the rocks all spoke of God's creative power. She took slow, mindful walks, noticing every detail, every nuance, every subtle shift in the light. Each rustle of leaves, each bird song, seemed to whisper a message of God's presence and His unwavering love. She found solace in the stillness of the forest, allowing herself to be enveloped by the beauty of God's creation. The silence of nature wasn't just absence of sound, but a different, richer way of listening to God.

One afternoon, she sat by a small, clear pond, watching the dragonflies dance across the water's surface. As she observed their graceful movements, a sense of calm washed over her. She realized that God's love was as boundless and pervasive as the sky, as steady and comforting as the earth beneath her feet. It was a love that surrounded her, permeated her being, and sustained her even in her deepest moments of struggle.

The retreat wasn't without its challenges. There were moments of doubt, moments of frustration, moments when the peace seemed elusive. But Sarah persevered, recognizing that spiritual renewal wasn't a passive experience but an active process that required effort, commitment, and faith. She learned to embrace the difficult moments, knowing that even in darkness, God's light could shine through.

As her retreat drew to a close, Sarah felt a profound sense of peace and fulfillment. She had spent time replenishing her spiritual wellspring, strengthening her connection with God, and deepening her understanding of His love. She carried with her not just a renewed sense of energy but a profound sense of purpose and direction. She knew that the journey of spiritual growth was a lifelong process, a continual striving toward a closer relationship with God, but the time spent in solitude and communion had revitalized her spirit and given her fresh courage to continue.

The journey back home was different. The everyday pressures seemed less daunting, the challenges less overwhelming. She had cultivated a deeper well of resilience, drawn from the inexhaustible source of God's grace. The retreat wasn't an escape from life, but a preparation for it. She had a renewed ability to engage with her responsibilities, her relationships, and her faith with a fresh spirit, a revitalized soul, and a quiet strength that only comes from intimate communion with God. The lilies of the valley, a symbol of peace and purity, bloomed vibrantly in her memory, their gentle beauty a lasting reminder of the transformative power of spiritual renewal and the enduring strength that comes from finding true rest in God. The journey continued, but she walked it now with a lighter heart and a surer step, her spirit renewed, her faith strengthened, and her soul refreshed.

The crisp morning air, scented with pine and damp earth, invigorated Sarah as she stepped onto the porch. The retreat had been transformative, a deep well of serenity she hadn't anticipated. But even as she felt the peace settle over her like a warm blanket, the quiet hum of daily life beckoned. The question lingered: would this newfound serenity endure? Would the refreshed spirit she carried within her withstand the onslaught of everyday pressures? The answer, she was beginning to discover, lay not in escaping the world but in integrating this renewed sense of self into it.

The benefits of rest and renewal weren't merely fleeting sensations; they were a profound shift in her perspective, a change that manifested in tangible ways. Firstly, her energy levels soared. The persistent fatigue that had clung to her like a shadow for months had lifted. This wasn't the frantic, caffeine-fueled energy she was used to, but a calm, steady, and sustained power. She found herself tackling tasks with renewed vigor, accomplishing more in a shorter amount of time, and approaching challenges with a newfound resilience. The exhaustion that previously characterized her evenings was replaced by a sense of peaceful contentment, a quiet hum of accomplishment that allowed her to truly rest and restore her energy for the following day.

Her focus, too, had undergone a significant transformation. Before the retreat, her mind had been a chaotic whirlwind of thoughts, a constant barrage of distractions that prevented her from truly concentrating on any one thing. Now, her mind was clearer, sharper, more focused. She could concentrate for longer periods without experiencing mental fatigue. She approached her work with a newfound efficiency, completing projects with a precision and attention to detail that had previously eluded her. This heightened focus wasn't just about efficiency; it was about presence – a deep engagement with the tasks at hand, allowing her to be fully present in every moment.

The change extended beyond practical matters. Her creativity blossomed. Ideas that had been dormant for years suddenly sprung to life, vivid and vibrant. She found herself sketching, writing poetry, even experimenting with new recipes— activities she had previously abandoned due to lack of time or energy. Her renewed spirit seemed to have unlocked a creative wellspring she hadn't known existed, reminding her of the power of stillness to unlock hidden potential. The silence of the cabin hadn't stifled her creativity but had fostered it, providing the space and quiet necessary for her imagination to flourish. The world around her, once a blur of obligations, now offered endless inspiration.

But perhaps the most profound benefit was the strengthening of her relationships. The renewed sense of peace within her radiated outwards, transforming her interactions with others. She found herself more patient, more understanding, more forgiving. The constant tension and irritability that had characterized her interactions with loved ones were replaced by a calm empathy. She listened more attentively, responded with greater grace, and resolved conflicts with a newfound maturity and understanding. Her relationships deepened, strengthened by the mutual respect and connection that flowed from her own internal peace. She discovered that true connection wasn't merely about superficial pleasantries but about a deep, genuine empathy and understanding that only comes from a place of inner wholeness.

As the weeks passed, Sarah diligently integrated the lessons of her retreat into her daily life. She consciously incorporated regular periods of rest and reflection into her schedule. She carved out time each morning for prayer and meditation, allowing the stillness to settle over her before facing the day's demands. Evenings were dedicated to relaxation and unwinding, avoiding screens and focusing on activities that nurtured her soul, whether reading a good book, listening to calming music, or spending time in nature. She understood that rest wasn't merely the absence of activity but a conscious choice to nurture her well-being.

This wasn't a rigid regimen but a flexible practice adapted to the demands of her busy life. She learned to prioritize rest not as a luxury but as a necessity, a vital component of her overall well-being. She realized that neglecting her spiritual and emotional needs had a ripple effect, impacting every aspect of her life, from her physical health to her relationships. Rest and renewal weren't an escape from life's responsibilities but a way of approaching them with greater resilience, clarity, and effectiveness.

She also made conscious efforts to cultivate mindfulness in her daily activities. She found moments of quiet amidst the chaos, pausing to appreciate the simple joys of life, the beauty of nature, the warmth of human connection. These fleeting moments of mindfulness became anchors of peace, helping her to navigate stressful situations with greater serenity. She learned to recognize the subtle signs of stress and fatigue in her body and mind, and responded by taking appropriate measures to restore her balance – whether through a short walk in nature, a few minutes of deep breathing, or a simple act of prayer.

Sarah discovered the importance of setting boundaries. She learned to say "no" to commitments that drained her energy or compromised her well-being. She prioritized her spiritual and emotional needs, understanding that she couldn't pour from an empty cup. This newfound ability to set boundaries not only protected her energy but also fostered healthier relationships, allowing for deeper connection and more authentic interactions. She found that saying "no" to some things opened up space for saying "yes" to what truly mattered.

The transformation wasn't always seamless. There were days when fatigue crept in, when distractions overwhelmed her, when the pressures of daily life threatened to consume her. But Sarah had developed a new resilience, a deeper well of strength to draw from. She had learned to recognize these moments as opportunities for self-compassion, acknowledging her limitations without succumbing to self-criticism. She had learned to treat herself with the same kindness and understanding that she extended to others.

She realized that rest and renewal were not static achievements but an ongoing process, a journey of continual growth and self-discovery. It was a commitment to nurture her mind, body, and spirit, a conscious choice to prioritize her well-being, and a testament to the transformative power of connecting with God in the quiet spaces of life. The lilies of the valley, a symbol of her renewed spirit, still bloomed brightly in her memory, a constant reminder of the enduring peace found in seeking true rest and renewal in God's grace. The journey continued, but her path was now illuminated by a renewed sense of purpose, a deeper understanding of herself, and a profound gratitude for the gift of rest. The world still held its challenges, but she faced them not with fear, but with a quiet strength drawn from the inexhaustible source of God's love.

Father God, as I stand at this crossroads, I humbly come before You, seeking Your wisdom and guidance. The journey thus far has been one of self-discovery, a pilgrimage into the depths of my own being, guided by Your unwavering love and grace. The peace I've found in stillness, the clarity I've gained through reflection, and the strength I've discovered in surrender—these are all gifts from You, blessings that I cherish and seek to deepen.

Yet, even with this newfound serenity, the path ahead remains unclear. The world's clamor continues its relentless pursuit, threatening to drown out the gentle whispers of Your Spirit. I feel the pull of competing desires, the weight of various responsibilities, and the uncertainty of the future. I find myself questioning what steps I should take, what choices I should make to live a life that truly honors You and fulfills my purpose.

Lord, grant me the discernment to distinguish Your voice from the cacophony of the world. Help me to silence the inner chatter of doubt and fear, so I can hear Your clear and gentle guidance. Open my eyes to the opportunities that align with Your will and close the doors on paths that lead away from Your purpose for my life.

I pray for the courage to embrace the unknown, to step out in faith, trusting in Your unfailing provision and protection. Grant me the strength to overcome obstacles and the resilience to weather storms. I ask for the wisdom to navigate complex situations with grace and integrity, always seeking to reflect Your love and compassion in my actions.

This journey is not a solo endeavor; I understand that I walk alongside You, hand in hand. Guide my steps, Lord, illuminate my path, and empower me to live with intention, purpose, and unwavering faith. I desire not to merely exist, but to thrive, to flourish, to live a life that is a testament to Your goodness and Your boundless grace.

Help me to prioritize Your kingdom above all else. Show me how to balance the demands of daily life with my commitment to follow Your call. May my actions speak louder than words, reflecting the transformative power of Your love in all that I do.

Lord, I also pray for protection from the pitfalls that await me. Help me to discern temptation and avoid the snares of the enemy. Surround me with Your love, Your peace, and Your strength, shielding me from harm and guiding me away from danger.

As I move forward, I ask for the wisdom to discern my priorities. Help me to identify the areas where my time and energy are most effectively spent, leading to both personal growth and serving Your purpose. Help me to recognize the fleeting nature of earthly pursuits and to concentrate on those values that will last an eternity.

Moreover, grant me the grace to be compassionate and forgiving towards others and myself. May I extend the same mercy and understanding that You have so freely bestowed upon me. Help me to approach my relationships with patience, kindness, and humility, always remembering that we are all flawed vessels striving to reflect Your glory.

I commit to cultivating a deeper relationship with You through consistent prayer, meditation, and the study of Your word. Help me to find joy in the simple acts of faith, finding the beauty in the everyday moments and acknowledging Your presence in all things. Help me to remain steadfast in my faith, even in times of uncertainty and trial.

Grant me the wisdom to be a light in the world, a beacon of hope and inspiration to those around me. Empower me to share Your love and compassion with others, reflecting Your grace in my words and actions. May my life be a living testament to Your transformative power.

Finally, Lord, I surrender my plans to Your divine will. I understand that Your ways are higher than my ways, and Your thoughts are higher than my thoughts. I trust in Your perfect timing and Your perfect plan for my life. I embrace the uncertainties that lie ahead, knowing that You will guide my steps and lead me into all truth.

I thank You, Father, for Your love, Your grace, and Your unfailing guidance. I pray all of this in the name of Your beloved Son, Jesus Christ, Amen.

This prayer is not a one-time event but a continuous conversation with God, a daily seeking of His will. It is a commitment to live intentionally, to align my life with His purpose, and to walk in His grace. As the days unfold, I will continue to reflect on this prayer, seeking deeper understanding of His direction and guidance.

This intentional living, I believe, will not be a smooth and effortless path; it will contain its share of struggles and setbacks. There will be moments when doubt creeps in, when the pressures of life threaten to overwhelm me. There might be times when I falter, lose my way and forget the promises made in prayer. But even in those moments of weakness, I will call upon God's strength, remembering His unwavering love and faithfulness. I will seek forgiveness, ask for guidance, and renew my commitment to His purpose.

The integration of faith into daily life is not merely about attending church services or saying prayers; it involves a conscious effort to make every aspect of my life a reflection of my beliefs. This means being mindful of my actions, words and thoughts. It means constantly evaluating if my decisions and choices are aligned with God's will, or if I am being influenced by my own desires and ambitions. This requires constant self-reflection, continuous prayer and a commitment to personal growth.

It's about choosing kindness over anger, forgiveness over resentment, patience over frustration. It’s about seeing others with God's eyes, extending love and compassion even to those who do not deserve it. It’s about recognizing the presence of God in every aspect of life and acknowledging Him in both the triumphs and the trials. It’s about living life with an open heart, a mind devoted to His teachings, and a soul dedicated to His service.

And it is not a journey done alone. This process of intentional living includes seeking support and fellowship within a community of faith. Spending time with fellow believers, sharing experiences and encouraging one another, reinforces our commitment and helps to sustain us during challenging times. The collective strength of the community offers encouragement, guidance and support, ensuring that we never feel alone on our spiritual journey.

Intentional living isn't a destination, but an ongoing journey of self-discovery and growth, a continuous process of aligning my life with God's will. It is a daily act of faith, a commitment to walking closely with God, seeking His guidance and trusting in His plan for my life. It's about continually striving to become more like Christ, reflecting His love, compassion and grace in every aspect of my life.

The prayer, therefore, is not just a request for guidance but also a commitment to living a life that honors God. It's a promise to actively seek His presence, to listen to His voice, and to follow His lead, no matter the challenges or uncertainties that lie ahead. It's a life lived in gratitude, knowing that every breath, every opportunity, every relationship is a gift from His abundant love. And it is a life lived with the unwavering belief that with God's grace, I can achieve anything He calls me to do.

Father, Your word speaks of a strength that surpasses all understanding, a courage born not of self but of Your divine Spirit. I come before You today, not in arrogance, but in humble dependence, acknowledging my own limitations and relying wholly on Your limitless power. The path I walk is not always smooth; it winds through valleys of doubt, climbs steep mountains of adversity, and crosses treacherous streams of uncertainty. I confess that my own strength often falters, my courage wanes, and my spirit feels weary under the weight of life's burdens.

Yet, You, Father, are the source of all strength, the wellspring of unwavering courage. You have promised to equip me for every challenge, to strengthen me in weakness, and to be my refuge in the storms of life. I cling to these promises today, Lord, claiming Your power as my own, trusting in Your ability to carry me through whatever lies ahead.

This journey of intentional living, as I've come to understand, is not a solitary expedition. It's a pilgrimage shared with You, a constant conversation, a dance of trust between Your divine will and my human striving. There will be moments, I know, when the path seems obscured, the way forward unclear, the burden seemingly unbearable. In these moments of discouragement, help me, Lord, to remember Your presence, to feel the warmth of Your embrace, to hear the gentle whisper of Your guidance.

Grant me the courage to face my fears, not with bravado or self-reliance, but with humble faith, knowing that Your strength is made perfect in my weakness. Help me to see the obstacles I encounter not as insurmountable barriers but as opportunities for growth, for refinement, for a deeper dependence upon You. Let each challenge become a stepping stone, propelling me closer to the life You have planned for me.

I pray for the courage to speak Your truth, even when it is unpopular, even when it is uncomfortable. Give me boldness to share Your love with a world that so desperately needs it, to be a beacon of hope in a sea of darkness. Grant me the wisdom to discern the appropriate time and manner, that my words may not only be heard but also received with open hearts.

Moreover, Lord, I pray for the courage to forgive, to extend mercy as You have extended mercy to me. Forgiveness, I know, is not always easy. It requires a letting go, a surrender of resentment, a release of the pain that binds us. Give me the strength to overcome the bitterness that threatens to consume me, to replace anger with compassion, to choose love over retribution.

I ask for the courage to let go of control, to surrender my plans to Your divine will. This, Father, is perhaps the most challenging act of faith, the ultimate expression of trust. It is a relinquishing of my own desires, my own ambitions, my own timeline, and an embracing of Your perfect plan, Your perfect timing. Help me to understand that Your ways are higher than my ways, Your thoughts higher than my thoughts. Grant me the humility to accept that my understanding is limited, and Your wisdom is infinite.

I also pray for the courage to persevere through discouragement. There will be times, I know, when I stumble, when I fall, when the weight of my struggles seems too much to bear. In these moments of despair, Lord, remind me of Your unwavering love, Your unfailing faithfulness. Help me to remember the victories of the past, the grace that has sustained me through previous trials, and the promises that await me in the future.

Furthermore, I pray for the courage to be vulnerable, to reveal my imperfections, my weaknesses, my struggles. This vulnerability, I believe, is not a sign of weakness but a testament to my faith, an act of trust in Your boundless love and acceptance. Help me to shed the mask of perfection, to embrace my true self, and to find strength in my authenticity.

Grant me the courage to say no to those things that distract me from Your purpose, that pull me away from Your path. Help me to discern the difference between true commitment and self-serving ambition, between genuine service and self-promotion. Give me the resolve to make choices that align with Your will, even when they are difficult or unpopular.

I pray for the courage to live with integrity, to be consistent in my faith, in my actions, in my words. Help me to walk the talk, to live a life that reflects the principles I profess, the beliefs I hold dear. Grant me the strength to maintain my moral compass, to remain steadfast in my commitment to Your truth, even when it's unpopular or difficult.

And finally, Father, grant me the courage to love unconditionally, to extend grace to all, regardless of their background, beliefs, or actions. Love, as You have shown us, is patient, kind, forgiving, and selfless.

Help me to reflect this kind of love in all my interactions, to see each person not through my own limited perspective but through the lens of Your infinite compassion.

This prayer, Lord, is not a one-time request but a continuous conversation, a daily seeking of Your strength and guidance. It is a commitment to walk in faith, to rely on Your power, and to live a life that honors Your name. I thank You for Your unwavering love, Your abundant grace, and the promise of Your constant presence. In the name of Jesus Christ, my Lord and Savior, Amen.

Father, in this journey of intentional living, I find myself yearning not just for strength and courage, but also for a deep, abiding peace—a serenity that transcends the chaos and anxieties of daily life. The world around me often feels turbulent, a tempest of conflicting demands, unmet expectations, and unforeseen challenges. The noise of competing voices, the pressure of deadlines, the weight of responsibilities—all these threaten to overwhelm me, to steal my joy, and to leave me feeling fragmented and depleted.

Yet, You, Lord, have promised a peace that surpasses all understanding—a peace that is not dependent on circumstances, a tranquility that remains unshaken even amidst the fiercest storms. This is not the absence of struggle, the avoidance of difficulty, or the illusion of a life free from pain. Rather, it is a profound inner stillness, a quiet confidence in Your unwavering love and sovereign control, a deep-seated trust in Your perfect plan for my life.

I pray for this peace today, Father. I pray for a serenity that settles deep within my soul, a calm that anchors me amidst the raging currents of life. Grant me the ability to find solace in Your presence, to feel the gentle touch of Your Spirit, to hear Your reassuring voice whispering words of comfort and hope.

Help me, Lord, to distinguish between the things that truly matter and the distractions that steal my peace. So often I find myself chasing fleeting pleasures, pursuing empty ambitions, and striving for approval from sources that cannot ultimately satisfy. Grant me the wisdom to discern Your will for my life, to prioritize Your kingdom above all else, and to find true fulfillment in my relationship with You.

Teach me, Father, the art of letting go. Release me from the burden of control, from the need to manage every detail, to anticipate every outcome. Help me to trust in Your perfect timing, Your sovereign hand guiding my steps, and Your unwavering love sustaining me through every trial. I confess, Lord, that I often cling to things that are beyond my control, fueling anxiety and hindering my peace. Give me the grace to relinquish my grip, to surrender my anxieties to You, and to find rest in Your loving embrace.

Grant me the ability to forgive, not only others but also myself. The weight of past mistakes, unresolved conflicts, and lingering regrets can be a heavy burden, a constant source of inner turmoil. Help me to release the bitterness, to let go of resentment, and to experience the freedom that comes from forgiveness. Show me how to extend grace to those who have hurt me, and to receive Your abundant grace for my own shortcomings.

Furthermore, Lord, I ask for the gift of mindfulness—the ability to be present in each moment, to appreciate the simple blessings that surround me, and to savor the beauty of Your creation. So often I am consumed by thoughts of the past or anxieties about the future, neglecting the present moment—the only time I truly have. Help me to cultivate a grateful heart, to focus on the good that You have given me, and to find joy in the everyday wonders of Your world.

Give me the strength to resist the temptation to compare myself to others. The insidious whispers of envy, inadequacy, and self-doubt can quickly erode my peace. Help me to embrace my unique gifts and talents, to celebrate my individuality, and to find fulfillment in my own journey, rather than measuring myself against the accomplishments or perceived successes of others.

I pray for the strength to resist the allure of instant gratification, the relentless pursuit of pleasure, and the seductive promises of the world. These things, Lord, often leave me feeling emptier and more discontented, further distancing me from the peace that You offer. Help me to seek lasting joy in Your presence, to find true satisfaction in fulfilling Your purpose, and to resist the deceptive promises of a fleeting happiness that ultimately leaves me wanting.

In times of adversity, Lord, help me to remember Your presence, Your love, and Your promises. When challenges seem insurmountable, when the weight of life's burdens becomes too much to bear, grant me the grace to find refuge in Your embrace, to trust in Your strength, and to experience the peace that only You can provide. Help me to see these difficulties not as obstacles but as opportunities for growth, for refinement, and for a deeper reliance upon Your guidance.

I ask for the courage to seek support and community. Isolation breeds fear, fosters doubt, and inhibits the peace of Your spirit. Help me to reach out to others, to share my burdens, and to allow myself to be strengthened by the love and fellowship of those who share my faith. Give me the humility to acknowledge my need for others, to accept their support, and to contribute to the well-being of the community.

Help me to cultivate healthy spiritual disciplines that nurture my peace. Through prayer, meditation, Scripture study, and fellowship, may I draw closer to You, deepen my relationship with You, and experience the transformative power of Your love. These practices will be my anchors during life's storms, helping me to navigate the unpredictable waters of life with grace and resilience.

Father, I know that this prayer is a continuous aspiration, a daily commitment to seek Your peace and to live intentionally according to Your will. I may stumble, I may fall, I may doubt, but I will always return to You, seeking Your guidance and trusting in Your unwavering love. For in You, Lord, I find the true and lasting peace my soul longs for, a peace that transcends all understanding and remains unshaken amidst the storms of life. In Jesus' name, Amen.

Father, as I stand before You, my heart overflows with a gratitude so profound, it humbles me to my knees. In the midst of life's complexities, in the face of challenges both great and small, Your unwavering love and faithfulness shine like a beacon, guiding my path and illuminating my way. I often find myself caught up in the whirlwind of daily existence, forgetting to pause and truly appreciate the myriad of blessings You lavish upon me. This prayer, therefore, is an act of conscious remembrance, a heartfelt expression of my deepest thanks.

I thank You, Lord, for the gift of life itself – the breath in my lungs, the beat of my heart, the strength in my limbs. These are not mere biological functions, but sacred gifts, evidence of Your creative power and sustaining grace. They are reminders of Your immeasurable love, a love that extends beyond my understanding, a love that holds me close even when I feel lost and adrift.

I thank You for my family, for the bonds of love that unite us, for the shared joys and the weathered storms that have drawn us closer. You have woven our lives together in a tapestry of unique relationships, each thread contributing to the rich and vibrant pattern of my existence. For the laughter shared, the tears cried together, the unwavering support and unconditional love, I offer my sincerest thanks. Forgive me, Lord, for the times I have taken these blessings for granted, for the moments when I have failed to cherish the precious gifts You have bestowed upon me.

I thank You for my friends, for the companions who walk alongside me on life's journey, offering encouragement, understanding, and a listening ear. You have placed these individuals in my life for a purpose, to support me, to challenge me, and to remind me of Your love through their presence. For their friendship, their kindness, and their unwavering loyalty, I give thanks.

I thank You for the opportunities You have provided, for the doors that have opened, for the paths that have led me to unexpected places. These experiences, both joyful and challenging, have shaped me, molded me, and brought me closer to understanding Your will for my life. For the lessons learned, for the growth experienced, and for the continuous opportunities to learn and grow, I offer my heartfelt gratitude.

I thank You for the challenges I have faced, for the struggles that have tested my faith, and for the trials that have refined my character. These experiences, while painful at times, have strengthened my resolve, deepened my reliance on You, and revealed the immeasurable strength that resides within me. For the lessons learned in adversity, for the resilience gained through struggle, and for the profound understanding that comes only through trials, I am eternally grateful.

I thank You for the beauty that surrounds me, for the wonders of Your creation, from the majesty of the mountains to the serenity of the sea, from the vibrant colors of a sunset to the delicate intricacies of a flower. In each creation, I see a reflection of Your boundless love, Your infinite wisdom, and Your awe-inspiring power. For the opportunity to witness Your masterpiece, for the inspiration found in Your artistry, and for the serenity that comes from contemplating Your handiwork, I give my thanks.

I thank You for the moments of joy and peace, for the times when my heart is filled with happiness and my soul is bathed in tranquility. These moments, often fleeting yet precious, remind me of Your ever-present love and Your boundless compassion. For the moments of pure joy, for the periods of tranquil serenity, and for the reassurance of Your loving presence, I am eternally grateful.

I thank You for my health, for the strength of my body, and for the ability to experience the fullness of life. I acknowledge that health is a precious gift, often taken for granted until it is threatened. I pray for continued health and strength, not just for myself but for all those I love.

I thank You for the roof over my head, the food on my table, and the clothing that keeps me warm. These basic necessities, often overlooked, are a constant reminder of Your provision and Your care. I pray for continued blessings of abundance, not for material wealth, but for the ability to meet my needs and the needs of those around me.

I thank You for forgiveness, for the grace that washes over me, cleansing me of my imperfections and allowing me to start anew. Your mercy is boundless, Your compassion unending. I thank You for the gift of repentance and the opportunity to make amends.

And finally, Lord, I thank You for the promise of eternal life, for the hope that lies beyond the horizon, for the assurance that my journey here is but a preparation for the glorious eternity that awaits. This hope sustains me through life's trials and strengthens my resolve to live a life worthy of Your grace.

Father, this prayer of gratitude is not merely a recitation of words, but an outpouring of my heart, a testament to the depth of my faith, and an expression of my unwavering devotion to You. Help me, Lord, to live each day with a heart full of gratitude, to appreciate the small blessings alongside the significant milestones, and to always remember Your unwavering love and unfailing grace. In Jesus' name, Amen.

Father, as I conclude this journey of intentional living, I come before You with a heart overflowing with gratitude and a soul yearning for Your continued blessing and protection. The path of mindful living, of diligently tending to my own responsibilities and resisting the temptations of gossip, judgment, and meddling, has been challenging yet profoundly rewarding. I have learned the power of silence, the importance of discerning wisdom from folly, and the immeasurable peace that comes from trusting in Your divine plan.

I thank You, Lord, for the clarity You have given me in understanding the principles of "minding my own business." It is not a retreat from engagement with the world, but rather a strategic positioning to maximize my effectiveness and impact. It is a recognition that my primary responsibility lies in cultivating my own spiritual garden, nurturing my relationship with You, and fulfilling the tasks You have entrusted to me.

Help me, Lord, to continue living quietly, not out of fear or passivity, but out of a conscious choice to prioritize peace and intentionality. Grant me the strength to resist the allure of gossip and the temptation to meddle in the affairs of others. I recognize that my words have power, and I pray for the wisdom to use them judiciously, always choosing kindness, compassion, and understanding over criticism and judgment.

Protect me, Lord, from the insidious whispers of negativity and the destructive forces of idle chatter. Help me to cultivate discernment, to recognize the subtle ways in which gossip and negativity can creep into my life, and to resist their destructive influence. Give me the grace to turn away from unproductive conversations and to redirect my energy towards activities that build me up and bring me closer to You.

Lord, I pray for Your protection over my heart and my secrets. Help me to be discerning in choosing those with whom I share my vulnerabilities and my deepest thoughts. Surround me with trustworthy friends who will offer me support and encouragement, not judgment or condemnation. Grant me the wisdom to recognize the difference between true friendship and superficial connections, and to build relationships that are rooted in mutual respect, loyalty, and faith.

I pray for the strength to resist laziness and foolishness. Help me to overcome procrastination and to cultivate discipline in all aspects of my life. Grant me the wisdom to make sound judgments, to resist impulsive decisions, and to align my actions with Your will. I acknowledge that I am prone to folly, and I ask for Your grace to guide me away from harmful temptations and towards choices that honor You.

Grant me the grace, Lord, to measure with mercy and to avoid the pitfalls of judgment. Help me to see others through Your eyes, to recognize their inherent worth and dignity, and to offer them compassion and understanding even when their actions disappoint me. I confess my tendency to judge and condemn, and I ask for Your forgiveness and the grace to cultivate a more merciful and forgiving heart.

Protect me, Lord, from the destructive power of uncontrolled passions. Help me to manage my emotions, to respond to challenging situations with grace and composure, and to avoid rash decisions driven by anger, fear, or frustration. Give me the strength to resist temptation and to pursue a life of self-control and emotional maturity.

Bless my friendships, Lord, and help me to cultivate relationships that are based on mutual respect, trust, and loyalty. Surround me with people who will lift me up, support me in times of difficulty, and encourage me to grow in my faith. Help me to be a faithful and supportive friend to others, offering kindness and understanding without compromising my own well-being.

Grant me peace, Lord, even amidst the chaos and uncertainty of life. Help me to focus on my own walk with You, to trust in Your plan for my life, and to find contentment in the present moment. Fill my heart with Your love, Your joy, and Your unwavering peace, knowing that You are in control and that all things work together for good for those who love You.

Father, I thank You for the journey we have shared through this study of intentional living. As I step out into the world, I pray for Your continued blessing and protection. Guide my steps, Lord, and help me to live each day with purpose, intention, and unwavering faith. In Jesus' name, Amen.

Discernment: The ability to judge well; the power to distinguish right from wrong, truth from falsehood.

Intentional Living: A conscious and deliberate approach to life, guided by faith and purpose, prioritizing spiritual growth and mindful engagement.

Mind Your Own Business: A call to focus on personal spiritual development and responsibilities, avoiding gossip, judgment, and meddling in the lives of others.

Peace: A state of tranquility and serenity that arises from trust in God's plan and a focus on personal spiritual well-being.

Self-Control: The ability to govern one's own conduct and emotions; a fruit of the Holy Spirit.

About the Author

Alander Pulliam is an american film producer,author, actor, writer, business owner and investor. Running for President of the United States 2024. Forming many corporations throughout his career, spending many years in the major label spectrum, he was responsible for several successes in the music industry. In 2015, Alander Pulliam was chosen as one of the Top 25 Marketing Innovators in the World. Serving as an Executive in the Entertainment Industry. Working on TV Shows and Movies, from Producing to Investing. He has made his mark in the industry. Now developing the ABM Streams APP which allows anyone to make money streaming anything and everything that can be streamed. Alander Pulliam is continuing to develop several empires throughout the world of Entertainment. Helping others establish themselves. Working with many of today's artist along with several of the most successful artist coming on the scene in the mid 2000's era of music. Serving as a major label executive, he gradually moved into the TV and Film spectrum.

About the Publisher

Alander Pulliam is an accomplished American film producer, author, actor, writer, entrepreneur, and investor. He is currently a candidate for President of the United States in the 2024 election. Throughout his career, he has founded numerous corporations and has extensive experience within the major label music industry, where he contributed to several notable successes.

www.ingramcontent.com/pod-product-compliance
Lightning Source LLC
LaVergne TN
LVHW090313210926
848480LV00001B/227
9798231631445